COMMERCIAL-INVESTMENT
REAL ESTATE:
MARKETING AND MANAGEMENT

COMMERCIAL-INVESTMENT
REAL ESTATE:
MARKETING AND MANAGEMENT

Lee E. Arnold, Jr., CCIM

REALTORS NATIONAL MARKETING INSTITUTE®
of the
NATIONAL ASSOCIATION OF REALTORS®
Chicago, Illinois

Acquisitions Editor: Barbara M. Gamez
Editor: Dawn M. Gerth
Associate Editor: Helene Berlin
Cover Design: Deborah Davidson
Interior Design: Diane Hutchinson
Composition: Set in Palatino and Helvetica by Typographic Sales
Printing and Binding: The Book Press

International Standard Book Number: 0-913652-53-9

Library of Congress Catalog Number: 82-062949

REALTORS NATIONAL MARKETING INSTITUTE® Catalog Number: BK161

Printed in the United States of America
First Printing, 1983

This book is dedicated to my inspiration and father,
Dr. Lee E. Arnold, and my mentor, Herbert G. Brown

Table of Contents

About the Author

REALTOR® Lee E. Arnold, Jr., CCIM, is founder of Lee Arnold & Associates, Inc. The firm specializes in the development, management and marketing of problem commercial investment real estate. He is an active principal in shopping center, industrial, mobile home park, and subdivision development. His Accredited Management Organization plays an active role in problem property workouts.

REALTOR® Arnold received his B.A. degree in finance from the University of South Florida. Arnold is a senior instructor for the REALTORS NATIONAL MARKETING INSTITUTE® and a member of the RNMI Commercial-Investment Council. He is also president of Lee Arnold Management Systems, Inc., developers of Realbase™, a commercial broker database system.

Preface

Originally, this work was never intended to be a formal, printed book. The expectation was that much of the research and procedures described herein would be used internally by the author's company with no vision of a final working product. As the years passed and the various chapters became more formalized, it was clear few had addressed the actual process of listing and selling commercial real estate as well as the all important office management process. In retrospect, it is my belief that this hesitancy to describe the process is because it is so broad and resists formal definition. Anyone so bold as to assume that he understands and can describe this business accurately is sure to experience deserved ridicule. Notwithstanding the potential for this work to seem outdated as it goes to press, I have agreed to take the risk, trying to describe and focus on the process and business known as "commercial-investment real estate brokerage." The keen awareness that there is no universal truth other than ethics in this business, dictated that the methodology used for the development of this work be flexible, yet fully defined.

The opportunity to interact with allied business professionals as well as the best brokers throughout the country was enhanced by my personal involvement in the REALTORS NATIONAL MARKETING INSTITUTE®. The theories, procedures and techniques described were developed through the solicitation and receipt of marketing techniques, procedures and policies as well as my own observation and personal experiences.

Because so much of this work is a result of many, many hours of discussions with other professionals, it is my hope that this book can be the catalyst for many other authors' future works on marketing and management of a commercial-investment real estate. We are truly on the verge of completely new approaches to our business resulting from computerization.

Through sharing of the insights you receive from this text as well as your personal experiences, including new marketing programs, policies and procedures you develop, you will greatly enhance the author's future text to be developed. A postcard or letter describing new procedures, policies or conflicts in the book would be greatly appreciated. For any ideas or marketing programs, please forward your thoughts and comments to:

Lee E. Arnold, Jr., CCIM
Post Office Box 5856
Clearwater, Florida, 33516.

Acknowledgements

This work has been touched by many. Without the free and open dialogue of hundreds of brokers, this work could not have been completed. Ten years in writing have caused the acknowledgement to reflect recent participation, but I must give particular thanks to major corporations who have elevated our trade to a profession. These companies that have contributed, some knowing and some not, include Coldwell-Banker, Cushman Wakefield, Grubb and Ellis, Sheldon F. Good Company, Baird and Warner and the Fuller Company. Numerous other firms should be included, but would create an exhaustive list. Many of these companies offered insight to marketing and management that have set the pace of our industry.

A particular indebtedness goes out to the leaders of the REALTORS'NATIONAL MARKETING INSTITUTE and its CCIM program. This program has offered the author unlimited opportunity to learn and to grow within our profession. Jack Pyle, CCIM, and President of the National Real Estate Exchange offered early guidance and inspiration throughout the writing of this book. His unusual gift for organization assisted in creation of many of the marketing plans and systems described throughout the book.

The book is like having a baby. First you experience euphoria, then a long and sometimes painful gestation period. Without the RNMI editorial and publishing staff's doctorial assistance, the book may not have made it to it's first birthday. Particular thanks goes out to Barbara Gamez, Dawn Gerth and Helene Berlin for their tenacity and creativity.

Through the years members of the Lee Arnold & Associates, Inc., staff have offered and aided in the development of our systems and the book. Giselle Forbes, our brokerage company's media coordinator, created graphics and offered key guidance in the marketing systems and overall company development.

A brokerage company is not a company without its independent contractors. My friends are my associates and my associates are my friends. For years they have been a part of and instrumental in the development of our policies and our procedures. Particular thanks goes out to James B. Davis, CPM, Joel Parker and John Gerlach. All played key roles over the last decade in the development of the Company.

No single person has worked harder on this book than my friend and secretary, Susan B. Dunbar. She survived the endless rewrites and changes with a smile and encouragement.

Further, I must acknowledge the patience of my dear wife, Debbie. The many times she unselfishly would allow the time for writing the book. There were many times when she packed my two young princesses, Alisha and Nicole, off to Louisiana so Daddy could work on the book. Without her support and love this material would have been only a company policy manual.

Introduction

In order to better understand the concept of marketing commercial-investment real estate presented in this book, one should understand this book's structure. The initial thrust will be to develop a business philosophy that will guide the creation of personal and office procedures. It will be the foundation that governs personal and corporate activity.

COMMERCIAL-INVESTMENT REAL ESTATE: BUSINESS PHILOSOPHIES

Once we have developed a business philosophy, the next step will be to understand how to get started in the real estate brokerage business. A thorough understanding of the steps necessary to place you in the mainstream of commercial brokerage is needed in order to fulfill your personal goals and achieve success in commercial-investment brokerage.

THE BROKERAGE BUSINESS: WHAT TO EXPECT

COMMERCIAL-INVESTMENT REAL ESTATE: BUSINESS PHILOSOPHIES

Once started in business, you will need products to sell. Programs and procedures for listing commercial-investment real estate are presented in Chapter 3.

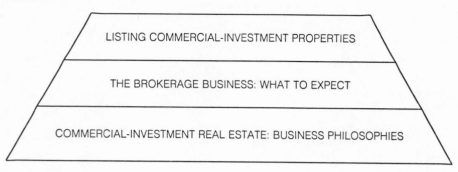

After listing exclusive right of sale properties, your immediate problem is marketing your inventory. Extensive marketing programs and policies are presented here to help you to profitably market your listings in the shortest amount of time. All too often it is perceived that upon reaching the status of a commercial real estate salesperson we no longer have to sell, that we are technicians rather than salespersons. Chapter 4 focuses on marketing and selling commercial-investment real estate with emphasis on basic selling philosophies that, when adopted, will assist the individual in selling efficiently and effectively. This completes Book One.

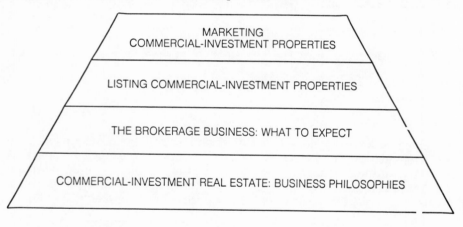

As we track the scenario of commercial brokerage into Book Two, Chapter 1 offers more insight into listing and marketing by presenting and explaining many useful forms and procedures and explaining how they can be best used. Once a property is successfully marketed, it will be necessary to write contracts or letters of intent and to facilitate the negotiations for that all-important contract. Chapter 2 focuses on writing tight, professional contracts. This is of supreme importance to the overall, long range goals, plans and success of the individual and the organization.

Chapter 3 will provide an extensive personal and company policy manual. It is based on ten years of research, and includes policies from across the country. It can improve profitability because it has been tested and developed for a commercial brokerage company.

The final chapter is a review of time saving office organizational procedures. It includes office procedures ranging from listing contracts to file inventory as well as how to interface marketing systems with today's word processor.

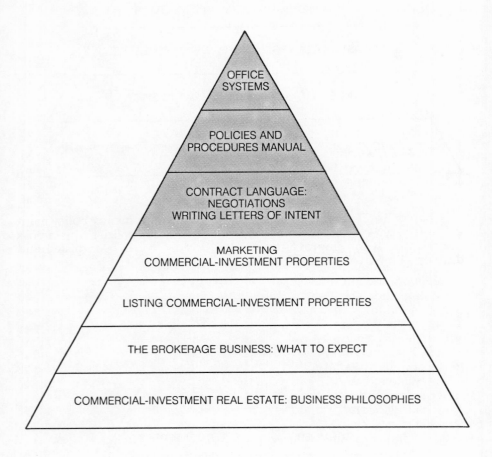

1

The Broker's Business Philosophy

The business philosophy is a very important, but neglected, ignored and misunderstood concept for the entrepreneur. For instance, a manufacturer must have a business philosophy stating how a product is manufactured and marketed and how employees are treated. However, many people entering the commercial-investment real estate business or even those who are currently in the business have given little significant time or effort to developing a personal business philosophy. Most business philosophies are functions of experience and perceived methods of facilitating sales and earning a living. Many times they are based on hearsay, observation and the interpretation of reference books. Basically, in the beginning, they are limited perceptions of the brokerage business. This author is confident that developing a philosophy is the most critical factor for success in the commercial-investment business. That is not to say there are not more technical areas that are possibly more complex and difficult to master. For example, determining an internal rate of return on a shopping center and the after-tax effect of a sale as opposed to a 1031 exchange, is a complex and rather difficult calculation to master. However, that is a much easier task than developing a business philosophy that is profitable, satisfying and successful. The end result of a well-developed business philosophy that is consistently updated, reviewed and modified will be continued personal and corporate success.

It has been said that successful people are people who do those things other people will not or choose not to do. Taking time to structure your personal business philosophy is just such an activity. A personal business philosophy is the most important, basic premise on which your success in this business will be predicated. At the end of Chapter 2, you will find a Business Philosophy Generator. After reading the various business philosophy topics covered in Chapters 1 and 2, stop and take the time to consider your business philosophy; then develop your own thoughts based on your own unique goals and expectations.

You will seldom find a lengthy discussion of business philosophies in "how-to-do" books. It is usually glossed over, given little or no attention. It is important to focus on a basic premise: *With few exceptions, there are no absolute right or wrong business philosophies.* There must be flexibility. There must be an awareness of different and changing markets as well as different and changing personalities and goals. Therefore, a constant vigil to ensure flexibility in your business philosophy will guarantee your own success as a commercial-investment salesperson and the success of your company. What works in one area may not work in another area and what works today may not work tomorrow. It is curious that 20 percent of the people in the real estate brokerage business earn 80 percent of the commissions. It would seem that there are unlimited monetary rewards in commercial real estate. There is strong, positive peer recognition for the successful commercial broker. It is an excellent vehicle for estate building and development opportunities. It is an almost constant challenge. Why are there so many failures? It seems to boil down to one basic underlying problem. The commercial-investment salesperson has not taken the time to develop his philosophy of business.

It is clear that to develop a business philosophy you have to focus on numerous topics that will dictate the manner in which you conduct yourself both from day to day and then over the lifetime of your career. There are three work-related topics that should be included in your philosophy to ensure both initial and continued success. They are: working ethically, working controlled and working smart.

Ethics

There is no more important element of a salesperson's philosophy than ethics. A salesperson who can create a relationship of trust with his clients is one who will create good will, have repeated referral business, a positive reputation and continued income from sales. An unethical salesperson is one who takes advantage of any party to the transaction, cannot consistently be profitable and will never be considered a true success by the community. In the REALTORS NATIONAL MARKETING INSTITUTE® CI 104 commercial-investment course, considerable time is spent discussing ethics. This includes discussions of both win-win relationships, in which all parties to the transaction win, and also win-lose relationships, in which one or more of the parties may lose or receive negative results in the transaction.[1]

Ethics help you develop your own personal business philosophy about representations and personal and co-brokerage relationships. It is impossible to attempt to give examples here of ethical behavior and the decisions you will have to make daily over the coming years. However, the following guidelines will help ensure an ethical method of work:
- Work from a foundation of goodwill.
- Ensure win-win relationships.
- Use the Rotary four-way test: Is it the truth? Is it fair to all concerned? Will it build goodwill and better friendships? Will this transaction be beneficial to all concerned?

---

1. CI 104, The Impact of Human Behavior on Commercial-Investment Decision Making. This course discusses methods of discerning and evaluating human motivations. Students learn to be consistently successful by combining client and property through the cooperative approach.

Here are three basic examples of how ethics become a part of everyday business.

If someone is going to be hurt or will lose as a result of a transaction, avoid the transaction. Do not attempt to collect a fee or be party to that transaction.

If there is a representation you would rather not make, if there is a rumor you know about the property, if you know anything and feel that if this were known by the client it would endanger the transaction, that same "I would rather not bring it up" attitude must trigger the desire to communicate the troublesome facts. In selling, it is amazing how positive the effect can be of an honest portrayal of a negative fact.

A third area in which ethics play a part involves dealing with co-brokers. Ethical questions arising over commercial-investment co-brokerage are some of the most difficult. Here is a case in point. How much time must elapse before a broker no longer has an ethical obligation to form a co-broker arrangement when dealing with a client introduced by another broker at some time in the past? For example, last week Salesperson Jones introduced me to Investor Smith. Two weeks later, Investor Smith comes back to me through no solicitation and inquires about an ad I have running in the paper. Is it ethical to sell Investor Smith without working out either a referral or a co-brokerage arrangement with my fellow broker? If at this point you are concerned and think that the broker would feel that you have been or will be unethical or that you have slighted him in some fashion by negotiating with his client, then it would be ethical for you to pick up the phone or take the fellow broker to lunch and discuss the problem. It is exactly this kind of situation for which you must build your own business philosophy.

Communication is always the best way to resolve a problem before it surfaces. For instance in this example, call up the broker and say, "Look, I did not solicit Investor Smith, he came to me directly and I know that under state law I probably do not have to pay a co-brokerage fee. However, I do feel that we may have a thin relationship ethically, how do you feel about it?" At that point, depending on the amount of control the broker feels he has over the client, you can probably resolve any ethical, co-brokerage questions. For example, you might suggest a minimal referral fee. Certainly, paying a referral fee is better than being involved in a law suit or getting a bad reputation.

Ethics is not a hard concept to sell, but it is a difficult precept to follow consistently, especially when big chips are on the table and it becomes easy to adjust the ethical parameters. So, set these ethical parameters before you need them.

Reputation

This author once used, "Our Most Important Asset Is Our Reputation" as his company slogan. It was intended to convey the belief that reputation means more than any one transaction and that he would go to any length to perfect and maintain it. When you are known in the market as a reputable, ethical broker—one who is knowledgeable, experienced and has a thorough understanding of the business—your sales, income and prestige will reflect this perception of you both as an individual and as a company. Place the importance on your reputation that it deserves.

Working Controlled

This concept is an absolute necessity if the principles contained in this text are to be used. If you are not going to work a controlled product, then the success of the many systems contained in this book will be severely limited. By working controlled in the brokerage business, a broker is given control of the property in one form or another. Many brokers control properties by options, outright acquisitions, joint ventures, syndications and a number of other methods. Such control can be called an exclusive right of sale. In an exclusive right of sale (a policy which is the basis of this text and the policies and procedures manual), the focus is on an exclusive right of sale agreement with a seller or a written buyer's agreement with a buyer. The main thrust of this system is on representing the seller.

This is not to say that successful brokers have not created significant success records by representing buyers. However, think of the typical buyer's broker scenario. The buyer contacts you with a specific request, a request for income property, for example, with a value of at least $500,000. The buyer has $100,000 in cash. Armed with this information, you immediately begin your search. At this point you have a buyer who has expressed a willingness to acquire property and has obligated himself only to the extent of indicating that he will come up with the money if you are able to find the suitable property. The $100,000 may or may not be available when the ultimate investment property is located. A typical buyer has no loyalty and will acquire property from anyone. Probably the most difficult part of working with buyers is that the seller pays the fee. The seller determines what it will be. For example, if the sale price of a listing is net $500,000 and your buyer says he will pay $505,000, your fee will not be between $30,000 and $50,000, but will probably be closer to $5,000. This of course assumes the presentation of an open listing, not another broker's exclusive right of sale.

Since the vast majority of commercial brokers deal with sellers, the focus here will be on the list and sell approach. Unfortunately, all too many of us are caught up in representing sellers on an open listing basis. This results in many of us being less successful than we might be. Test the validity of this thesis by calling ten *top* commercial brokers in different markets and determining what percentage work only when they control the property in one way or another. This author is sure you will find that the successful brokers insist on control of the property. This is because you cannot take listings and set up a successful marketing system unless you work only on exclusive right of sale listings or some form of control, e.g., an option.

The exclusive right of sale is the bread and butter of the commercial-investment broker. Opening a commercial-investment real estate division or office without these listings is like opening a supermarket without products. The entire marketing system used to sell commercial-investment properties is based on control of the product for an amount of time sufficient to develop not only a sophisticated marketing program, but also to develop the problem-solving techniques necessary to create large commissions. The real estate sales cycle starts with a good listing and a motivated seller. The more complete the salesperson's inventory of fairly priced listings owned by motivated sellers, the better he is able to serve his clients.

Never get yourself in the position of telling the seller that "Yes, I will show the property and if I do, will you pay me?" Never be in the position of presenting the contract and having the seller say, "I've changed my mind, it is not on the market." Never get in the trap of presenting an offer only to be reminded the listing was "net." No longer will it be to the advantage of the buyer and the seller to negotiate with all the financial flexibility being found in the broker's fee. No longer will there be the possibility of being in the embarrassing position of being asked a question about a product for which there is not a basic answer ("How's the property zoned?").

Getting Paid

Through the exclusive right of sale concept, you will consistently be paid more cash, more often, with fewer disputes, and have better long-range client relationships. You will see that by working on one or more exclusive right of sale properties and focusing on just exclusives you will develop a better understanding of the product and have a better opportunity to create a sophisticated and satisfying sale. If you are not hired by the buyer or seller, do not work the property. If a fellow broker tries to share an open listing with you, your business philosophy will dictate that you not be interested in open listings as you may be asked to exclusively list it in the future; you do not want to become involved in an ethical conflict with the open listing agent. Your response should be, "We appreciate your considering us, but we do not work open listings."

This is not to say that there are no exceptions. The operations that are successful in working open listings have a very strong market influence through name recognition or the length of time they have been in the market. New operations and new salespeople are at an extreme disadvantage on open listings and for the most part have difficulty competing in an open listing market. When you develop your control philosophy and believe in it, you will not only be able to develop the listing, but you will also be able to market it consistently and profitably. Veterans in the business will tell you that you just do not have time to work on all the pie in the sky transactions that are available to you. Some of the most difficult decisions you will make involve deciding which transactions to work and which transactions not to work. This may not seem a problem if you are beginning in the business, but it becomes an increasingly difficult decision as you are exposed to more and more real estate opportunities.

You must perceive yourself as a professional. How many professionals can you name that work when they have not been hired? Does your doctor work when he has not been hired? Does your attorney, C.P.A. or certified property manager? Without exception, the professionals in the marketplace know they are going to get paid if they perform the service. Why, then, do commercial brokers work on open listings when there is a low probability of getting paid? It is this author's perception that this is a function of risk and return. There are certain occasions when you will not be able to close on an exclusive listing. In these cases, the return may be so high and the risk so minimal in terms of time, that you may want to take a shot at an open listing. Said another way, "Hey, I have got to present this once. I have the exact fit." Have at it, this business requires flexibility; but remember your work controlled philosophy.

Between ten and 20 percent of this author's company's gross commissions are usually derived from open listing sales. For the most part, these commissions are a function of focusing on a property in an attempt to take an exclusive right of sale. At some time, either during the exclusive listing attempt or at some later time, an obvious match with a known buyer is made and it makes good economic and business sense to proceed with an open listing presentation. These shots in the dark or pie in the sky transactions must be limited, however, or the systems outlined within this text will be ineffective and your income stream will be subjected to peaks and valleys—the simple feast or famine syndrome.

An agent working only open listings is a communicator rather than a problem solver. The top commercial-investment salesperson is paid for solving problems and not just for the communication effort. Often the salesperson who is a good communicator, has good market knowledge, and works open listings will have success one year and failure the next. For example, in a strong buyer's market, the communicative, open listing broker tends to see fairly positive results, but when the market tightens up, an agent's percentages drop dramatically. The communicator who is not able to create sophisticated marketing programs and fall back on the skills and organization necessary to move problem properties in difficult times, usually will be at a loss to compete against the broker working under the controlled exclusive right of sale concept. In good economic times, in a seller's market or in a market in which there are numerous buyers looking for all types and classes of sellers' properties, it is more difficult for the controlled product broker to take listings to maintain his inventory of exclusive right of sales. However, in all times, whether a buyer's market or a seller's market, there is always product available that requires professional commercial brokers' services. The results of the controlled property business philosophy is to have a rather consistent trend line of continued success with good, planned, predictable growth in income. This program results in security in the commercial-investment business.

Working controlled is best defined as offering services to sellers (sometimes buyers) who need professional service. Said differently, you work for sellers who are *motivated* to pay for professional service. By motivated, this author means sellers who are motivated to use a broker; sellers who need a broker. The key words are seller, motivated and control. Empathize with the seller. Why pay a broker $50,000 or $100,000 to sell property when you get three letters and four phone calls a week soliciting the property? If the seller perceives that he can sell the property at any time without the assistance of a broker, then the broker should be aware that the seller will not perceive the need for using the broker's services and therefore, will attempt not to pay the broker fee or at the very best, pay only a marginal or small fee. If many investors in the marketplace want shopping centers, the broker should be looking for listings that everyone does not want. Look for the product which is relatively difficult to sell, more complex to sell or requires more skill and in-depth knowledge of the product. Find those products which require a skilled, professionally trained person who works for a marketing-oriented company. The bottom line is, work on properties the sellers are *motivated* to sell. Facilitating, measuring and judging sellers' motivations are important skills to develop. Learn to determine that there is a true motivation to sell and that the seller perceives the need for professional service. Figure 1-1 is a form that can be used to determine the owner's goals and motivations.

Figure 1-1

OWNER'S GOALS AND MOTIVATIONS

1. PRIMARY MOTIVATION: Cash out, negative pre-tax cash flow, long-term equity growth, estate building, move to new property, 1031 tax-deferred exchange, land lease, installment sale, reduce risk, pride of ownership, people problems, partner problems, etc.

_____

_____

2. WHY IS OWNER SELLING PROPERTY?
In owner's words

_____

_____

3. WHY IS THE OWNER SELLING PROPERTY?
As *you* perceive owner's motivation

_____

_____

This concept of controlled marketing is crucial to deriving maximum benefit from the systems that are presented in this text.

Working Smart

There is an almost mysterious quality or aura surrounding successful, experienced commercial brokers. They know which properties to work, how to market those properties and whom to contact. They do it consistently, effectively and successfully. The successful commercial-investment real estate broker works smart as well as hard.

Visualize a shopping center. At the time of this writing, shopping centers are in high demand. Typical financing is running 80 to 90 percent. Cash into the transaction runs ten, 20 or 30 percent. If, for example, we were to look at a $1,000,000 shopping center investment property with an 80 percent loan, we would have some 20 percent or $200,000 cash coming into the transaction. What are the odds on the commercial-investment salesperson receiving 50 percent of the cash into the transaction or any other large commission? Most likely the fee will be considerably less because the seller is not willing to allow the salesperson to earn half of the equity in the transaction for marketing property that is in such high demand.

Assume the salesperson had an opportunity to work on a vacant piece of land owned by a motivated seller who had held the property for a reasonable period of time and would like to take his profit. It too is now worth

$1,000,000. The mortgages are usually considerably less on unimproved property. For example, if the mortgage is $300,000 there is $700,000 worth of equity. It is reasonable to take this listing rather than the shopping center listing in order to:

1. take the exclusive right of sale,
2. get paid a larger fee at closing,
3. get a larger portion of that fee in cash at closing.

The bottom line is working smart. Look for properties in which you earn the *largest fees* and look for property owners who are *motivated*. Not working smart is working open listings, working for property owners who are not terribly motivated and working on properties on which the fees are typically negotiated at much lower rates. You either have to sell more properties at higher fees or sell larger properties in order to earn a higher income.

Another factor in working smart is dealing with those properties that are not typically co-brokered in order to make a sale. In general, most part-time commercial brokers in your marketplace work open listings. If this is true, they usually are not looking for the properties that are in low demand and are relatively complicated and difficult to sell. When you choose to sell these more difficult properties, you will find that you co-broker less and earn larger fees consistently. This is not meant in any way to discourage co-brokerage arrangements. But, it is important to plan and choose the properties that are worked.

Working ethically, working controlled and working smart are parts of the basic business philosophy. The working smart category involves planning and consistent goal organization. The only way in which one can work smart is to think about the process by which he is attempting to earn his living, the philosophy under which he is operating and the goals for which he is striving.

Goals

Almost every sales book you read includes a discussion of goals and planning. This is because goal setting is the basic premise on which most successful salespeople operate. But, for the vast majority of people, goal setting is only a topic of conversation, not something that they would take time to think about during the day-to-day competitive pressures. An important part of a business philosophy involves taking the very minimum amount of time each week to plan your business activities, to set goals and to adjust long-range objectives.

Goal setting is a conscious effort to address where you want to be five years from today in terms of income, status in the community, educational level, personal desires, family, bank balance, investments and portfolio, church, leisure time, travel, hobbies and numerous other important categories. Where do you want to be in the future relative to your objectives? Goal setting is relatively simple. If I know where I want to be five years from today, what must I have accomplished four years from today? If I know where I want to be four years from today, what must I do to reach my three year goal? And so on, right down to, "What must I do today in order to reach my six month goal and my one year goal?" For example, perhaps after developing a business philosophy you decide that you will be a CCIM two years from today. To meet this goal you must be a candidate for one year. Then, all five of the CI courses must be scheduled over the next two years in order for you to reach your two year goal. Figure 1-2 illustrates a form you can use to write down your goals.

Figure 1-2

GOALS

5 Years _____

_____

4 Years _____

_____

3 Years _____

_____

2 Years _____

_____

1 Year _____

_____

6 Months _____

_____

_____

3 Months _____

_____

_____

1 Month _____

_____

_____

1 Week _____

_____

_____

Today _____

_____

_____

Goals should be structured not in terms of just business, but in terms of what you are trying to accomplish as a total person. All of your goals need to be integrated into the business philosophy. Once you determine your one year goals, set six month goals, six week goals, one week goals, and daily goals. Attempt to set goals that can be achieved, yet still will meet your long-range planning goals. Set realistic goals; consistent failure to meet goals is not only depressing but is counter-productive.

Time Management

Most individuals who are aware of the importance of goal setting soon become aware of the importance of time. Most success systems and sales manuals have at least one chapter on goals and one chapter on time management. There is no magic to the concept of time. It is obvious that once it has been spent it cannot be recovered. The curious point is how unaware some people are of the use of their time. Or even more frightening, how many salespeople allow others to rob them of their time: idle conversations over coffee, socializing in the hallway, principals who continually drop by for additonal hints on the market and on how to sell their property, family members who make continual phone calls to the office and disrupt concentration and work trends, distracting horseplay in the office. Other examples of wasting time are driving two or three hours for a 20 minute meeting when a simple request for the client to meet with you at your office would have saved over two hours, failing to confirm a meeting prior to leaving the office that results in cancellation upon arrival at the client's office, failing to schedule several meetings in the same vicinity when driving time is involved.

The salesperson who is aware that he has approximately 2000 working hours in a year, and, if he is to earn $100,000 a year, that each one of those working hours is worth at least $50 per hour is on track to jealously protect his time. There are few merchants who would allow $50 to be taken from their cash register without a fight. But so often the salesperson, because he is unaware of the importance of his time, will allow an associate or a client to take several hours from him through frivolous conversations.

Typically a time management system will include setting the ten most important projects that must be handled each day. From this priority list, the salesperson starts at the top and tries not to move on to the second priority until he has completed the first. Through a well-organized day, one can minimize the down time and maximize the productive use of each hour.

A very fruitful approach to time management is to constantly analyze your use of time. Your most productive time is when you are actually meeting with buyers and sellers. Less productive time, but important time, is that time you use to prepare contracts or prepare to meet with buyers and sellers. Even less productive time would be time that is spent doing routine maintenance activities such as maintaining your listing manual, going to meetings, performing market research and other clerical duties.

A salesperson in a slump or having difficulty getting started would do well to keep track of how he is spending his time using half-hour increments, a difficult but always productive procedure. After three or four days of this, trends can be seen. This simple procedure forces you or your associate to spend what is commonly called "Class A Time," that time during which you are most productive, with buyers and sellers. This not only will enhance self-image but also will create an atmosphere in which more listings can be taken and more properties can be sold. If 80 or 90 percent of the salesperson's time was spent taking listings and meeting with buyers and sellers, he would not only create more activity, he would increase the numbers of closings. Obviously, it is impossible to spend that much time meeting with buyers and sellers. The main thrust of the time inventory is to place more emphasis on meeting with buyers and sellers and less emphasis on routine matters. It is important to meet with clients during those periods when they are available, specifically from 8:30 a.m. to 5:30 p.m. Do the routine activities after hours, or when other appointments cannot be arranged. Time management is an all-important aspect of a business philosophy that cannot be overlooked or minimized.

Now, if you are a salesperson who is ethical, has a good reputation, works controlled and smart, has focused on goals and has a strong awareness of time, it is necessary to focus on the business of being a selling broker.

2

The Brokerage Business:
What to Expect

I t seems important at this point to make some generalizations about the business of commercial brokerage and becoming involved in it. As previously discussed, there is no absolutely right or wrong way to carry on the business as long as it is ethical. The concepts discussed in Chapter 1 are the basis for the remainder of the book. Even if you were to adopt them and begin working, starting at virtually ground zero, you could expect that the first six months would be less than exciting. It would be eight months at the very minimum before you would see a relatively decent income. Do not expect big dollars during the initial period of this program. As you will see later, it takes a considerable amount of time to build a reputation, to become educated in commercial brokerage, to develop and know in-house marketing systems, and to become knowledgeable about the marketplace. Many times it takes up to two years before the monetary rewards seem adequate. The entire system is predicated on developing control of product, which takes time—time to develop centers of influence. Typically, this time can be cut down if the individual has extremely good contacts in the marketplace in which he is working.

Expect to experience extreme frustrations with the business. Upon entering the field, you will find that it is extremely difficult to understand the complexities of the business. You will find it is difficult to consistently get paid if you do not work controlled products. When you are at a loss, go back to the basics of time management. Try to plan your work and work your plan as closely as possible. If things are not going well in the early stages, take the advice offered in Chapter 1: Look toward those properties that are not in demand and have sellers who are motivated to sell their properties. If you have been in the residential business, you will note that the feedback and immediate gratification in the commercial business is considerably less. The transactions take a great deal of time as compared to residential. Complexities and contingencies are numerous. There are few quick transactions. Be prepared for a considerable amount of detail work in the commercial-investment business. As in the residential business, expect to be turned down numerous times especially in the beginning when your credibility level is relatively low. There is no substitute for the first 12 months in this business. It is difficult; it is depressing; it takes good training and broker leadership in order to make it through this period without any permanent scars.

Try to affiliate yourself in an atmosphere of success with good leadership and office organization. Remember that you must have a commitment to the business full time. You cannot continue to operate your other businesses and slowly move into the commercial business. You must constantly work toward your goals, reassess your plan and jealously protect your time. Go into your new commercial brokerage business with the expectation of spending at least a year before seeing consistent gratification. This is an extremely complex, competitive business that requires a great deal of catch-up time for the new associate. Sixty to 70 hours a week of intense real estate activity in the office and study out of the office are necessary in the first year in order to come on line with any kind of successful record. A good portion of this time should be spent on self-education, going to courses, reading books, reading periodicals and doing market research.

It takes several years of following trends in the marketplace before you can sound knowledgeable to your clients and have enough background information to be convincing in the listing process. Ask your sales manager or broker for help in those early listing pitches. It takes several more years to build the contacts and the reputation necessary to generate the kind of referrals that make life flow a little smoother later in your career. This is not a short run, immediate gratification business. Conquering it involves not only understanding, but consistent and constant reinforcement of the business philosophy. A weakness in one area can destroy the strong points in other areas. You cannot really conquer the business, but you can control it and profit from it.

Despite all these somewhat negative statements, there is really nothing quite as satisfying as the realization that you can solve a very complicated problem and serve the client in a profitable and rewarding manner. The business actually becomes rather simple with experience and proper planning, marketing and business philosophies. It is a matter of understanding the business of brokerage and of maintaining your marketing system, your contacts and your personal energy. Commercial-investment real estate is financially rewarding, it is psychologically satisfying, and there is good, positive peer recognition.

Now to focus on the business activity called brokerage.

Creating the Successful Business Environment

The first step in developing a successful, profitable brokerage is to create the business environment. This is a difficult area to describe, but by examining some of the various elements that make up this environment, you will begin to understand it.

Visibility in Your Community

Part of your business philosophy should include interaction with your community. High visibility in community affairs is an important variable and almost a necessity in the commercial brokerage business. To accomplish this you must get involved. Getting involved means becoming a joiner. Join and take leadership roles in the local civic organizations, such as the Chamber of Commerce, the Downtown Development Club, your church and even the city government. At this writing, this author's associates hold the following positions in civic organizations: president-elect of the Chamber of Commerce, president-elect of the Rotary Club, secretary of the Committee of 100, member of the City Code Enforcement Board, member of the City Variance Committee, president-elect of the local certified property managers chapter, and the list goes on. Visibility is born out of involvement.

Centers of Influence

There are people surrounding you who will influence your professional life by the reputation they create for you and by the referrals they send your way. This referral network is probably the most important vehicle for taking listings. Those people who are in regular contact with you refer various buyers to you. These centers of influence are the ones with whom you need contact. If you are stalled in a slump, not happy with your production, can't find financing, just cannot seem to get anything closed, get out and circulate. Get out and talk, and talk positive. Surround yourself with an atmosphere of self-motivation and success.

Centers of influence are everywhere. Look for them in church, Rotary clubs, Kiwanis clubs, the Chamber of Commerce, Committees of 100, hobby groups and in your office staff. Some of the most profitable centers of influence are those that have businesses parallel to the commercial-investment business, specifically, property managers, attorneys, C.P.A.s, developers and contractors. Cultivating the attorneys and C.P.A.s in town as your centers of influence, making certain that they know who the top commercial broker is, will most likely do more for you in creating listings than any other activity. Normally the C.P.A. and the attorney are the first to know when a client has a severe problem. Many times, the C.P.A. or attorney can recommend or will be asked to recommend a broker to handle marketing property. This first line of referral is the foundation of your commercial-investment listing program. In order to develop a long-range listing program, you must also develop a long-range referral contact program. When you receive a referral, even if you do not choose to handle the property, it is important that you thank the referring person and that you at least make certain that the referral is handled properly by another broker and tell the referring person why you did not handle the prospect.

The Real Estate Industry

The local Board of Realtors is always a good starting point for contacting other people in real estate. You know the commercial-investment people in your market. Meet those who have an impact in the market. You should know the most successful commercial-investment brokers in the market and be on a first name basis with the ones who have the most impact and create most of the sales. There are many types of listings that other brokers will not attempt to handle for one reason or another and will refer to you. Many, many listings will be referred from residential brokers, since most residential brokers have attempted at one time in their careers to handle a commercial listing and found it unprofitable. Cultivate your broker contacts. It is a very important center of influence.

Attorneys

There is no more important center of influence than attorneys. Cultivate them, try to become involved with the local bar association by offering your services at broker-bar interface meetings. Lawyers are just as interested in maintaining contact with brokers as you are in maintaining contact with lawyers. Be the catalyst for that contact.

Property Managers

Get to know the managers of the types of properties that you handle. Make sure that they know your name and understand your specialized business. Try to contact them on a regular basis. Ask them if you can give them help or referrals.

Public Relations and the Press

Does the local press know your commercial-investment activities? Are they prepared to write favorable articles, reference your activity and look favorably on you as a professional? Proper utilization of the press plays a big part in creating a positive business environment. Learn how to successfully communicate your successes to the market. Focus on the very candid, soft sell. Stress your personal attributes to your centers of influence verbally as well as through press releases.

NEWSLETTERS The newsletter, a method of communicating monthly with centers of influence, is an effective means of public relations and marketing. There are numerous types of "canned," or prepared, newsletters that can be purchased with company logos and name affixed that may meet needs during the early stages of developing a mailing list and a formal newsletter. After your business is established, an in-house newsletter is an extremely effective vehicle for communicating the company's successes and properties available for sale. Many firms throughout the United States prepare newsletters on a monthly, quarterly, and semi-annual basis. The newsletter presented in the policy manual, Chapter 3 of Book Two, is a monthly newsletter and once the logo mask has been prepared, the remainder of the newsletter can be prepared in-house and easily reprinted by local printers. The listings can be produced on a word processor and then reduced down efficiently and inexpensively by a local printer. This is an extremely useful listing tool and an excellent vehicle for communicating new listings and past sales.

PRESS RELEASES The press release is an important public relations vehicle that for one reason or another is often overlooked by the commercial broker. Public relations firms can be hired to prepare press releases; however, most press releases of major sales and significant activities of public interest performed by members of the firm can be prepared in-house. Press releases will be accepted and printed in newspapers when they are short, concise and of genuine public interest. A flood of insignificant press releases will only serve to mitigate the significance of an important press release from your firm at some future date. Choose carefully the press releases that you wish to distribute. When possible, include a rendering or a photograph of a major real property that has been sold or is about to be developed.

WRITING FOR THE NEWSPAPER An excellent time-tested vehicle for exposure is writing articles for the local newspaper when requested. Offering insight to various reporters and becoming familiar with local business reports is an important way to communicate your successes as well as to foster name recognition of the personnel in your firm. Reprint any article that is printed with the newspaper's name and date, then print it in your newsletter.

LETTERHEAD AND BUSINESS CARDS The commercial REALTOR® today is as technically advanced as many of the other professionals on his team. His letterhead and his business cards should reflect his professionalism. Letterhead and business cards should be compared to other professionals in the market and should include clean, decisive lines without excessive promotional material.

SIGNS The commercial broker has the advantage of placing signs on well-traveled streets and on significant properties. Indeed, signs can°be the most important promotional tool the broker has. A careful, well thought-out sign is important for effective marketing and public relations impact. Signs should be uniform in color and design. The sign's most important variables are the company name, the colors and the phone number. A clean, consistent logo and a simple, easy to recognize company name and phone number with appealing colors will enhance sign recognition.

The commercial broker should not use a residential size sign when promoting commercial properties. A 4 by 4 foot standardized logo sign should be developed and used on a uniform basis, in order to enhance public recognition. Larger specialized signs may be created for significant parcels on well-travelled streets. However, for the most part, a double-faced 4 by 4 sign, perpendicular to the road, will give as much sign impact as the broker needs. Also, by standardizing the sign and silk screening them en mass, the company can save sizeable expense. When signs are installed, an extra touch is to paint the legs of the sign to be consistent with the sign colors. Unpainted legs tend to give an unfinished appearance to a promotional sign that reflects on your company's image. Old signs should not be placed on properties and all signs should look fresh and new. As soon as a listing sells or expires, the sign should be removed and destroyed. If reusing signs, repaint them. A fresh sign is important to enhance the public image of the company. Old, beat up signs give the impression of a cost-cutting organization and have no place with a professional, finely tuned marketing team.

Restrict your signs to the minimal amount of detail necessary to get the call. More than eight words on a sign cannot be read and as a rule, most billboards are very ineffective when more than eight words are included. Sold signs should be attached by the listing and selling associates as soon as the property is sold. Early application of a sold sign terminates the marketing effort and can be fatal, causing hard feelings with the seller. Once the sale is imminent, a sold sign might be added a week or so before closing if the closing is deemed to be firm. Sold signs are an effective marketing tool that should be used whenever possible.

OTHER POSSIBILITIES There are other effective vehicles for exposing your firm to the public including direct mail, outdoor advertising, novelties and color brochures. One of the most effective vehicles is a professionally prepared four-color brochure describing the specialities and benefits of your corporation. Depending on the sophistication of your market, an effective handout brochure will promote the company effectively.

Another idea is to send out the synopses of new tax acts that many publishing companies publish. The commercial broker can distribute these to his clients and make a positive impact during the confusing period following the enactment of a new tax law. For example, Commerce Clearing House produces a synopsis that can be personalized with your company's name and logo.

Thank-you notes, also carrying your logo, should be sent to all people referring customers to you. Another public relation tool is "In the News" cards. These are preprinted cards sent to people who receive publicity in the newspaper. For instance, when you read the newspaper, keep track of notices of promotions, successful business deals, etc., and send these congratulatory cards to the people mentioned. In other words, do everything you can to keep your name in front of your influence base.

All your public relations efforts affect your centers of influence. Other than generating these centers of influence, you must convince them that you are the person to refer their potential prospects to. Offer your library or various research collateral materials at your firm to these people on a friendly basis. Always send a thank-you note for even a casual referral. An extra special thank you in the form of a plant, a bottle of wine, a personalized pen or even a very fine dinner goes a long way toward enhancing your image in that person's mind. One referral of the proper listing can more than pay for all of the premiums or gifts given away in a year's time.

"How Is Business?"

One question you will always be asked is, "How is business?" The response should always be "Business has been excellent." Be prepared to quote some sort of a success level based on the "best 30 days we have ever had, the best six months we ever had, the best year we ever had," or "Our firm has sold over __ million dollars worth of properties," or "I really cannot believe how much activity and how much success we have had in the last __ months." The bottom line is the atmosphere that creates a listing environment is one of success. Success breeds success. A negative environment and attitude create negative results and hence, a very difficult listing environment.

Put yourself in the position of the seller who has two different agents come through the door proposing to list his property. One is obviously a very successful individual, one who speaks with confidence and has good market knowledge and contacts and exhibits all of the previously described aspects for a positive business attitude. The other associate comes in, not well groomed, without a strong positive attitude and unprepared for the listing effort. Which one do you think you would list with if you were the seller? Furthermore, if you are going to refer a friend or a client to a broker, which broker would you refer to?

Specialization

It is important to develop a business philosophy, which on a long-range basis, indicates some level of specialization. The very minimum level of specialization is becoming a commercial broker. There are some successful commercial brokers who are also residential brokers, but for the most part, successful commercial brokers are exclusively commercial brokers. This is because residential and commercial brokerage are very different. Both brokers may be marketing real property but at that point the similarity ends. The residential broker is typically not qualified to handle most commercial properties; and, the commercial broker is not knowledgeable in the residential market. It is extremely difficult to stay informed of changing market values, trends, rates of return and rent in both the commercial and the residential markets.

Certification in a specific specialty is required to reach higher levels of professionalism. For example, the Real Estate Securities and Syndication Institute offers the SRS (Specialist in Real Estate Securities) designation; the Society of Industrial REALTORS® offers the SIR designation for specializing industrial REALTORS®. The REALTORS NATIONAL MARKETING INSTITUTE®, of course, has the Certified Commercial Investment Member (CCIM) designation. Within the realm of the CCIM designation there are many possible specializations: free standing restaurants, apartments, industrial parks, industrial buildings, shopping centers, mini-warehouses, etc.

Another aspect of specialization was discussed under "working smart," page 7, that is, when looking for a specialization, look for the product which is relatively difficult to sell, more complex to sell or requires more skill and in-depth knowledge of the product. Again, discover those products which require a skilled, professionally trained salesperson, and a marketing oriented company.

For example, some brokers market themselves as specialists in problem properties and vacant land. Any property that is or will be difficult for the seller to sell is a "problem" property—it may not be a problem to the new buyer. So the objective is to make certain that in the marketplace, all potential sellers realize that when they are having difficulties selling their property, or, better yet, when they want to sell their property, that they should call the "problem solvers," the people who are familiar with solving their problems. This author promotes the marketing of vacant land, as there is a direct correlation between selling vacant land and solving problems. The types of marketing plans and approaches, variations and alternative uses for problem properties are very similar.

In order to deal in a profitable specialization, you must know how to specialize and this always involves education.

Education

What part will education play in your future as a commercial-investment broker? In this extremely competitive time with new computers, sophisticated marketing models, new marketing tools and ideas and quickly changing financial markets, the process of education is never ending. The responsibility of the commercial broker to his client is growing geometrically, as is his liability. If you are starting out in this business, the only way to shortcut the time period for experience is through the educational process. How important this is to you is determined by your goals and your total business philosophy. There are few truly successful and consistently profitable commercial operations that are not based on a foundation of education, re-education and more education. A basic business philosophy should include both continued self-education and formal education.

Personal Appearance

A sometimes neglected but important part of your business environment is your appearance. The way you carry yourself, the way you walk, the way you talk, the way you present yourself to clients, the public, your employees, your associates, all play a big part in your success.

As you are sitting here developing your philosophy in your own mind, think of those people in your marketplace who you believe are the most professional. Think of the most professional doctor, the most professional attorney. Who is the most professional commercial broker you have met in the last three years? What does this person look like? What kind of clothes is he wearing? How is his hair cut? How does he carry himself in public? What kind of physical shape is he in? How important is health to that success-oriented person? It is interesting to note the positive correlation between people who are extremely successful and who are also healthy.

It is difficult not to respect the professional who walks into your office with good posture, and has a pleasant and convincing voice. So often the beginning salesperson is not aware of the importance of the voice. But, the salesperson is just one step away from the professional actor, who is also a professional communicator. The abilities to sound convincing, to be interested and interesting, to ask questions and to control tone, diction, vocabulary and the enthusiasm of the voice play a big part in the success of the professional broker. Have you taped your own voice lately and listened to it? How does it strike you? Put a tape recorder beside your phone as you talk to your next client and play it back to see how you sound. Did you sound enthusiastic? Did you sound like you were glad to hear from him? Did you use a monotone? Did you sound concerned about his problem and questions? Is there room for improvement in your voice? Your business environment includes an awareness of your body, your mind and your entire psychological self.

Take one moment and consider your appearance in relation to the next person you will meet. If you are sitting in your office and a client calls you unexpectedly, are you prepared to meet him? Every contact you meet will look at your posture, your appearance, the way you carry yourself and then establish a mental vision of how successful you are. Not everyone can or should drive a Rolls Royce; however, everyone can drive a clean, well-maintained car. Remember that you may not get past the first impression if your first impression is not a professional one.

Associates and Staff

Are your associates professional? Are they the most professional associates in the market? If you are not associating yourself with professionals, then people will associate you with the unprofessional atmosphere in which you have chosen to work. Are the people around you also striving for a high level of professionalism? If they are, are you the most professional in your group? If not, what makes the other people more professional? How can you better improve your level of professionalism?

Does your staff create the environment of business success you are trying to communicate? Is your staff well qualified and are they well paid? Are they happy in their work? Are they given the equipment necessary to do their jobs? When people visit your office is the appearance of the staff professional and well mannered?

Office

The office itself is a testimony to both your success and the environment in which you work. It makes a first impression on your prospects and your sellers, and it forms the basis of how your associates and staff perceive your business environment. If you choose to keep a messy, sloppy office, expect both your staff and your associates to keep messy, cluttered offices. The old saying, "A cluttered desk makes way for a creative mind," has no place in the professional, winning environment.

Tools of the Professional

To create the environment of success, you must have the tools for success. These can be both sophisticated and expensive. They may range from a jet helicopter to a fountain pen. If you are aware of the value of your time, it becomes increasingly important to surround yourself with the necessary tools to operate your business. A commercial broker must allocate funds for these necessary tools, whether they include a word processor for those operations that can support one, an extra telephone line to avoid lines that are always busy, or the proper furniture for your office. An adequate and well-established library is another example. It is impossible for the professional commercial-investment salesperson to remember everything he needs for his daily activities. A library will play a big part in creating the image of success as well as improving the potential for success by helping you provide suitable service to your clients.

Put It All Together

If you have a businesslike appearance and attitude, and communicate the image of success, it will assist you in creating the environment for success. When you are asked what you do for a living, your response should be "I sell commercial-investment real estate." It should not be "I am in the real estate business," or "I am a broker," or "I list and sell property," or "I work for Lee Arnold & Associates," your response should be "I sell commercial-investment real estate." Don't beat around the bush, let people know *exactly* how you can benefit them.

The aspects of a basic business philosophy that have been covered in Chapters 1 and 2 are important in understanding the thrust of the marketing systems described later in this text and in Book Two. It is important at this time that each category of the business philosophy be developed, at least on a preliminary basis, prior to going on with the remainder of this text. Ethics, working controlled and working smart are extremely important components in the understanding and development of your own business philosophy and policy manual. Take the time to study each category of the business philosophy and write yours out on a form similar to the one in Figure 2-1 on the following page.

Figure 2-1

BUSINESS PHILOSOPHY GENERATOR
WRITE OUT YOUR PERSONAL THOUGHTS FOR EACH CATEGORY.

Ethics _____

_____

Reputation _____

_____

Working Controlled _____

_____

Getting Paid _____

_____

Working Smart _____

_____

Time Management _____

_____

Visibility in Your Community _____

_____

Centers of Influence _____

_____

Public Relations and the Press _____

_____

Specialization _____

_____

Education _____

_____

Personal Appearance _____

_____

Associates and Staff _____

_____

Office and Tools _____

3
Listing Commercial-Investment Properties

The exclusive right of sale is the bread and butter of the commercial-investment sales associate. Opening a commercial-investment real estate division or office or beginning your career as an independent contractor or a salesperson without these listings is like opening a supermarket without products. The entire marketing system used to sell commercial-investment properties is based on control of the product for an amount of time sufficient not only to develop a sophisticated marketing program, but also to develop the problem-solving techniques necessary to create large commissions. The real estate sales cycle starts with a good listing and a motivated seller. The more complete the salesperson's inventory of fairly priced listings owned by motivated sellers, the more he is able to serve his clients and reach his goals.

There are three categories involved with taking exclusive right of sale listings. The first, creating the business environment, was covered in Chapter 2. Now, the other two—selecting the property to be listed and properly offering the exclusive right of sale listing contract to the seller—will be examined.

There are many types of property which the commercial-investment associate may work. Some of these categories include, but are not limited to, apartment houses, vacant buildings, houses, raw land, shopping centers, farms, net lease properties, industrial buildings, mobile home parks, government leases, commercial strip centers and even such investments as restaurants, marinas and nursing homes. There is almost an endless variety of commercial-investment real estate to sell. As stated in Chapter 1, an important and basic premise for success in your commercial-investment listing program is choosing the type of product you want to list. At any time, in any given market, there are certain listings which are in high demand.

If the seller is being inundated with contacts from potential buyers and real estate brokers to list his property or to sell his property or if the seller is fighting off buyers on a regular basis, will the seller perceive that he really needs professional assistance in marketing his property? It is not always true, but as a generalization, if the property is in high demand, the seller will not perceive the necessity of hiring a professional broker, especially at the higher fee structures.

Attempt to find sellers who are motivated and who are trying to sell a product but are having difficulty selling or leasing. Any seller who is having a problem marketing his property has a "problem property" in his mind. Therefore, by listing problem properties, you are actually saying that you are specializing in motivated sellers who are having difficulty selling their product.

At this point, do not be concerned with how you are going to market this "dog" or "lemon." If the seller believes that he has a problem and he is unable to market the property, then he will look for and agree to list with the most qualified commercial-investment broker he can find. People will look to the professional broker and be more than willing to pay when they cannot solve their own problems. They are not willing to pay when they can solve their own problems. So, a basic premise when looking for listings is to look for sellers who are motivated and who have a problem.

Locating Sellers

There are endless vehicles for finding sellers with problem properties. Some of the best sources are the most obvious: the newspaper that has a for sale by owner, trade journals that reference problem properties or potential problem properties, your referral network—the Rotary Club, the Kiwanis Club, fellow brokers, attorneys, and local commercial bankers. If the chief executive officer of your local commercial bank or savings and loan and his board of directors are familiar with your specialty, you can bet you will receive a phone call prior to the completion of a foreclosure.

Sellers with problems typically fall into two categories: 1) property problems, including market and physical problems, that is, physical obsolescence and financial structure, 2) personal or people problems including health, family and partners. These two general categories give rise to many creative listing approaches. You must look for and discover the problems. Many times the problems are brought to your attention through very casual and almost unrecognizable sources. A problem may be very difficult to identify unless you are a careful listener.

For example, a builder-developer who actively buys vacant land to build strip centers is having trouble marketing his newly developed center. He may hesitate to tell you that he is having this marketing problem. The amount of time that he continues to hold the product indicates that he may be ripe to list his property so that he can realize his profit and move on to the next project. Another good indication that a problem may exist is the

For Lease sign or the rental sign. After owners have attempted for several months to sell or lease their property, they may be more than willing to discuss using the assistance of a professional broker.

Sometimes problems present themselves in the most subtle ways. Perhaps a growth motivated seller interested in maximizing his future wealth may not be having the slightest difficulty proving his success in his individual business; however, he may not be maximizing his investment wealth. He might not have the time or the experience to properly maximize his wealth by marketing his real estate and reinvesting his equity in larger properties with a higher overall growth rate of return. This problem can be used by the listing associate to motivate the investor-client to list his property. The investment based concept is by far one of the best approaches to taking a commercial-investment listing from an investor.

Taking the Listing

Taking listings is an art that cannot be perfected through memorizing a canned pitch. A well thought-out listing presentation can enhance your listing success record. The following is a guide to the listing effort, but should always be used only as a framework to be creatively modified in order to obtain the best results.

Look for the basic approach:

- The warm up
- The listing presentation
- The close: countering negatives
- Asking for the listing

There are two ways you can expect to take listings:

1. the absolute cold call,
2. when you have asked to take the listing or can reasonably expect to take it if you are successful in your presentation.

Basically both require the same techniques; however, entry into the listing presentation should be modified to fit the individual program. The spontaneity necessary to close an exclusive right of sale cannot be reduced to writing. Since the act of listing and closing takes place verbally, the most effective training is a live dialogue. This written guide cannot be substituted for the inspiration and imagination or actual exposure to a listing prospect. You must adapt the following to your own personality, the particular environment in which you are operating and the variables, such as whether or not you are cold-calling, that you are faced with when you make the listing presentation.

If you are cold-calling, your first attempt is to get a physical meeting with the seller. Any approach which gets you the meeting is, of course, acceptable, but one which is almost consistently successful is:

"Mr. Seller, I noticed that you have your property on the market."
or,

"Mr. Seller, I was advised that your property is for sale and I would like an opportunity to update my records, take a look at your property and also give you some information on the services of our company."

At no time imply that you just want to look at the property or that you are a prospective buyer and then try to flip into a listing pitch. You must let him know that it is your intention to take a few minutes of his time to describe your services in the event that he chooses to, at some time in the future, list the property. Cold-calling can be difficult. No one can minimize the difficulty of convincing a seller on your first meeting that he should list with you if he has already made up his mind to try to sell the property himself. However, if he is unsuccessful in selling his property or has been trying to sell it for some time and is now desirous of trying to list the property, timing is everything. Once you have made your initial pitch, follow up because you know that if the seller does not successfully market his property within a reasonable time, he will list his property, and you want it to be with you.

Another typical listing scenario involves the referral property owner or the property owner who knows you as a result of your listing activity or the company's listing promotions and makes contact with you or your firm for discussions about a listing. At this point, you would use the following presentation techniques.

Warm-Up

At the beginning of the meeting take time to warm up or, as it is commonly called, "spit and wittle." In the land sales business this is called neutralizing. It is almost impossible to get into a selling posture without the warm-up period. This can be done through a series of generalized questions, but typically the best approach is to discover a key question which will encourage the seller to talk. Remember, you cannot sell if you do all the talking. The best salesperson is almost always a good listener. One of the best ways to get a seller talking is to ask some pointed questions that demand something other than a yes or no response.

- "Mr. Seller, how did you come to own this property?"
- "Mr. Seller, how long have you owned this property?"
- "Mr. Seller, why are you selling this property?"
- "Mr. Seller, how long has the property been on the market?"
- "Why has the property not sold?"
- "What kind of offers have you generated in your own attempts to sell the property?"
- "What do you think the benefits of this property are?"
- "What do you think are some of the negatives we will have to overcome?"
- "What kind of marketing presentation have you put together for the sale of this property?"
- "Has the property ever been listed with a broker?"
- "What other properties do you own?"
- "Do your partners also want to sell?"
- "How many people have to join in the decision of making the sale?"

Any of these questions will get the seller talking. And you will gain enough information to creatively modify your listing approach in order to best present the benefits of listing. After you feel the seller has told you basically everything that you need to make an adequate marketing pitch and you have encouraged the seller to talk about his prize asset for the last ten to 20 minutes, it is time for you to begin your listing presentation.

A good lead-in to your presentation is to suggest to the seller that you describe how your company markets real estate. It is through this description of the marketing system that you can best sell your company's professional abilities. The following is a typical scenario that you should modify, adjust and adapt to each individual selling and listing presentation and also to your personal style. By the time you make your presentation, you should have developed your listing manual. It will include your basic listing approach along with the descriptions of the marketing programs you use to sell property plus various current brochures, flyers and marketing tools, including the monthly newsletter. Book Two includes an example of a well planned listing manual.

Listing Presentation

The intent of this presentation is to make the marketing of commercial-investment real estate appear as it really is—complicated and requiring special skills. Few sellers truly understand the difference between marketing commercial-investment real estate and marketing their latest automobile. They don't realize that there are more programs than the classified ads so commonly used by most sellers. It is important to emphasize the numerous ways in which you and your company market properties. If you do not feel comfortable with your ability to sell to a certain listing, try to obtain the assistance of a manager or someone else in your firm who has that experience. Now, using the Marketing System Flow Chart, Fig. 3-1 (which should be included in your own manual), follow along through this typical listing presentation.

Stress to the seller that you would like to explain your marketing approach. *Try to avoid interruptions by the seller* or attempts to discuss the seller's property or a specific marketing plan for his property. Your objective is to show the seller you have the best company, that it is the most organized, the most professional and that you are the salesperson to do the job.

"Mr. Seller, I would like to take just a minute to show you how our firm markets commercial-investment real estate. The first step is developing the range of value for your property. There are five key elements in developing a value range for your property:

1. the property itself,
2. the competitive market conditions,
3. the financial structure,
4. the owner's motivation,
5. buyer appeal."

Figure 3-1

MARKETING SYSTEM FLOW CHART

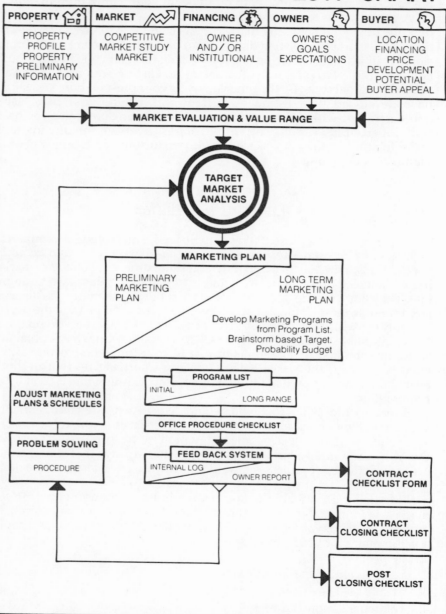

PROPERTY	MARKET	FINANCING	OWNER	BUYER
PROPERTY PROFILE PROPERTY PRELIMINARY INFORMATION	COMPETITIVE MARKET STUDY MARKET	OWNER AND / OR INSTITUTIONAL	OWNER'S GOALS EXPECTATIONS	LOCATION FINANCING PRICE DEVELOPMENT POTENTIAL BUYER APPEAL

MARKET EVALUATION & VALUE RANGE

TARGET MARKET ANALYSIS

MARKETING PLAN

PRELIMINARY MARKETING PLAN

LONG TERM MARKETING PLAN

Develop Marketing Programs from Program List. Brainstorm based Target. Probability Budget

PROGRAM LIST

INITIAL

LONG RANGE

ADJUST MARKETING PLANS & SCHEDULES

OFFICE PROCEDURE CHECKLIST

PROBLEM SOLVING

PROCEDURE

FEED BACK SYSTEM

INTERNAL LOG

OWNER REPORT

CONTRACT CHECKLIST FORM

CONTRACT CLOSING CHECKLIST

POST CLOSING CHECKLIST

Property

"We study the property on a preliminary basis in order to develop a full understanding of not only the land use, topography, zoning, water, sewer and construction, if any, but also to understand such detailed information as current income, expenses, financial structure, owner's adjusted basis and physical layout." (Point to the property symbol on chart.)

Competitive Market Study

"After careful review of the property, we develop a competitive market study. For this competitive market study, we locate at least five properties—currently on the market—that are comparable to yours and will compete against your property as we begin our sales effort. We also locate at least five properties which are truly comparable that have sold recently. After gathering this competitive market information, we develop a better understanding of what your property should sell for." (Again, point to chart.)

Financial Structure

"In today's market, the financial structure of the property plays an important part in telling us at what price and in what range of value we will be able to sell your property. Members of our firm have gone through extensive financial training in order to understand and analyze alternative investments and financial structures."

Owner's Goals and Motivations

"Mr. Seller, your expectations and goals play an important part in helping us establish the value of the property. The terms which you expect to realize will guide us in our judgment of the value range and market evaluation. If, for example, you desire all cash above the existing mortgages, you can expect a lower price than if you are willing to offer terms and secondary financing. For example, even if you really believe the value of your property is $500,000, we believe we can sell it for $700,000 if you let us set the terms. Instead of $100,000 down and a first mortgage of $400,000, a $700,000 purchase price might be possible if you will take $10,000 down and have the purchase money mortgage paid off over the next 30 years at an extremely reasonable interest rate. Obviously, your expectations and goals will play a big part in the value we are able to realize."

Buyer Appeal

"We will also grade your property based on buyer appeal. This category examines the variables from the buyer's standpoint. [Figure 3-2 illustrates this.] How does the property appear in the eyes of an objective buyer? Each one of the categories is allowed 20 points for a total of 100 points or 100 percent.

"1. How does the property location affect the value? Is it a 10 percent or 50 percent location or is it 100 percent location? If it is a 100 percent location, it would receive 20 points.

"2. Terms and financing? Will the seller help finance? A no is a zero rating; a yes will give points ranging from one to twenty. The more positive the effect of the potential financing we have, the higher the rating.

"3. Is it priced under the market? If it is priced under the market, how far under the market do we think it is? If it is priced at the market, how many points will you give it? If it is not listed in our range, we would have zero points.

"4. Development potential? Does the property have potential for development, expansion, modification, conversion, etc? Water, sewer, zoning are all taken into consideration. Are there any major problems in developing the property? If it is vacant land, for instance, are water, sewer, zoning

Figure 3-2

VALUE RANGE & MARKET EVALUATION

BUYER APPEAL: (How does subject appear in the eyes of objective buyers?)

1. Location ___%

2. Terms, financing ___%

3. Under market price ___%

4. Development potential (water, sewer, zoning, etc.) ___%

5. Area market conditions/property appeal ___%

TOTAL RATING ___%

MARKETING POSITION: (Evaluation of saleability)

1. Seller motivation (reason) ___%

2. Time period in which sale must be completed ___%

3. Seller will help finance   Yes___ No___ ___%

4. Property listed at market value   Yes___ No___ ___%

5. Seller will consider *alternatives*—lease, exchange, build-to-suit ___%

TOTAL RATING ___%

Each item represents a maximum of 20%. Yes can be 5, 10, 15 or 20%; No is zero.

Assets/Benefits _____

_____

Negatives/Drawbacks _____

_____

Area Market Conditions _____

_____

Recommended Terms _____

_____

RANGE OF VALUE: Top Listing Price   (Terms) $_____

Probable Final Sale Price $_____

Cash to Mortgage Sales Price $_____

This recommended listing price is a measure of the top value at which Real Estate, Inc. estimates the property should be offered. There is no absolute value for any one property. Our estimate is based on generally acceptable valuation techniques but is not intended to be a formal appraisal.

and land use available and consistent with each other? If so, it might get 20 points, because the development potential is good.

"5. What are the area market conditions? We will analyze the property's marketing position and evaluate the saleability of the listing. We will estimate how fast the property will sell. Some listings require over a year to complete a sale. Usually the longer the listing period, the higher the sales price. If we are asked to market the listing in six months or less, the time we have to expose the property to the potential buyer is even less.

"Buyer appeal plays a big part in the buyer's decision. We will study and grade all these variables. When we total the number of points in all five of those categories, it will give you an idea of the property's buyer appeal. What is your motivation? How strong do we perceive your motivation? We will estimate and grade this and give you an idea of how we perceive your motivation. These are all subjective evaluations that are important to us in trying to come up with the value."

Market Evaluation and Value Range

MARKET EVALUATION & VALUE RANGE

"Once we have determined our analysis, we mix the art and science of our group experience to arrive at a market value range. We will estimate as of the date of our recommendation the range of value based on a top listing price and cash to mortgage sales price. We will also tell you what we expect to be the final sales price."

No Absolute Price

"Mr. Seller, I must tell you that there is no absolute right price for your property. There is a *range of values*. We estimate the value that we believe to be the highest value the property should be marketed at in order not to severely limit potential buyers for your property. At some point of value, the price is so far out of the market, it will discourage even the most bullish of potential buyers. You should place a reasonable value on the property and expect some negotiations within the top value range."

This is a very good time to try to bring the seller in line with his request for either sales price, purchase money price, seller financing, listing period or, perhaps having the seller just fix up the property or make it more marketable. This is a very candid way of illustrating to the seller how he affects the marketability and buyer appeal of his property. At this point in the value range and market evaluation, describe the asset benefits, any negatives and the market condition (see Figure 3-2). It is through this step by step approach that it is possible to recommend terms and give an estimate of the value range.

Emphasize that there is *no absolute value* and that the seller plays an important part in the valuation estimation. Also stress that this is not intended to be an appraisal. Many appraisers will come out with values considerably less than the estimate. The estimate is based on what the property should be listed at in order to derive the highest price for the seller. One of the key variables to consistently stress throughout your listing presentation is that your most important objective is to get the *seller the highest price in the shortest period of time*.

If the seller insists on an inflated value, suggest to him that you would be more than happy to test the market at the higher value if he is willing to put up the money necessary to market his property. In other words, you have no qualms about risking your time if he is willing to risk his dollars at the higher price. And if he is correct and the property sells, then you would be willing to deduct the front-end costs off the top of your listing commission at time of sale.

Onward with the listing approach. You have described how you arrived at the property value and how, though this value may be above or below that of the appraisers, it will be based on the keen awareness of the seller's goals, the property's benefits, the competitive market and the financial structure. You have explained that many times such variables are not considered by professional appraisers because they are not responsible for marketing the property. Now, you must stress that you are an *expert* on marketing. At this point, you are selling not only yourself, but you are also selling the firm, your training and your ability to describe how you go about the business of selling commercial-investment real estate. A keen understanding of the procedures of marketing real estate will not only assist you in the marketing, but also will be a valuable asset in closing the listing contract.

Target Market Analysis—The Next Step

Returning to the Marketing System Flow Chart, it is time to discuss the target market approach to marketing commercial-investment real estate.

"Mr. Seller, if you have ever sold your own home or observed others selling homes, you have seen many people advertise for their prospects using classified ads. The classified ads are an effective marketing tool but they are only one marketing program. The classified ad is very expensive and has a very limited market. In commercial-investment real estate, we use target marketing. We study the property, the financial structure, the tax structure and your objectives, but more important, we study the market for the property and then we determine the target that we are going to sell to. This is a completely different approach than you might expect because it is not used in marketing a single family home. When selling the single family home, you are not certain who the buyer will be and you must expose the property to the general market and hope that the buyer contacts you. A very small percentage of properties in commercial-investment real estate sell through our local multiple listing. Most of the property sold in our office is sold through what we call the target market approach. We have developed a system called the Target Market Generator [Figure 3-3]. Let me take a moment and explain how this works."

It is important to focus on a conceptual approach to marketing when discussing your marketing plan. There is a mystique in most people's

Figure 3-3

TARGET MARKET GENERATOR

A. Listing Code _____   Date _____

Property _____ Listing Price _____

Owner's Desired Terms _____

Owner's Stated Reason for Selling _____

1. PROPERTY CHARACTERISTICS (BASIC)

Zoning _____ APOD Owner statement _____

Land Use _____

Size _____ APOD Broker's Forecast _____

Topography _____

Water _____ Specialized Information _____

_____

Sewer _____ Construction _____

_____

2. FINANCING	Assumable Existing	Owner Pur. Mon.	New Institutional
Current Balance	_____	_____	_____
Annual Interest Rate	_____	_____	_____
Payment Am't & Frequency Remaining Term	_____	_____	_____
Assumption Provisions	_____	_____	_____
Prepayment Penalties	_____	_____	_____
Personal Endorsement	_____	_____	_____
Release Clauses	_____	_____	_____
Subordination Clauses	_____	_____	_____
	_____	_____	_____

Figure 3-3, continued

a. What alternative financing approaches are available?

_____

_____

b. What is the likely final financial structure or approach that will be used to close the sale?

_____

_____

B. DEVELOP TARGET MARKET

1. How does the property relate to the market? Based on market price, property characteristics and financing, what are the best uses that will result in the highest price in the owner's time frame?

_____

_____

2. Based on market conditions, what real need could the property meet?

_____

_____

3. Describe and define the size and scope of the effective market for the subject property: local, state, out of state, world, investment/user, etc.

_____

_____

4. What use or user is missing or limited in the market?

_____

_____

5. What are the benefits this property offers?

_____

_____

6. Define the highest & best use of property.

_____

_____

7. Given the above, list in order of priority the potential target prospects, in general.

_____

_____

minds about how the properties are really sold and the number of potential prospects you have at your beck and call. Play upon this mystique and develop the presentation that is best suited for the seller. By going over this form, the client should develop a better understanding of how you develop your target market. After showing him how the information on the property is detailed on the first part of the form, turn to Question 1 of Develop Target Market, Figure 3-3, "How does the property relate to the market? Based on the market price, property characteristics and financing, what are the best uses that will result in the highest price in the owner's time frame?" Explain, again, that you are trying to get the highest price for the seller in the shortest period of time.

As an example, we will examine a vacant land listing. Are we looking at a 40-acre commercial tract that would be best suited for a shopping mall or is this land better zoned, needed and sought after in the market as a mobile home park? Question 2 deals with this aspect of the market. Focus the seller on the benefits that the property offers, and how you are going to use those benefits to develop a target market.

Point 3 asks that you describe and define the scope of the market. Play up the market size potential for the property. Most sellers can only think in terms of the local market, or at best, the state market. Few can think of how to contact users or even investors for the property outside of a classified ad program. Sell your ability to understand and deal with the market conditions because you have been analyzing this market over a period of years, are very familiar with it and have staff and research department resources available to you.

Working through the form, explain some of the benefits of his property. Try to avoid talking about any negatives. Remember, he acquired the property originally. He may now perceive negatives or for one reason or another, is desirous of moving the property, but he certainly does not want you to make negative comments about his property.

Define the best use of the property, Step 6 in developing a target market. It is not desirable to actually develop the target market in front of the seller; only go through the process that best describes your ability to meet his needs, that is, your ability to get the highest price in the shortest period of time. Part of this process is listing in order of priority the potential target market prospects in general. You point out that, at this point, you would develop some prospects who are best capable of buying the property based on the target market you are developing.

The Marketing Plan

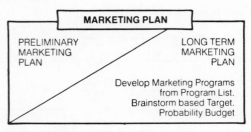

MARKETING PLAN

PRELIMINARY MARKETING PLAN

LONG TERM MARKETING PLAN

Develop Marketing Programs from Program List.
Brainstorm based Target.
Probability Budget

We next explain to the seller that at this point we start thinking in terms of developing the marketing programs. Probably there is no better time to emotionally close your listing than when you start discussing how many different ways there are to skin the cat. Marketing programs, which will be discussed at length later in the marketing chapter, are your strongest selling point and yet they are the most difficult to explain. Examples of marketing programs include using co-brokers, the MLS, classified ads, direct mail and personal contact, etc. Point out to the seller that the primary focus of your marketing effort is to target a prospect and then try to personally contact him with a presentation. However, there are many ways to develop and contact those prospects. We develop a plan based on the needs that the property can satisfy. We list all the various programs that can logically facilitate the sale. Figure 3-4 (page 38) illustrates a very useful Marketing Plan Generator.

First, develop the marketing budget. It's important to ask the seller about this. The more dollars available, the better able you are to obtain the highest price. Therefore, ask the seller to provide funds to assist you in marketing his property. For example, you might explain that if there is a high probability that the property will be co-brokered, the seller must realize that the broker is going to earn a $10,000 fee and $5,000 of that is probably going to go to the co-broker. That leaves only $5,000, $2,500 of which goes to the selling salesperson who has his own expenses, and the other $2,500 goes to the office. You therefore cannot afford to spend $5,000 on advertising, special signage, direct mail, etc. Emphasize, as you are talking about the budget, that an actual budget will be set up at the front end of the marketing program. This budget will estimate how many dollars are available for the various marketing programs. Go through the complexities of marketing his real estate over and over, showing him that it is beyond what he had ever dreamed. Explain to him where his dollars are going and how you earn the fee he will pay for your professional services.

Marketing Programs

At this point, turn to the marketing program section of your presentation manual and go through some of the programs with him.

"For example, Mr. Seller, we may set up a preliminary market development plan on your property. We would review the possibilities of a higher and better use than the current zoning allows and examine the possibilities of that better use. We may recommend that you give a cocktail party on site for a select number of brokers in an effort to better expose the property to the brokerage market. We may attempt to get certain certificates of need necessary in order to obtain federal financing. We may offer a bonus commission for quick sale. We may adjust the price and terms in order to better motivate certain buyers' interest. We would use exciting programs to generate interest including our direct mail program and our sign programs.

"As you know, having seen our signs all over town, the sign plays a big part in bringing a sale to your property. Many times the sign on your property will not generate the ultimate sale for your property, but signs on other properties will collectively bring us the prospect who will eventually buy your property. The sign program plays a big part in the overall marketing for a brokerage company of our size."

Again, play up the impact of your firm whether it is large, small or medium.

"What we do, Mr. Seller, is list all the programs that are best suited to your property. Those with the highest probability of success and the lowest

Figure 3-4

MARKETING PLAN GENERATOR

A. DEVELOPING MARKETING PROGRAMS

1. Marketing programs should be developed based on time and cost.
2. Primary focus on target prospect/market.
3. Develop plan based on needs that property can satisfy.
4. List ALL of various programs that logically should facilitate a sale.
5. Schedule programs:
   a. Highest probability first.
   b. As schedule is developed, choose programs with highest probability that fall within budget until allocated funds are exhausted.

B. LIST PROGRAMS BEST SUITED FOR PLAN—HIGHEST PROBABILITY VS. COST.

1 _____ 10 _____
2 _____ 11 _____
3 _____ 12 _____
4 _____ 13 _____
5 _____ 14 _____
6 _____ 15 _____
7 _____ 16 _____
8 _____ 17 _____
9 _____ 18 _____

C. DEVELOPING MARKETING BUDGET

- What is estimated fee?
- What is percentage probability of co-brokerage?
- What is total dollar to be expended in marketing?

Allocate to Programs:
Gross Fee	$_____
Co-brokerage	$_____
In-house salesperson	$_____
Company	$_____
Classified	$_____
Direct mail	$_____
Signage	$_____
Other (special publications, etc.)	$_____

D. BASED ON NEEDS THAT CAN BE FULFILLED BY PROPERTY, WHAT PROSPECTS COME TO MIND?

1 _____ 19 _____
2 _____ 20 _____
3 _____ 21 _____
4 _____ 22 _____
5 _____ 23 _____
6 _____ 24 _____
7 _____ 25 _____
8 _____ 26 _____
9 _____ 27 _____
10 _____ 28 _____
11 _____ 29 _____
12 _____ 30 _____
13 _____ 31 _____
14 _____ 32 _____
15 _____ 33 _____
16 _____ 34 _____
17 _____ 35 _____
18 _____ 36 _____

cost are listed first and then as the listing time period passes, we use our more costly marketing programs as necessary.

"When we reach Point D of our Marketing Generator, we enter the prospects that come to mind as we develop our marketing plan. Mr. Seller, we have an in-house computer that keeps track of all prospects. Each week every salesperson who gets a call puts the name into this system. The staff organizes these prospects within categories according to what their needs are. When I get a listing, I will go through all of our prospect lists in that category and generate the prospects who are best qualified to buy your property. The sophisticated marketing system we have developed over the years saves a great deal of time, effort and money."

To further elaborate on the sophistication of your marketing programs, explain your company's use of the various media that are available.

"Now, Mr. Seller, I would just like to show you a few unique variables in our marketing system. Our monthly newsletter features a listing each month. One month your property will be a featured listing. Notice all the different exclusive rights of sale we have available both in the commercial and the leasing departments. Notice all the sold signs in the month of June. Certain listings such as this one downtown require color brochures. Industrial listings like the one you see here have black and white photos in the flyers. We put together not only a flyer for more massive mailings and distribution, but we also put together what we call our property profile, a marketing tool which has gained us recognition in the market. It is a fairly complete selling tool that answers almost any question a potential purchaser might ask. We have experienced media and graphics people on our staff to develop these in-house. Our advertising department handles and assists us in developing these marketing packages. I would like to show you a couple of them." (Adjust presentation to fit your company.)

At this point, thumb through two or three selected property profiles that best exemplify the type of property profile you would develop for his property. Again, emphasize not only the medium itself, but the complexities of the property profile and how you have developed them to help you sell. It would not hurt to jump into a little discussion about any diversified services your firm offers and how they are vehicles used to solve problems for clients. At this point, you can show them one of those brochures and move into your closing techniques.

You have spent no less than ten minutes, maybe as many as 20 minutes, talking about your company and your approach to marketing commercial-investment real estate. This pitch should be relatively polished, not too lengthy, but elaborate enough to impress upon the seller your capabilities in marketing commercial-investment real estate. Most of all, your objective is to get the highest price in the shortest period of time. Nothing is left to chance; it is a very deliberate and professional marketing program.

Program List

At this point in explaining the marketing approach there is one negative that is consistently heard, "I once listed my property and the broker did not do anything except put a sign on it and run a few classified ads."

The best response to that is to explain your program schedule (See Figures 3-4, 4-1 and 4-2. Also, a detailed list of programs is presented in Chapter 1 of Book Two).

"Mr. Seller, I can understand your concern over this particular problem. Let me explain how our company keeps all listings on a fast track. We set up marketing schedules. We set up the date, the program—we have already talked about how many different programs there are—and what action is to be taken. Right here you can see that we have a three-part marketing schedule, [See Book Two, Chapter 1, for example] white copy goes to you, the canary copy goes to my manager and the pink copy goes to the sales associate. We set up both initial programs and long range programs. This is very important in keeping track of how your property is moving through the marketing plan. Also, we discuss your property every week at our weekly sales meeting. From these meetings we generate quite a few sales as we have some of the best trained, top associates in the area. I would like you to take the time to come down and meet my fellow professional associates after I have the staff type up our listing agreement."

OFFICE PROCEDURE CHECKLIST

You have just made your first close. You assume you are going to type the listing agreement. At this point, you should discuss the Office Procedure Checklist. The Office Procedure Checklist (Figure 4-3, page 61) is a rather extensive start-up checklist that the staff uses to generate all the systems that back you up in your marketing effort (An example of all of the forms mentioned in this discussion are included in Book Two.) It is important, again, to stress the *complexity* of the marketing system, the amount of *work* and the *people* who are necessary to effectively market a property as important as his property. Reinforce this to the seller and confirm that you are not going to just sit on his listing.

Feedback System

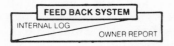

Moving along on the Marketing System Flow Chart:

"Mr. Seller, we also have what we call the Active Market Listing Feedback Report. Every two weeks I am going to give you a written personal report on the direct action taken to market your property. It will contain the prospects contacted and how they were contacted, why I believe the listing has not sold to this point, what would help your listing sell and what adjustments to the marketing plan are necessary in order to sell your property. Now, Mr. Seller, it is quite obvious that a property as challenging to sell as yours is, will from time to time need adjustment to the marketing plan. For this we have another procedure.

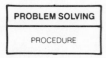

"What we will do is constantly reassess our marketing programs. We will find any problem and determine alternatives. We will reintroduce a listing to our group of associates, some of the best professionals in the market, and we will free associate. We will come up with ideas about how to market your property. We will evaluate the alternatives. We will select the alternatives that seem best.

```
┌─────────────────────┐
│ ADJUST MARKETING    │
│ PLANS & SCHEDULES   │
└─────────────────────┘
```

"We will choose an optimum solution and then we will adjust our marketing plans, schedules, targets and budgets based on our problem-solving technique. This is all part of the service you get when you list your property with us.

"Now, Mr. Seller, at some point in this system we are going to get into writing contracts. We have spent a considerable amount of time developing elaborate contract-writing procedures that give us excellent language for enhancing your negotiating position."

As you can see, we have come to the end of the system flow chart. This means that you have thoroughly discussed your entire marketing system with the client.

If at any time you feel like you are expanding in an area in which you do not personally have expertise, for example, negotiating a 1031 exchange, you might emphasize that your office has handled more 1031 exchanges than most firms in the area. However, you would not necessarily lock yourself into having to discuss a 1031 exchange if you did not feel comfortable enough in this particular area.

The Close to the Point of Verbal Commitment

As you know, you usually do not have enough information to take the listing on the first meeting. However, some listings will be given to you after this pitch. If the seller is motivated, and you feel the price is reasonable, take the exclusive on the first meeting. But, it would seem in poor taste to say that by walking through a building or looking at a piece of land in an aerial that you can give a valuation or even discuss intelligently how you would market the property. Unless the seller offers to sign the exclusive right of sale, you are not attempting to gain a signature. More than likely, you will ask the seller for a second visit, hopefully, within a day or two after you have evaluated the property and discussed it with several of your associates. It will help if you get their ideas prior to taking the listing.

By the end of the first visit you should have virtually convinced the seller to use you and your firm as his representative. However, if he is not convinced, you should confront as many of the negatives as you can now, before going through your entire individualized property evaluation (discussed on pages 30–33 and in Figure 3-2) during the second visit only to find that you cannot close on the exclusive. After you have finished your marketing pitch, ask a positive question of the seller.

"Mr. Seller, you have obviously talked to several other brokers. Have you ever seen a more complete approach to marketing your property?"

Say nothing else; try to say no more until the seller opens up with any negatives he might have about listing. If the seller has been favorably impressed, he will give you several positive indications. The most common is, "I think we want to go ahead and list the property. Can we get together tomorrow on the paper work?"

Countering Negatives

Often the seller will give you some negative indications. At this point, when you try to close on the final objection, you must really turn on the polished closing approach.

The "final objection to close" is the hardest close to learn, but it is by far the most important of all. It is one that must be practiced. It is not uncommon that a few sellers will simply say no when you attempt your first close. They may give you a simple objection. What do you do? You answer the objection. Does this get you the close? Almost never. All that you get when you answer an objection is another question. You begin to get involved in a contest of wits. Can the seller think up more objections than you can answer or can you answer more objections than he can think up? As fast as you kill one of his objections, another one will be coming. However, closing on the final objection can be done if you will memorize this formula:

1. Hear the seller out.
2. Confirm the objection.
3. Question it.
4. Answer it.
5. Confirm the answer.
6. Close.

Hear Him Out

How many times have you heard a salesperson jump in and try to answer the question he thinks the seller is going to ask after hearing only two or three words. Even if he is correct in knowing what the seller was going to say, the seller is going to be irritated and odds are the salesperson has not answered the right question. So, listen to the objection.

Confirm the Objection

After you have listened to the objection, confirm it; that is, expand upon it. First of all, use body language. Look defeated.

"As I understand, Mr. Seller, you want to think about it for a couple of weeks, is this right sir?"

Now, what have you done? You look a little defeated, you have expanded upon his question and you have confirmed it. New statement: "That is the only thing standing between us, isn't it? Well, that's fine, Mr. Seller; obviously you wouldn't take the time to think it over unless you were really interested, would you? I am sure you are not saying this just to get rid of me so may I assume that you will give it careful consideration."

At this point the seller thinks he is going to be able to let you go. So he agrees with you all the way. Yes, he is going to give it consideration. *Listen for the yes.*

Question the Objection

When he finally has agreed with you, question his objection.

"Sir, what part of our marketing program do you want to think over? Is it the integrity of the company? Is it my personal integrity? Or, is there a specific problem?"

You need to ask the seller what his specific objection is. Is it this? "No." Is it that? "No." All of a sudden he is going to wake up and say, "That's it." Now for the first time, you have identified the *final objection* and you can go into the final close effectively.

"Yes, if it was not for [final objection], I would go along."

Answer the Objection

At this point you should attempt to find the vehicle that will satisfy his negative. If the seller's final objection is:

"I cannot afford to list and not have action and a sale."

Your response might be:

"Mr. Seller, if at any time during the listing period you do not feel I am doing an adequate job of marketing your property, I will return the listing to you. However, Mr. Seller, I will not feel obligated to return the listing just because you have a buyer whom we generated through one of our marketing programs."

If the final objection is, "I will do it myself," use your for sale by owner techniques to persuade the seller that he needs your services as a real estate broker. A real estate broker knows how to advertise properties to the best advantage and for the highest price. The broker knows how to qualify prospects, show property, secure financing and has the experience to negotiate and close complicated transactions. Few owners have spent as many years developing the expertise necessary to handle complicated real estate transactions.

Promise only what you can deliver. Explain the firm's advertising program. Many people do not understand the difference between classified and institutional advertising, the value of the latter in selling real estate and the limited effectiveness of advertising a single property. Tell how the institutionalized strength of your office is the base of your daily efforts and how they attract buyers to our office. Do not promise to advertise during a certain period of time unless the seller is willing to put up an advertising budget.

There will be plenty of objections and it is impossible to cover them all. However, since the thrust of this listing presentation is to take the exclusive listing, here are some answers to objections concerning this topic.

CERTAIN PROSPECTS SHOULD BE EXEMPT FROM EXCLUSIVE RIGHT OF SALE Typical sellers will have at least one or two potential buyers—people who have expressed an interest—in mind. An exclusion from an exclusive right of sale sets up the seller as a competitor against you when you bring in your first offer. Suggest to the seller that you will not compete against him but you will work with him as a team. In some cases, the seller is fairly close to an offer or feels that you will not have done anything to bring in the contract. Experience shows that as soon as you present a valid marketing program and show him considerable activity, the seller will be quick to communicate this to his prospect who is not included in the exclusive. Furthermore, when you submit that contract, he will, of course, give one last try to his prospect because he can pick up $20,000, $30,000, $40,000, or whatever your fee is, in savings by selling it direct. Express that it is the company policy that there shall be no exclusions from the exclusive right of sale contract even for a limited time.

It is a business decision of the listing associate, however, to consider an exclusion. In the event it *is* the business decision of the listing associate to exclude a particular buyer, it should be only for a very limited time. For example, the exclusion should last no more than the two weeks during which time you are gearing up the listing. The listing agent should negotiate a reduced fee in the event the excluded party acquires the property even during this two week limited period. Specifically, the fee could be 25 percent of the normal fee if sold during the first week and, 50 percent of the normal exclusive right of sale fee if sold in the second week. In the event the excluded party acquires the property after the two week limitation, the full fee would be payable. Do not put yourself in a position of taking properties with exclusions.

"OTHER BROKERS WILL NOT WORK ON THE PROPERTY IF I LIST EXCLUSIVELY!!" This is another negative that you will hear. An answer to this is:

"Mr. Seller, I am a professional broker specializing in commercial real estate. I can look you in the eye and tell you that the only listings I will work on are controlled listings. I have no qualms about working on another broker's exclusive right of sale. I emphatically refuse to work on a listing that has a seller who has not been qualified to the extent that he is willing to sell and that the property research has not been done effectively on. It is extremely important that the professional take the time to generate the collateral material necessary to market your property."

"I JUST DON'T, NEVER HAVE AND NEVER WILL LIST WITH A BROKER." "Mr. Seller, a few moments ago you advised me that if I were to successfully sell your property you would be more than willing to pay me a fee. Most of the inquiries you have had on your property have been from brokers, have they not? So it is quite reasonable to assume that there is a very high probability that if your property sells, you will pay a brokerage fee. If you agree that you will pay a brokerage fee, does it not seem reasonable that you should get the services that you are paying for, including all of the marketing systems and services I have previously described? Wouldn't it be nice to know that you have someone representing you rather than the buyer? If you are going to pay the fee why not get full, just service?"

"I WOULD LIST WITH YOU, BUT MY BROTHER-IN-LAW IS IN THE BUSINESS." "It is important to cooperate with your family, but you have to agree that business is business. When it comes to your equity dollars, even your "brother-in-law," would not want you to do what would not be in your best interest. Is your brother-in-law capable of describing how he is going to market your property in the same detail I have just given you? Your brother-in-law can still earn 50 percent of the fee by selling the property, but at least you know that you have full time commercial-investment salespeople working on your behalf.

Closing Techniques

All answers to objections should lead to the close. Ask for the contract. The following are additional responses to objections that can be used to close on the exclusive right of sale listing.

A Broker Is the Best Negotiator

There are many psychological nuances in selling property. All are facilitated by using a third party as a sales intermediary. The owner may feel that he cannot consider the prospect's suggestion of a lower price, certain that if he makes one concession, he will be asked to make two or three. Therefore, he must brush aside, any suggestions of a change in price or terms unless he is prepared for a substantially larger concession.

It is almost impossible for a seller to effectively negotiate his position unless he professionally negotiates day in and day out. He is at an extreme disadvantage for getting the highest price in the sale of his property. The same reasoning applies to the buyer's position.

Using professional brokers, the principals can reach a satisfactory agreement with far greater ease. The broker can negotiate an offer between the prospective buyer and seller that can be considered by the seller with all the available facts at hand. The seller has the assurance that if he accepts the sale as presented or if he has another possibility in mind, the prospective buyer will be able to consider the counter-offer intelligently and make a prompt and wise decision.

Face-to-face negotiations can create an environment of gaming that does not always benefit either party. A buyer may be reluctant to talk frankly with the seller, but many will talk effectively with a broker. The buyer may avoid bringing up criticisms that must be answered before the sale can be made. He may be too proud to discuss his financial resources with the seller or ask for the terms he needs to close the transaction. If the seller cannot overcome these problems the broker can act as an intermediary.

Seller's Sensitivity

Many times the owner of the property may be inclined to be extremely sensitive about the property. Sometimes he might be offended if a prospective buyer criticizes it. The professional broker knows that criticism is the first step to the ultimate close. He can effectively handle criticisms and communicate the benefits to the potential buyer.

Sell Your Service

Brokers need to memorize the objections commonly voiced by owners. The seller must be convinced that the broker not only earns his fee, but in many, many cases has saved sellers considerable losses through effective and professional marketing.

"Mr. Seller, do you have computerized lists of prospects? Do you have access to numerous buyers and are you constantly on the phone generating buyers? Do you qualify and eliminate the lookers from the buyers? Can you show potential buyers other properties as comparables? Can you take a prospect to another property to show him the benefits of your property?

Are you familiar with the techniques of selling real estate? Do you know what the stamps cost on the deed? Are you familiar with title insurance? Can you show the property as effectively as we can as third party negotiators? Are you prepared to expose your property to any stranger that knocks on your door to see it? When we meet with someone, we meet in a business location and qualify the prospect prior to seeing your property. In today's world, doesn't it make sense to have the safety of a qualified prospect? Are you available on a full time basis until the property is sold to show the property, negotiate and prepare the contracts? Can you answer objections and criticisms without losing your temper? Do you have the time to call back prospects without placing yourself in a poor bargaining position? Can you draw a legally binding contract and include all the customary conditions necessary for your protection? Are you familiar with today's financing and do you have several sources of financing available in order to consummate the transaction? But most important, do you have the time to handle all these details?"

How many of the above reasons for using a broker can you repeat without looking?

Not one of these questions suggests that you already have a buyer for the property. You have not even developed your preliminary marketing plan or identified your target market. What you are selling is your real estate services, your company and yourself. Most of all, the seller must like and trust you and your company. You must build a trust relationship based on your ability to sell. A seller who believes you have done a good job in selling him on the listing will trust you. You will have created the trust relationship necessary to close future offers and counter-offers. Many owners may agree to an appointment simply to pick your brain in order to find the eventual buyer himself. If you identify the buyer on your first meeting, use caution not to involve your buyers or prospects until you have the exclusive right of sale. It is a risk talking about your buyers to your sellers first hand without the exclusive, but it is the best opportunity to persuade him to list his property with a professional.

Ask for the Listing

At the end of any listing presentation and, in this case it is assumed that you have seen the seller twice and have made your evaluation presentation, your listing agreement should be typed in full on a type-set standardized form. After you have made your final close, go through the physical effort of reaching down, grabbing your pen, holding it out and saying:

"Mr. Seller, please give me your okay so we can begin our marketing effort."

You have not asked him to sign a contract, you have asked him to give his okay so you can begin the action.

Listing Contracts

Standard residential listing agreements do not usually meet the needs of today's commercial-investment broker. The many methods the commercial broker uses dictates different fee structures. It is usually best to quote a rate or fee structure and reach a meeting of the minds with the seller prior to beginning a marketing effort. A standard listing agreement with a lease commission paid up front can be found in Book Two.

Summary

Here are some general comments that will help you in taking exclusive right of sale listings.

1. Create the business environment necessary to take listings.
2. Recognize the importance of having a neat, clean professional appearance when visiting any prospect.
3. Make certain that the seller needs professional marketing assistance and is motivated.
4. Review your listing pitch before you go into the presentation so that you are confident that you have the proper supplies, presentation manual and are mentally prepared for the listing.
5. Arrive on time. Arriving five or ten minutes late is not only irritating, it is rude.
6. Prepare and present your services and marketing plan with confidence.
7. Try to be attentive and look the seller in the eyes at all times if possible.
8. Keep a calm, low-key professional voice.
9. Be prepared to greet the seller's objections with humor, levity and cheerfulness.
10. Do insist that your clients sit in the seats you have determined to be best suited to the sales presentation. Lead the conversation by asking questions. Direct questions to all parties involved in the decision.

Practice your listing presentation on tape and/or video, if available. Have reasonable responses planned for each potential negative or objection you might encounter. Do not go into any listing presentation unprepared. Assemble enough market information to sound convincing and professional. At the bottom line, know you can take the listing, will take the listing and then *ask for the contract*.

4

Marketing Commercial-Investment Properties

The basic function of the commercial-investment broker and his company is to market commercial-investment real estate. When an exclusive right of sale listing is taken, the focus is on the act of selling the owner. The needs of the seller are emphasized: getting the highest price in the shortest time through constant marketing activity and the use of a selling system. However, when the property is marketed, the focus is on the needs of the buyer.

The marketing process itself is long-range and future oriented. The process started during the listing presentation when you defined the services to be offered by you and your firm. The *formal* marketing effort on that property began when you formally took the listing.

Once the listing is taken, the process of marketing begins with focusing on certain premises and targets. These premises and potential targets or prospects are then transformed into marketing activities. From this list of activities, a marketing plan is generated or established. The plan is used to guide the scheduling of operational activities—activities that will identify and locate buyers and sellers and then create and stimulate demand. As with any well thought-out plan, feedback from the marketing activities is needed. This feedback as well as a flexible plan allows for new and better marketing efforts until the objective of the effort is reached.

Jack Gale, in his *Introduction to Commercial-Investment Brokerage*, states: "There are three simple and easily understood steps to marketing any property. They are found by asking and answering the following questions:

1. Who is the potential buyer of the property?
2. Where is he now?
3. How do we reach him?"[1]

First, the potential needs that the property will satisfy must be identified in order to then identify the target or prospect. Then, a method of ascertaining how to contact that target must be found.

---

[1]Jack L. Gale, CRB, CRS, AFLM *Commercial-Investment Brokerage—An Introduction with Case Studies* (Chicago: REALTORS NATIONAL MARKETING INSTITUTE®, 1979), p. 40.

The flow of commercial-investment marketing tends to follow a consistent scenario:
1. planning the marketing,
2. contacting prospects,
3. solving problems,
4. closing the transaction.

The first two steps, planning the marketing and contacting the prospects will be dealt with in this chapter; items 3 and 4 are covered in Chapters 5 and 6.

Planning the Marketing

What makes a fast-track, successful marketing team is a marketing plan that is buyer and goal oriented. All the steps in planning your marketing efforts are logical and necessary. Taking the time to plan will make a big difference in your marketing success.

Keep Your Planning Simple

Your plan should be one that can be referred to with ease in spite of the day-to-day pressures. Marketing commercial-investment real estate is complex and competitive. Planning will help identify the most feasible approach in a maze of alternatives.

Make the Plan Flexible

A hard and fast rule in marketing is, "Do not rely on any one program." For example, do not expect the site sign to make all the contacts with prospective buyers. In addition, your plan should allow you to regroup, retreat and make variations as more information becomes available. However, avoid making more changes than necessary. Constantly changing your marketing programs will result in constantly changing feedback that cannot be relied on.

Form a Marketing Plan Team

Form a team, committee or group with fellow salespeople or with an informed member of management. The group synergism is dynamic. Your best targets are created from the enthusiastic participation of the members of your marketing team.

Keep a Loose-leaf Manual

A three-ring note book with each page devoted to a specific program allows easy reference for weekly and daily planning and allows convenient revisions.

Minimize Paper Work

Do not put all your planning in writing. Try to improve group communication, improve the environment of marketing creativity and improve individual relationships by discussing your marketing plan with your associates. Work in outline form as suggested in the Target Market Generator and the Marketing Plan Generator (see pages 34–35 and page 38). Discuss your marketing outline. Do not write essays.

Use Time Productively

Do not delegate the marketing plan. The person responsible for execution must review and improve the plan. Decisions should be made either by him or by someone very close to the situation. To create a marketing plan, the team must allocate uncommitted time—not time between phone calls or during high-energy periods such as negotiations or closings.

Get out of the office, if necessary. Fresh air helps some people open up. Avoid phone calls, distracting pressures and other responsibilities. Plan to meet during a productive period—late afternoon is good for some, early mornings work for others. Great plans can be developed over a long, scheduled lunch hour. Saturday mornings work best for the author. In fact this author has found that a bottle of wine in the park or on the property itself does wonders for the creative process. Tension narrows our ability to perceive; it is difficult to be creative when you are not relaxed and committed to the project at hand.

Answer Six Questions

All good marketing plans answer six basic questions:

1. Where are we now? This focuses on the product, the market, the seller's needs and the financial structure.

2. Where do we want to go? Are we looking for a cash sale, a 1031 exchange, an installment sale, or fast liquidation?

3. How will we reach our goals? Which programs will be used? For example:

- Sign program
- Broker programs
- Personal contact
- Direct mail
- Flyer

4. How should the programs be scheduled? When do we want the programs to take effect? Do we want to create 5,000 four-color brochures in the first week of a six-month exclusive right of sale? Or should we first contact, in person, the best prospects or targets on our marketing plan?

5. Who will implement the program?

Sign program	— Office manager
Broker program	— Salesperson and marketing department
Personal contact program	— Sales manager and salesperson
Direct mail	— Staff, with follow up by a salesperson

6. How much will it cost? We have a $10,000 commission. Can we spend $5,000 of the company's marketing dollars for this listing?

A close review of the marketing plan strategy that follows will demonstrate the creative process that experienced commercial salespeople follow either consciously or unconsciously. There is a strong inclination to create a standardized marketing plan, and to suggest that it is gospel, but there is no one sugar-coated pill that will solve all problems. A plan so standardized that a broker need only fill in the blanks to set up a sale does not lead to or reflect creative thinking.

Using the Target Market Generator

The salesperson has a choice; he can try to generate ideas with help or he can try to do it without help. The Target Market Generator presented on pages 34 and 35, can be used either as a tool to foster creative thinking or it can be passed over as just plain busy work.

Creativity comes from within, but it may be stimulated by an organized approach to planning. Feel free to add or subtract steps or processes within the Target Market Generator. This tool is like all tools—it will not fit every job exactly. It should be used along with your past experiences and those of others to market today's listing. It will help you focus on the key variables in planning the marketing.

The concept of planning the marketing and target marketing will be demonstrated here. Each step in the process will be examined and one example will be used throughout to demonstrate the thought process. This example will be a 40-acre tract of land. The importance of the example is in the thought process, not the specific sample conclusions reached about the 40 acres.

Where Are We Now?

The first step is to review and focus on the property itself and the motivations of the seller. This is easily done by referring to Section A of the Target Market Generator.

A. Listing Code _____   Date _____

   Property _____ Listing Price _____

   Owner's Desired Terms _____

   Owner's Stated Reason for Selling _____

   1. PROPERTY CHARACTERISTICS (BASIC)

      Zoning _____ APOD Owner statement _____

      Land Use _____

      Size _____ APOD Broker's Forecast _____

      Topography _____

      Water _____ Specialized Information _____

      _____

      Sewer _____ Construction _____

      _____

The section on property characteristics is brief and basic. It is intended only as a catalyst to get the marketing team tuned in to the property. The listing salesperson, who is usually the team leader, should supplement the basic information suggested with extensive background data on the property as well as on the owner's motivations. The team should use this to try to answer the question, "Where are we now?"

Financing is included in this step. Existing owner purchase money and new institutional money will both play important roles in the planning process.

2. FINANCING	Assumable Existing	Owner Pur. Mon.	New Institutional
Current Balance			
Annual Interest Rate			
Payment Am't & Frequency Remaining Term			
Assumption Provisions			
Prepayment Penalties			
Personal Endorsement			
Release Clauses			
Subordination Clauses			

a. What alternative financing approaches are available?

_____

b. What is the likely financial structure approach that will be used to close the sale?

_____

Financing will affect the potential target and the marketing plan. For example, a user-priced tract of vacant land (land priced for immediate use rather than for appreciation and future resale) may appeal to a speculator client if the owner will take five percent down and hold the balance over five years, interest only paid annually at ten percent. How would your marketing plan change if the owner of a $250,000 restaurant building said, "I'll sell to an operator, $10,000 down, balance over 20 years." Both examples illustrate how the financing structure opens up ideas of new prospects.

Question "a" should foster group thinking on alternative financial structures to meet the seller's objectives. Look down your list of financial structure problem-solving vehicles (presented in Chapter 5) for fresh new ideas. Free association demands an open mind.

Never, never "neg out" or throw out a negative such as, "It won't work because . . ." to your team. Encourage members to open up and be creative. This should result in an answer to Question "b," "What is the likely financial structure or approach that will be used to close the sale?"

Where Do You Want to Go?

After all the open—and sometimes wild—thinking about how to structure the sale, temper your enthusiasm in order to come up with the best approach, given all the variables and all the current information available to you. This step helps keep your programs from straying too far from the real world.

For example, a dealer who sells subdivision lots might offer all paper to the seller of the 40 acres. The seller, however, wants 20 percent cash, plus the income created from a purchase money mortgage. A more real world approach might be to suggest the dealer offer:

10% cash
10% paper (purchase money mortgages for sale of his lots)
80% purchase money mortgage to seller

This structure is between 20 percent down and an all paper offer.

In the example above, we have identified as a target prospect for our listing, a subdivision developer who has acquired paper from the sale of inventory or lots. We matched his need of vacant land with his financial structure going into the transaction.

The next small step is to convince the seller of the land that ten percent cash and ten percent paper meet his needs. If the seller must have 20 percent cash, we need only discount the paper for the cash. Keep in mind there are endless financial structures if we know where we want to go.

How Will We Get to Our Goals?

The step that requires the most creativity, experience and market information is developing the target markets. The 40 acres of vacant land might be best suited, based on zoning, characteristics of location and our perception of demand, for a subdivision. Therefore, we will target subdivision developers. Our marketing goal then is to contact subdivision developers.

The Idea Generators

The preliminary goal has been identified. Now, to focus even closer on the property, we will use the Idea Generators. These help us identify specific tactics to use in the marketing plan.

Idea Generator 1

How does the property relate to the market? Based on market price, property characteristics and financing, what are the best uses that will result in the highest price in the owner's time frame?

How the property relates to the market is impossible to determine if you have not studied the market and gathered the necessary background information. If our hypothetical seller's 40 acres of vacant land is a beautiful, rolling, tree-filled property, zoned eight units to the acre, across from the area's finest subdivision, targeting a mobile home park developer may be futile.

The owner's price is $30,000 per acre for the 40-acre tract. Your comparable market studies (sales of vacant land to other subdivision developers) indicate that this price works. The property characteristics are ideal for a single family subdivision. Trees bring big prices and the subdivision is located in a prestigious area. Determining the highest price that can be obtained within the owner's time frame may be a more difficult question.

Perhaps, for example, the zoning permits zero lot line housing, that is, housing built in clusters, usually contiguous. Your studies show that zero lot line developers can pay up to $4,500 per unit or $36,000 per acre.

40 acres × 8 units per acre = 320 units
320 units × $4,500 per unit = $1,440,000
$1,440,000 sales price (40 acres = $36,000 per acre)

What we have discovered is that we apparently have a target market that can pay up to $36,000 per acre for the same land. If single family subdivision developers are paying $30,000 per acre for comparable land and zero lot line developers are paying $36,000 per acre for comparable land, the best use that will result in the highest price in the owner's time frame is zero lot line development.

However, if the property requires rezoning for the zero lot line and this would take six months, the owner's time frame may dictate sale at the $30,000 per acre price.

This same thought process works for most types of property: investment property, improved commercial property, vacant land or whatever.

Idea Generator 2

Based on market conditions, what is the most sought after use—need—that the property could meet?

The marketing concept suggests that we satisfy needs, not sell just vacant land. As a salesperson becomes more proficient and knowledgeable about the market's needs and wants, he becomes a better planner and therefore a more successful salesperson.

Assume that our 40-acre tract of vacant land meets the needs of both zero lot line developers and subdivision developers and, at $20,000 per acre, would also meet the needs of a mobile home park developer.

Your market research tells you that the supply side of the zero lot line housing market is overbuilt and that inventory of zero lot line parcels exceeds the existing market's needs. However, your information from developers tells you there is a need for single family home acreage. Market conditions dictate that a plan that will meet with the highest probability of success will be directed at the conventional subdivision developer rather than the zero lot line developer market. Therefore, Idea Generator 2 focuses the marketing team on the needs that could be met by the property.

It is easier to empathize with the buyer's needs if you are willing to identify and understand the economics of various users, buyers, or investors. A salesperson must be or must become familiar with current market demands for the type of property he is marketing. This can be done by reviewing past market studies and marketing plans of similar properties and by calling developers and buyers to determine the economics of their needs.

Idea Generator 3

Describe and define the size and scope of the effective market for the subject property: local, state, out of state, world, investment/user, etc.

There may be a possible buyer in Japan for the 40 acres of vacant land; however, it seems unreasonable to try to contact a prospect in Japan if a more probable buyer is closer.

The number of potential prospects for a 300,000 square foot shopping center with 80 percent AAA credit tenants is significant on the world market. However, the number of qualified prospects within 50 miles in urban markets is usually sufficient to sell a product with such obvious international appeal.

Most experienced salespeople are constantly amazed by how obvious the prospects are once identified (targeted) and contacted. Your most logical and probably best buyers for most properties are usually closest to the property (there are exceptions to this rule). Contiguous property owners are usually good for a high percentage of sales each year; buyers within one mile represent an even higher percentage of annual sales. This is because most people are sold on the market they bought in before. The number of potential buyers for the hypothetical 40-acre tract of vacant land would drop significantly if it were exposed to buyers outside the state; within the county or the region, the number of prospects is much greater.

There is one other consistent reality that amazes experienced salespeople. Most sales are to people who have been sold to in the past or who are known by the broker though personal or market contact. And if your company maintains an active "want system" or mailing list, of course, a high percentage of prospects will be found on this list.

What this means is that many of our marketing approaches skip the obvious buyers. A salesperson may use a direct mail program to a new, specially designed list or undertake expensive ad campaigns only to sell the property to a member of his civic club three months later. Always attempt to focus your marketing as close as possible to the property and keep it even closer to your personal contacts.

Idea Generator 4

What use or user is missing or limited in the market?

This is a marketing question that especially lends itself to creative thinking about vacant land or vacant user property. As with all the Idea Generators, this is intended to provoke thought and discussion, not give pat answers. Perhaps the 40 acres of vacant land might best be used for a number of very exclusive five-acre ranchettes or a Nob Hill type development, a use that may be missing in the market.

A smaller, user out parcel (a tract, usually frontage, sold to freestanding users), on a shopping center parking lot would surely focus on what user is missing in the marketplace—a McDonalds, a Burger King or a Ponderosa Steak House, for example.

Idea Generator 5

What are the benefits this property offers?

There is a close correlation between needs and benefits. We communicate benefits and the property we sell fulfills needs. Our 40-acre tract of land fulfills a need for basic raw land that is necessary for building a subdivision. It may also fulfill the needs of water, sewer access and drainage. But what is important is how we translate the fulfillment of these needs to benefits. For example:

"Mr. Deserving Developer, we just listed the most beautiful, heavily treed profitmaker you ever laid eyes on. It is ready to go, zoned proper land use, water on site—ten-inch line and gravity feed sewer; and I have a plan to get it for just ten percent cash down."

Needs	Benefits
Land	Most beautiful, heavily treed
Water	Ready to go
Sewer	Gravity feed, no lift station
Minimum Cash Down	Plan to need minimum cash
Profit	Profit maker

Try to focus on the benefits you will communicate that meet the needs you have identified. Determining how to communicate benefits is part of the process of planning your marketing effort.

Idea Generator 6

Define the highest and best use of the property.

This is a concept that helps formulate a marketing plan. Highest and best use is commonly defined as "reasonable and profitable use that will support the highest present value."[2] A second definition specifically used for the highest and best use of land is "that use from among reasonable, probable and legal alternative uses, found to be physically possible, appropriately supported, financially feasible and which results in the highest land value."[3] In cases where the site has existing improvements on it, the highest and best use may very well be determined to be different from the existing use. The existing use will usually continue, however, unless and until land value in its highest and best use exceeds the total value of the property in its existing use.[4]

Close review of the highest and best use of a property will foster new and creative thinking about the property and prospects for the property.

Idea Generator 7

Given the above thought process, list in order of priority the general potential target prospects.

This list should be general, not as specific as listing the ABC Land Development Company of Dr. Jones. The thrust of Generator 7 is to focus on

---

[2]Byrl N. Boyce, *Real Estate Appraisal Terminology*, (Cambridge, MA: Ballinger Publishing Co., 1975), p. 107.
[3]Ibid
[4]Ibid

general markets suggested by Generators 1–6. Markets for our 40-acre tract might include:

1. Subdivision Land Developer

Developers who develop lots to sell to users and builders in the $85,000 + home price range.

2. Zero Lot Line Developer

Developers who develop for the $65,000 + zero lot townhouse projects.

Using the Marketing Plan Generator

Idea Generators 1 through 7 only help the marketing team identify goals and potential targets for contact. The question of what programs should be used to make contact with the targets is all important.

A "program" as loosely used in the context of this marketing plan is an activity to contact potential prospects and generate new contact ideas. At this stage in the marketing process, an attempt is made to identify specific prospects to contact and programs to generate prospects. Some methods of identifying prospects are:

1. Study sales of similar properties. Look at terms and transaction structures. Call sellers or their brokers. Ask how contact with the buyer was made and what motivated the prospects to buy the tract. Call the buyer; ask if he is looking for another property.

2. Approach the local zoning department for prospects that have made use of similar properties.

Programs to contact prospects are numerous:

- Signs
- Personal contact
- Classified ads
- Direct mail
- *Wall Street Journal*

A detailed list of contact programs can be found in Book Two; however, Figure 4-1 serves as an example. You should have a three-ring, loose-leaf

Figure 4-1

CONTACT PROGRAMS
PROGRAMS TO GENERATE NEW PROSPECTS
1. Joint venture—start one, sell interest in-house
2. Auction all or part—worst or best
3. Contact building supply company managers for prospects, i.e., lot users
4. Contact tenants in existing properties managed by company
5. Press release on new listing
6. Complete "Marketing Plan Generator"
7. Contact site selection departments of major franchises
8. Check local universities—real estate, business departments
9. For sale by owner—look for exchange potential
10. Call CCIM in another market to hash out ideas

---

marketing notebook that includes a similar marketing idea list covering programs for generating new prospects as well as programs to contact these prospects. The Marketing Plan Generator, Figure 3-3, page 38, will also help you to focus on all the various programs available to you as a broker.

How Should the Programs Be Scheduled?

There is an obvious limit to how much time and money can be spent in establishing programs to contact prospects. Once you have selected a group of programs at random using the team approach, the next step is to assign a priority number on the program list.

In scheduling programs, the most logical target should be personally contacted first. In other words, the marketing programs should be scheduled so that the highest probability programs that are within the budgeting constraints are scheduled first (Item 5, Developing Market Programs). Less

---

A. DEVELOPING MARKETING PROGRAMS
  1. Marketing programs should be developed based on time and cost.
  2. Primary focus on target prospect/market.
  3. Develop plan based on needs that property can satisfy.
  4. List ALL of various programs that logically should facilitate a sale.
  5. Schedule programs:
    a. Highest probability first.
    b. As schedule is developed, choose programs with highest probability that fall within budget until allocated funds are exhausted.

B. LIST PROGRAMS BEST SUITED FOR PLAN—HIGHEST PROBABILITY VS. COST.

1	10
2	11
3	12
4	13
5	14
6	15
7	16
8	17
9	18

---

specific, more general programs such as large, direct mail campaigns should be scheduled later in the marketing strategy. When an excellent prospect has been identified, it is logical to contact that specific prospect prior to attempting programs that will generate new prospects. Why direct mail 100 targeted developers with a flyer on the subdivision when we have already identified at least ten specific developers who are potential takers of the listed property?

The list of marketing programs developed to generate prospects should be implemented only after actual primary or specific targeted prospects have been contacted personally by the salesperson. The programs and prospects should be scheduled on a marketing schedule (Figure 4-2). It is

Figure 4-2

```
+---------------------------------------------------------------+
|                    MARKETING SCHEDULE                         |
|                                                               |
|     DATE              PROGRAM              ACTION             |
|   _____         _____           _____            |
|   _____         _____           _____            |
|   _____         _____           _____            |
|   _____         _____           _____            |
|   _____         _____           _____            |
|   _____         _____           _____            |
+---------------------------------------------------------------+
```

useful not to put a specific date at time of scheduling because the actual date that the program is implemented will often be governed by the response and success of previous programs. Flexibility is often useful when it comes to specific dates for program implementation. This open schedule requires a great deal of self-discipline on the part of the person responsible for the marketing effort. If you cannot keep a continuous flow of activity on a listing schedule, use specific date deadlines as mini-goals and personal motivators.

The most common cause of failure to sell a listed property is not lack of sales expertise, but lack of consistent well thought-out marketing efforts. The hit and miss approach results in a hit and miss sales record and income. Steady, intelligent, continuous effort gives steady income.

Who Will Implement the Program?

In a small office, the salesperson is responsible for most marketing activities. In larger operations, many such activities are handled by staff and management personnel. Careful scheduling and follow up by the salesperson is necessary to guarantee a satisfactory response no matter what the size of the operation, however. (The Office Procedure Checklist, Figure 4-3, helps keep track of this information.)

How Much Will It Cost?

Most companies have a set policy for marketing and promotional expenses. Management governs most policy, but this can be influenced and directed by the sales and marketing team. Section C, illustrated on page 61, from the Marketing Plan Generator, can be filled in to help develop the budget.

The number of dollars that can be spent on a listing is, for the most part, a function of the number that will be earned. Therefore, it is important that the fee be entered on the form.

If the probability of a co-brokerage sale is high, it means there will be fewer company dollars—there will be less available to promote the listing. Sometimes the listing agreement provides for owner participation in the promotion of the property. Once the total amount of available money is known, the agreed upon discretionary dollars available for marketing should be allocated to the most effective programs first until all budgeted dollars are expended.

C. DEVELOPING MARKETING BUDGET
  • What is estimated fee?
  • What is percentage probability of co-brokerage?
  • What is total dollar to be expended in marketing?

Allocate to Programs:		
	Gross Fee	$_____
	Co-brokerage	$_____
	In-house salesperson	$_____
	Company	$_____
	Classified	$_____
	Direct mail	$_____
	Signage	$_____
	Other (special publications, etc.)	$_____

Write Down Prospects as They Are Identified

Throughout the marketing plan process, the names of various potential prospects should come to mind. If you are in your car, write them down. If you are in the shower, write them down. As a prospect is identified, transfer the name of that person or firm to the Marketing Plan Generator, see Figure 3-3 page 38. When you have completed your schedule, contact prospects based on highest probability.

Many of your best prospects will come early in the market research phase when you are fresh and not influenced by the negatives encountered later in the listing period.

Initiating a Feedback System

Let's stop a moment to see where we are in the market scenario. The basic product and its apparent position in the marketplace have been discussed and are understood by the marketing team. Programs to contact known prospects and programs to generate or identify new prospects have been scheduled. Certain programs will be long term and require a defined and thought-out plan.

Once the programs are developed, it is time to initiate the individual office start-up procedure. If you do not have a procedure, establish one to avoid missing important steps and basic marketing programs. **Figure 4-3** illustrates a useful office procedure checklist.

Figure 4-3

OFFICE PROCEDURE CHECKLIST

LISTING CODE: _____
PROPERTY: _____
DATE: _____

Marketing Startup

	Responsi-bility	Initials	Date Completed
Establish Action File	Staff		
Establish Listing Code	Staff		
Add to Master Inventory	Staff		
Add to Current Listing Inventory	Staff		
Place on Sales Meeting Agenda	Staff/SP*		
Sign Placement Ordered	SP		
Notify Front Desk of Listing	Staff/SP		
Complete Marketing Plan	SP		
Complete Property Flyer	SP		
Complete Property Profile	SP		
Newsletter Narrative	SP		
Add to Local MLS	Staff		
Establish Marketing Team Meeting	SP		
Confirm Marketing Budget with Management	SP		

*Salesperson

Any professional marketing effort requires a good feedback system—a system that identifies prospect responses and records the problems encountered in the sales presentation. This is also part of the all important seller education/information processs. Figure 4-4 illustrates a helpful feedback form that also serves as a log to help identify any marketing problems that might occur.

From this internal log you should report back to the owner regarding the success or failure of various marketing programs you have tried.

Figure 4-4

ACTIVE LISTING MARKET FEEDBACK

LISTING NAME _____   CODE _____

WEEK OF _____

Direct action taken to market property:

_____

_____

_____

Owner contacted by phone, in person, letter, etc. (at least once a week)

_____

_____

_____

People contacted and how contacted:

_____

_____

_____

Why hasn't listing sold?

_____

_____

_____

What would help sell listing?

_____

_____

_____

What adjustments should be made to marketing plan (see Problem-Solving
Procedure)?

_____

_____

_____

                                        _____
                                        Salesperson

Owner Education

A secret to selling commercial-investment real estate is the owner education/information process. Too many salespeople assume the owner knows what the salesperson is doing. If the owner has not heard from you, he assumes you are doing nothing even if you have been knocking yourself out trying to sell his property. Educating the seller is also part of the marketing program.

Owner, or seller, education includes informing the owner of buyer or prospect response, supplying him with activity reports and filling him in on market conditions and the economics of the sale. Many times elaborate presentations about how the property relates to the market need to be used to educate the seller. These presentations have little to do with the potential buyer, but this client information and education is the step that closes many transactions.

Many transactions require an overt planned approach to owner education. This formal information presentation is especially effective with bank and corporate boards of directors and trust departments where many people affect a decision. Even the most knowledgeable real estate seller needs current information on the market. If you skip the education phase, you should be prepared to go unpaid.

Information is power and is necessary to counsel a seller. People do not make poor decisions intentionally. They make decisions based on information, which may be erroneous (a poor appraisal perhaps), or out of fear—fear that a decision will be wrong. The belief that a decision is a correct one eliminates that fear. Fear is usually caused by the unknown. You can eliminate the unknown with information. Show your client the list of showings of his property. Discuss the responses, show comparable sales, produce engineering reports, soil tests, investment analysis and any other information that will support your marketing plans and the contract offers and counteroffers.

To Review

Marketing commercial-investment real estate requires a balance of product knowledge, market knowledge and people knowledge. An absence of proficiency in any one of these three categories leads to low sales volume, frustration and sometimes even a new job.

Think about the marketing process described in Chapters 3 and 4. The early stages dealt with product and market knowledge. The process that involved creativity was the interplay between information on the product and information on the market.

As the marketing plan was developed, programs that would help us identify prospects were focused on. Then programs were chosen that would make contact with these prospects. Examples of contact programs include direct mail, personal contact and signs. These programs for thinking of and contacting prospects are personal and may even be regional in terms of how well they perform.

The marketing plan was designed around specific, probable and feasible methods of making contact. The intent of the market planning process is to brainstorm and develop targets or best potential prospects.

Despite all your efforts to market a property and educate the seller, you will sometimes run into a real problem—a listing that just won't sell. Chapter 5, "Problem-Solving Techniques," will attempt to help you effectively market these properties. But first, here is a short discussion of that important marketing tool, the property profile.

Appendix to Chapter 4:
Preparation of a
Property Profile

T he effective communication of property information may take several forms. Two popular categories for this communication are the property brief and the property profile.

Property Brief

A property brief, somtimes referred to as a property flier, is not intended to provide enough information to close the transaction or to answer all or even most of the potential purchaser's questions. The purpose of the brief is to stimulate inquiries. The brief should focus on the anticipated target or prospective users/investors. It is intended to be an overview and should not give out any more essential information than is necessary to generate the call. The flyer or brief should make contact and arouse curiosity. It is relatively inexpensive to produce on a mass basis compared to the more extensive property profile. *Showcasing Commercial Properties*[1] is an excellent reference for preparation of the property brief.

Property Profile

Unlike the brief, the property profile is intended to give detailed information and descriptions of the property beyond the scope of what you would normally expect to give to a casual observer. The property profile is a rather complete presentation of the salient details necessary to make a decision about acquisition. It is also considerably more expensive to produce and therefore should be given only to selected and qualified purchasers.

A profile is an essential marketing tool that should normally be prepared on all exclusive right of sale listings. It is an ongoing public relations tool as well as a communication device. The property profile is designed to provide the inquiring party with sufficient information upon which to base his conditional acceptance or rejection of a property. Buyers need all the facts to make the big decision.

Usually, the opening page of the profile should include information on

---

1. Jerome S. Metzger, *Showcasing Commercial Properties*, (Chicago, REALTORS NATIONAL MARKETING INSTITUTE®, 1980).

the company, either a letterhead sheet or a standard sheet with detailed phone number and address information for easy reference. In preparing the property profile itself, the first page should be devoted to an introductory narrative. This should be no more than a paragraph in length and should include a sales pitch directed toward your target market. This pitch is intended to excite the reader so he will go deeper into the property profile. All profiles will include maps featuring the city, county and sometimes the state, if marketing is planned for outside the general area. Usually it is most cost-efficient to limit such maps to one page each. Plot plans and floor layouts should also be reduced to 8 ½ by 11 inches, if possible, when they are included in the property profile. These standardized sizes will increase the reader's ability to absorb information quickly by allowing him to see the maps, plans, etc. at one glance, without having to unfold and refold pages. For property profiles of less than five pages, it is not necessary to include an index as it adds to the preparation costs.

Profiles should be limited to approximately ten pages. An overly long profile results in extensive photo copying which takes up staff time and results in an uninviting package for the reader. Preparing these overly cumbersome property profiles is probably the most common error made by the professional broker. It is not the intent that the profile bury the reader, only inform him. For example, most people are not interested in the entire zoning code, only that portion that directly applies to the acquisition.

All property profiles (and flyers) should be produced by one person in the organization in order to maintain consistency, especially in regard to logos, disclaimers and the general quality of the presentation. The listing associate should prepare the detailed original draft and layout and give this information to the person in charge of producing the profile. The profile should be standardized using all possible cost-cutting steps including utilizing company equipment. For instance, the text of the profile can be produced on a word processor or typewriter and transferred to either letterhead or high quality paper by using a dry copier machine. The profile may be bound in-house by using a punch and a spiral binding system. Maps, other graphic details and photographs may also be attached and bound into the profile. This is an effective way to quickly produce the necessary information for a professional presentation.

There are properties that require more sophisticated property profiles. A shopping center or office complex would demand very complete profiles in order to provide a complete analysis. These sophisticated property profiles, more expensive to produce than simpler ones, should be distributed on a very limited basis, only after the prospects have been qualified with the preliminary presentation. Properties warranting custom brochures, profiles with extensive marketing information or detailed technical information, should be prepared professionally. In any case, if more than 25 profiles are to be distributed, it will usually be less expensive to have a professional brochure prepared and printed. It is very expensive to continuously prepare numerous extensive property profiles by hand, in-house.

In all profiles, whether prepared in-house or professionally, the following information must at least be addressed, if not discussed fully.[2]

---

2. Credit must be given to Jack Pyle, CCIM, of the National Real Estate Exchange for his development of the property profile format.

1. A basic physical description of the property
2. A statement of the highest and best use of the property
3. Address, including city and state, and/or directions to the property
4. Maps (both state and local) showing the location of the property
5. Legal description of the property (shown exactly as on the deed)
6. Name(s) of the title holder(s) (shown exactly as on the deed)
7. A summary of assumable loans including:

   a. Current principal balance

   b. Annual interest rate

   c. Payment amount and frequency

   d. Remaining term

   e. Assumption provisions

   f. Prepayment penalties

   g. Participation clauses

   h. Release clauses

   i. Subordination clauses

8. A summary of purchase money financing available incuding terms and conditions
9. A summary of any new institutional financing available including:

   a. Length of commitment

   b. Amount

   c. Annual interest rate

   d. Payment amount and frequency

   e. Maximum term available

   f. Estimated loan closing costs

   g. Special loan qualification requirements

10. A description of the physical condition of any improvements on the property and estimated cost of any repairs and/or maintenance needed
11. A complete rent roll, incuding:

    a. Current actual unit rents

    b. Tenant identification (except residential tenants)

    c. Terms of lease

    d. Lease escalation clauses

    e. Lease renewal options

    f. Lease insurance currently in force

    g. Unit square footage

12. Properties with income (including agricultural properties) require the following income and expense data:

    a. An owner's statement showing the actual performance of the property for a minimum of the past 12 months

    b. A broker's forecast, based on current information, showing a realistic projection of how it should perform for the next 12 months

13. A survey, plat or sketch showing dimensions
14. A minimum of one ground level photo of the property
15. A summary of current taxes including assessments and allocation to land and improvements
16. A statement regarding zoning, including:

    a. Current zoning classification and a copy of appropriate sections of the current zoning regulations

    b. If the property is vacant and/or a change of zoning is indicated, the zoning for the highest and best use, including a copy of the appropriate sections of the current zoning regulations

17. A statement regarding the availability of utilities, including:
    a. Sewer
    b. Water
    c. Electricity
    d. Telephone
    e. Natural gas
    f. Costs for connection
18. A statement regarding the availability of transportation, including (as applicable):
    a. Highway
    b. Railroad
    c. Port facilities
    d. Airport
    e. Mass transit
19. A description of any "will add" paper (third party mortgages owned by seller, available to be added in form of additional equity), including:
    a. Current principal balance
    b. Annual interest rate
    c. Payment amount and frequency
    d. Remaining term
    e. Assumption provisions
    f. Prepayment penalties
    g. Participation clauses
    h. Release clauses
    i. Priority of the lien, if it is secured
    j. Type, location, and current market value of the property encumbered, if secured
    k. Payment record of the mortgagor
    l. Personal liability of the mortgagor
    m. Discount from the face value of the paper acceptable to owner.
20. Depending upon the specific type of property being offered, much additional specialized information may need to be included in order for a potential taker to give conditional acceptance of the offering.

An example of what can be included in a property profile is presented in Chapter 7.

5

Problem-Solving Techniques

I t goes without saying that there are properties and transactions that try the patience of even the most experienced veteran salesperson. You planned your work and worked your plan. You scheduled and then followed the schedule religiously. And for this you drew a big zero: zero contracts, zero offers! Your seller is starting to smile less and may even mention the expiration date on your exclusive. Your sales manager is sure to bring up the problem in the general sales meeting. You may have made the unconscious decision to avoid working on a loser. The salesperson who can continue to face rejection over and over is one of a rare breed.

There are two types of problems, the first, involves marketing, the second, transaction problems. When you hit a listing that is tough and your personal inclination is to avoid working on it, it is time to look at the Problem-Solving Procedure. In the overall listing and marketing procedure described on page 49, this is step number 3. This will help you determine where your problem is. Is it with marketing? Or, do you have plenty of prospects but can't close?

There is no magic to the problem-solving procedure. This procedure simply directs your attention back to the planning stage. Yes, back to the marketing plan. A salesperson will continue to work a listing for which he has exciting prospects; but to work a property that he is burned out on is tough. The best way to break a slump is with a sale. The best way to get a sale is to get the marketing program moving again. The best way to do this is with a new, or even an old, hot prospect. The alternative is to do nothing and hope for a call on the sign or a co-broker sale.

Figure 5-1

PROBLEM-SOLVING PROCEDURE

STEP 1—Define Problem

_____

_____

_____

STEP 2—Determine Cause

_____

_____

_____

STEP 3—Determine Alternatives (Free Association)

_____

_____

_____

STEP 4—Evaluate Alternatives

_____

_____

STEP 5—Select Alternatives

_____

_____

STEP 6—Choose Optimum Solution

_____

_____

STEP 7—Adjust Marketing Plans, Schedule, Targets, Budget

_____

_____

_____

White Copy—Client, Canary Copy—Manager, Pink Copy—Sales Associate

The procedure outlined in Figure 5-1 is not magic, but it is time-tested and has worked on many properties. We will go through the steps one by one.

Step 1—Define the Problem

Sixty to 90 days into a listing, you have enough information and market experience to make some assumptions about why you think the property has not sold. Write out these various problems.
- Is the problem seller inflexibility on price or terms?
- Is it a zoning problem?
- Is there a problem connecting to a sewer plant?
- Is there an access problem?
- Are prospects turned off by the topography?
- Is it a parking problem?
- Is just finding a prospect to show the property to the problem?

The variations to the problems are endless.

As you can see, most problems are either people problems or physical property problems. For example, if the seller's price is at the top of the market range and he wants all cash, seller education may be the order of the day. If your property is priced as if a sanitary sewer were available, but in fact, it is a mile away, find out the cost of running the sewer in and then try to get a price cut allowance for the sewer run. In other words, define the problems and then write them out.

Step 2—Determine the Cause

Once the problem is identified, the next step is determining the cause of the problem. For example, a pricing problem or problem with terms may be the result of a poor appraisal or an error in an appraisal upon which the seller is relying. The seller may have called a few broker signs in the market and made an erroneous judgment of market value. The seller may perceive his purchase money mortgage as a bank mortgage and may want the prime rate. A sewer problem may be just a matter of a salesperson having accepted the utility department's verbal statement over the phone that no sewer is available in that area. Further investigation might show that an error was made and a sewer may be available just 200 feet west of the property.

What is the cause of the problem? Determine this and write it down.

Step 3—Determine the Alternatives

This is where the marketing team can work for you. Toss the problems out on the floor and sit back and make notes on possible solutions and ideas. Never respond, "That will not work because . . ." Hear out your team, then offer feedback. Free association uses many minds in open synergism to create solutions.

For example, a pricing problem may be handled by having a short meeting with the appraiser to discuss the error in the appraisal. It may be necessary to make a frontal attack on the validity of the appraisal based on new or updated information.

The example of a sewer problem is one that almost always can be solved. The solution usually depends on how much money can be spent and how much time is available. Both questions can be addressed by a professional engineer. For example, he could suggest a new lift station and a mile of force main. A sewer moratorium might require a request for a hardship variance. Another solution might be building special holding tanks to hold effluent which would be released at night during non-peak hours. And you can sometimes build a sewer plant. Both economics and time will play an important role in the process. As always, information will help make the sale both from the seller's and the buyer's perspectives.

Step 4—Evaluate Alternatives

Simply stated, this step involves determining the alternatives that will be most likely to lead to a successful conclusion based on time and cost. In Step 4 the results of the creative process are discussed.

In the pricing problem example, calling the appraiser to tell him he was given the wrong size tract of land may solve the problem caused by an error in the appraisal if such an error has been made. With the sewer problem, you may want to suggest to the seller that he contract with an engineer to estimate the cost of a lift station and force main. If the seller's property is priced as if a sewer is available, adjust the price by the cost of the lift station and force main. Or even better, promote the property at the higher price and advise prospects that the seller will install the sanitary sewer. From the buyer's perspective, this eliminates all fear of the sewer cost.

All these solutions are evaluated; the pros and cons are determined. Evaluating the alternatives is really a grading process used prior to selecting the best alternatives.

Step 5—Select the Alternative(s)

This selection is usually based on many variables including the personalities of the people involved. Choose the two alternatives that fit your situation best. You may want to attack from two or more directions, then select the right alternative. Step 5 requires a formal selection of an alternative to pursue.

Step 6—Choose the Optimum Solution

What results are you looking for? If the alternative of, for example, showing the appraiser the error, is chosen, what is the expected solution? You want the seller to realize that a price reduction on the appraisal is necessary. In the example of the sewer problem, if an engineer is hired to solve the problem, the risk to the buyer is eliminated and the seller will know the impact of the sewer on the value of his property.

After finishing Step 6, we have chosen a path and made a judgment as to the desired results and the expected destination.

Step 7—Adjust Marketing Plans, Schedule, Targets, Budget

Often the problem is identified, the solution is selected and it all ends there because there is no follow through. Who will contact the appraiser and when will he be contacted? The top MAI[1] appraiser in your market might better be approached by your sales manager than by you. The cost of consulting a sewer engineer for the sewer problem has to be paid by some-one. Is it the brokerage firm's or the owner's cost? Yes, the firm may see that incurring an engineering cost is a valid marketing expense, usually when the owner will absolutely not pay. The successful broker does what has to be done to consummate a sale. This is where the marketing budget comes back into the picture. More dollars may be necessary to sell the property. These dollars are for problem solving, not just promotion. While the selection of alternatives is in progress or after it is complete, schedule the *new* marketing plan.

Then, back to the prospects who rejected the property based on pricing or terms. Back to the developers who said, "We need a sewer." As you can see, we have gone full circle in our marketing plan flowchart. The creative commercial-investment salesperson plans programs, studies responses and persistently looks for solutions.

Structuring Transactions to Solve Problems

Your review of the Problem-Solving Procedure may indicate that your marketing plan *has* worked, and you have prospects but need to find a suitable transaction structure to solve the problem. Many new salespeople try to make decisions for the client or cut the transaction close to the seller's stated expectation, whether it be all cash, 30 percent down, balance in three years or whatever. Close observation of successful commercial brokers reveals a subconscious thought process that says simply, "What I need in order to make money is a 'haver' [someone who has property] and a 'taker' [someone who will take the property]." Stop and think about that thought process. Are your creative juices blocked by, "Where are we going to get financing," or "My seller said bring just the cash-only offer."

---

1. Member, Appraisal Institute. This designation is awarded by the American Institute of Real Estate Appraisers to members who have proven their ability to appraise all types of real property.

Open up your brokerage potential and look for someone who wants what you have, not always someone who wants it with a predetermined transaction or with the particular financial structure you have. With the "I need a taker" attitude, your first goal is to identify and make contact with a taker; then you will worry about the transaction.

Now, for the fun part. We have made contact with a prospect who says, "I will take the property at _____ terms." (Take means lease, joint venture or simply steal.) What is your response to the taker? "Sorry, zero down will not work with my seller,"—wrong, wrong, wrong. Your response should be, "That seems like a difficult transaction structure. How about five percent down, (or ten percent or whatever)." Remember, you only asked— you did not decide for the seller. Your taker says, "100 percent purchase money mortgage or I am not interested." Your response, "Good, let's go to contract and make an offer." First, get the taker emotionally involved and then solve the structural problems of the transaction.

Not all problems can be solved, but most can if you have the basic ingredient: a motivated seller. The process of solving problems has not changed. Grab a problem-solving form (Figure 5-1) and think. Then all you have to do is identify the problem, find the solution and close. It looks so good on paper and was so easy to write down but it is so hard to do. But, if everyone could do it (solve the problems), sellers would not pay us as much as they do.

The transaction and negotiation problems that brokers encounter just do not fit into nice, little, easy to remember categories. There are hundreds, if not thousands of transaction structures that will help solve people problems. For lack of a better method of indexing problem solving transaction structures, 25 typical or common transaction problems have been identified in Figure 5-2. Figure 5-3 offers 106 possible solutions.

Because this business depends on the proper use of time, there just is not time to read 20 pages of potential solutions. In addition, most people do not have the ability or experience to apply all of the financial structures suggested. Therefore, the potential solutions to each of the 25 problems are numerically listed under each problem. Choose the one that will work best for you. In this way, you will not have to read through all the solutions to find the one that you need. After you have read the following transaction problems, think of a transaction problem not covered. If you think of one, add it to your own list of transaction structure problems.

As an example of how to use the problem-solving list, suppose our taker says he can afford the property based on an all purchase money mortgage structure. Our seller wants all cash. Go to the list of common transaction problems on pages 76 and 77. Find the one that fits your problem. Look for a solution number; go to the proposed solution and look for a potential fit or perhaps come up with a variation. Read all proposed solutions with an open mind to the many variations or combinations of solutions that are available.

Often the salesperson can forecast the seller's response. Part of presenting the offer is to have both a recommendation for the counteroffer and a plan for implementing the recommendation.

The taker we found offered no cash down and the balance in a purchase money mortgage. The problem-solving list would suggest that this problem falls within category D:

"Qualified buyer or developer wants property, but is short of cash or wants to put cash in project or property work-out, not in down payment."

Suggested solutions include 1, 2, 6, 7, 8, 9, 10, 11, 12, 13, 14, 15, 16, 17, 18, 19, 20, 21, 22, 23, 24, 25, 26, 32, 34, 46, 70, 80, 81, 82, 100.

There are 31 potential solutions to this problem listed. One of them should give you an idea for a contract presentation, a negotiation strategy or some other action. Solution 32 looks like a good place to start. You could suggest to the seller that he sell the land under the building to an investor for cash at closing and hold the balance of the purchase price in a purchase money mortgage. This new land buyer would simultaneously lease the land(s) to the original buyer who was interested in the property. The investor gets a cash flow from the landlease; the buyer gets the building and the depreciation plus other benefits associated with owning the improvements; the end result is effectively 100 percent financing to the new building owner (buyer). The seller gets cash down resulting from the land being sold at closing.

Here's another example. The landlease buyer, described above, has a net leased land investment. This buyer may have to subordinate and is afraid that it is too much risk. In this problem, the land buyer has a question of risk. Reviewing the common transaction problems, we look for problems that deal with risk. This problem falls into category G:

"Seller thinks sale is too risky. He is concerned that he will get property back or be foreclosed. Does not want risk, hassle or aggravation."

Solution 25 suggests offering a letter of credit from the buyer which should secure the landlease buyer.

Most problems can usually be solved by using new, creative approaches especially when the buyer is a taker and the seller is a serious "don't wanter." It is also helpful to study various problem-solving tools on a regular basis, perhaps monthly, just for reinforcement. This may seem complicated, but the problems we solve are complicated. To solve problems, you need a "never die" attitude.

Figure 5-2

COMMON NEGOTIATION AND TRANSACTION PROBLEMS

A. Price or terms are a problem. Broker unable to bring buyer and seller together.

35, 36, 43, 47, 48, 49, 50, 51, 52, 53, 57, 58, 59, 60, 67, 75, 81, 82, 85, 90, 94, 95, 101

B. Cash flow from property is low, nonexistent or negative during early ownership period.

45, 60, 67, 93, 95, 101, 105

C. Seller wants larger down payment.

25, 27, 35, 46, 57, 58, 68, 105

D. Qualified buyer or developer wants property, but is short of cash or wants to give cash in project or property work-out, not in down payment.

1, 2, 6, 7, 8, 9, 10, 11, 12, 13, 14, 15, 16, 17, 18, 19, 20, 21, 22, 23, 24, 25, 26, 32, 34, 46, 70, 80, 81, 82, 100

E. Property has questionable future cash flows and property or price is based on specific cash flows that are subject to change or challenge.

3, 5, 6, 35, 47, 58, 67, 85, 93, 94, 95, 105

F. Property is a big problem property. Seller wants out. Seller may be willing to take a loss.

6, 19, 47, 57, 58, 79, 97

G. Seller thinks sale is too risky. He is concerned that he will get property back or be foreclosed. Does not want risk, hassle or aggravation.

4, 25, 31, 35, 38, 39, 42, 78, 91, 102

H. Buyer wants lower purchase price and will give additional security to seller.

18, 21, 25, 31, 32, 33, 84, 102

I. Buyer needs more cash for down payment. Seller wants additional collateral or letter of credit.

30, 31, 32, 39, 46, 82

J. Seller needs cash, wants to discount mortgage. Also, he wants installment sale.

29

K. Need financing? Need a private lender or a financial institution?

7, 12, 13, 14, 15, 16, 17, 18, 20, 23, 25, 38, 39, 40, 41, 44, 54, 55, 56, 58, 69, 70, 81, 85, 86, 87, 88, 89, 94, 97.

L. Due-on-sale clause problems.

41, 73(a,b,c,d,e)

M. Subordination requested. Seller says no.

24, 38, 39, 74(a,b,c,d,e,f,g)

Figure 5-2, continued

N. New first mortgage needs to be obtained by buyer, and seller wants installment sale.

61, 63

O. Buyer or tenant needs to occupy property. He has no down payment or says he cannot afford it.

27, 99, 102, 103

P. User wants to lease, not buy. Seller wants to sell, not lease.

28, 102, 106

Q. Developer/user needs property for development. Seller wants installment sale.

37, 62, 63, 65

R. Need fast sale.

46, 47, 57, 84, 86, 105

S. Parties want S 1031 Exchange. No like-kind property available.

60, 66

T. Tax problems: capital gain recapture problem or income tax problems on sale or exchange structure.

60, 64, 65, 67, 68, 71, 72

U. Seller wants out of personal property (boat, camper, airplane).

35, 47, 105

V. Seller decides not to sell.

98, 102

W. Personal liability or personal guarantee required by seller.

38, 39, 96

X. Landlease on property.

83, 102

Y. Attorney or other advisor is a "deal killer."

76, 77

Z. Broker needs control of property to:
   1) conduct research on feasibility, marketing, engineering
   2) pre-lease
   3) obtain financing
   4) re-sell
   5) structure a 1031 exchange.

92, 104

Figure 5-3

TRANSACTION STRUCTURE SOLUTIONS

1. Acquire 100 percent purchase money first or assume first. Seller holds second mortgage.

   D

2. Mortgage 100 percent—obtain first mortgage for development based on appraisal. Keep cost below acquisition and development cost.

   D

3. Refinance existing mortgage. Seller holds second mortgage, creates cash in transaction for seller. Down payment is net between old first and new first mortgage.

   E

4. Use additional collateral for cash. Give home or other property. Create secured paper guaranteeing seller that note will not be defaulted.

   G

5. Use performance purchase money mortgage. The purchase money mortgage payments are a function of asset cash flow. Good vehicle to test seller's faith in income representations.

   E

6. Pledge future income as down payment. In turn-around project, it is useful to make down payment in a series of installments as project turns around.

   D, E, F

7. Exchange other property for down payment. Other real property such as: listed and unlisted stock, bonds that may have fallen below face value, partial interest in other real estate or personal property.

   D, K

8. Use broker's commission as a down payment.

   D

9. Use sweat equity, also known as effort equity, as ownership interest. Expertise in assisting partnership or help in property work-out, contractor fees, legal fees, engineering fees, plumbing may be used in lieu of cash, any other service, partnership or property that the owner values.

   D

10. Look to the private lending market. Investigate individual or small pension fund.

    D

11. Joint venture—offer interest, profit participation and preferential return.

    D

12. Advertise for a loan from private lender.

    D, K

13. Call credit union if a partner is a member in good standing.

    D, K

Figure 5-3, continued

14. Borrow against inheritance of trust or future income of a controllable trust.

    D, K

15. Loan from family or close friend—get better rates and/or invite family member into deal.

    D, K

16. Have employer co-sign note as a bonus or incentive.

    D, K

17. Use either broker as lender or his commission as part of the down payment.

    D, K

18. Pay a fee to a co-signer to get the loan. Example: $40,000 fee to co-sign a note for the down payment of $300,000. The co-signer has a mortgage on the property until released from mortgage.

    D, H, K, W

19. Seller puts up cash to close or pays buyer to take over liability. Seller could agree to mortgage for buyer.

    D, F

20. Borrow against paper or mortgages you hold. At least 45–60 percent of face value is not uncommon.

    D, K

21. Give the sellers stock in the corporation that is acquiring the property as down payment.

    H, D

22. Spread the risk by getting a series of small personal notes from several of the buyers. These can be used as down payment or additional collateral.

    D

23. A line or signature loan is one of the most common methods of raising down payments. Banks will make unsecured loans up to ten percent of net worth for credit worthy customers.

    D, K

24. Broker/salesperson takes commission in form of receivable. It is then discounted to a broker, salesperson or bank for cash.

    D, M

25. Offer letter of credit as down payment or as guarantee; no actual cash flow to seller, but guarantees future performance of buyer.

    C, D, G, H, K

26. Split or staged down payments—if $150,000 down is required, pay part down at closing, say, $50,000, another $50,000 in six months, and another in six more months. Balance is amortized as a mortgage.

    D

Figure 5-3, continued

27. Lease payments can be applied toward down payment.

O

28. Seller gives two months free rent which buyer uses as down payment. Sale is consummated. If a tenant does not buy, get investor to take advantage of free rent.

P

29. Use separate notes—a mortgage that allows seller to sell separate notes for cash. This reduces tax payment cash flow when reporting under installment method as to notes sold or until cash is received from other notes.

J

30. Use insurance, its cash value or loan policy.

I

31. Seller keeps land and the purchaser buys improvements subject to mortgage and land lease.

G, H, I

32. Sell land to investor and improvements to buyer for the cash flows net at closing simultaneously with sale of improvements to buyer. Buyer leases land and gets cash as part of down payment.

D, H, I

33. Buy property with first purchase money mortgage; give second purchase money mortgage to seller. Make deal contingent upon sale of first mortgage to an investor in mortgages. Buyer puts up a letter of credit guarantee as additional collateral for the second mortgage.

H

34. Use buyer's purchase money mortgage from sale of another property as down payment.

D

35. Offer personal possessions (car, boat, camper) as down payment alternative. Broker takes one item as commission. However, value is hard to ascertain.

A, C, G

36. Seller wants higher price than fixed lease will support. Have a seller make a new sandwich lease and pay the difference to support the higher price. Makes sense if cost of lease is less than opportunity cost of funds.

A, E

37. Set up a distant closing date. This gives time to accumulate down payment, or better, sell an out parcel prior to closing.

K, Q

38. Use tax refunds as security for a loan.

K

39. Pledge personal assets or securities.

G, K, M, W

Figure 5-3, continued

40. Buy REO (Real Estate Owned) property from lending institution with the lender giving a commitment to loan on another property.

K

41. Need a loan? Transfer funds to the bank you need a loan from. Compensating balances will get the bank's attention. Move your own escrow or get a friend or relative to move accounts.

L, K

42. Need extra collateral? Try a blanket mortgage over several properties.

G

43. Buyer should buy paper or mortgages on open market; discounts are 30 percent to 50 percent. Example: In a $200,000 transaction, the buyer buys a $100,000 note and first mortgage on the real estate. Buyer purchases it for $50,000. The seller gets this note at face value plus another $100,000 so $50,000 price reduction.

A

44. Obtain a personal loan that will pay part or all of down payment and will be renewed year after year until repayment is possible.

K

45. Any mortgage may be written to reflect the cash flows the parties want.
    - No interest or an interest moratorium first two years.
    - One-half interest paid during year one and two, balance accrues.
    - All interest accrues first three years. This is added to the principal; the mortgage is amortized over a specified period, for example 20 years at 12 percent.

B

46. Buy real property with credit card. Yes, limits up to $10,000 are available and some banks have made higher limits for preferred customers.

C, D, I, R

47. Discounted buy-back option—seller sells property at a discount and has option to buy back within specific time period for an increased price. Very good for fast sales in vacant land.

A, E, F, R, W

48. Automatic pay off or option to pay off, at a discount. Mortgagee has the option to pay off or discount mortgage based on a percentage of unpaid balance any time during first 12 months. Good for getting higher price when it is known that buyer will pay off soon.

A

49. Have seller reduce price and buyer pay fee under acceptable formula.

A

50. Lease commissions owed on a project. Buyer may wish to purchase these commissions on an installment basis from broker, creating potential favorable deductions for buyer as part of his investment in the property. This also creates a new point of discussion when a price agreement cannot be reached.

A

Figure 5-3, continued

51. Certain noncompete clauses can offer buyer incentive to pay more for a property. Check out tax ramifications with buyer's and seller's advisors.

A

52. A buyer could pay a portion of the purchase price for a bona fide option on other property owned by seller. If buyer subsequently does not exercise the option, the option money is deductible by the buyer as an ordinary business loss.

A

53. An on-going fee could be paid to seller for cross easements and/or sign rights or anything else of value that would adjust terms and/or price.

A

54. Have the buyers of either a condo conversion or a development of a highly desirable project pay all up-front money except the profit to developer or convertor. This creates cash for development at closing at no interest. Buyer knows he got that super buy he wanted.

K

55. Finance transaction with Industrial Development Revenue Bonds from state or local government. This results in lower interest and can include equipment—100 percent financing at 62 percent–68 percent of prime rate.

K

56. Industrial development revenue bonds with a twist. Developer or seller buys bonds from issuing entity. A ready market lowers administration and underwriter cost.

K

57. Use no interest loan, just straight amortization, perhaps over 60 months. Incentive to seller is a larger down payment, perhaps 40 percent down. Often, present value looks better with higher front end cash.

A, C, F, R

58. Write a purchase money participation loan at a lower interest rate or for a soft term (nine percent–12 percent). Give seller half of cash flow after debt service and half of sales proceeds or refinance. The increase in purchase money mortgage amount lowers cash requirement. Use any combination that works.

A, C, E, F, K

59. IRC Section 501 C-3—Charitable organization—get a higher sales price when selling to charity by gifting part of sales price. This is then a charitable deduction. The government, a church or any charity that qualifys under Section 501 C-3, Charitable Gift Deduction, offers a great negotiation potential. Part of the property can be sold at a lower price to charity as an incentive to buy. You can create more cash flow after tax with this formula.

A, F

60. If accelerated depreciation recapture is a problem and, as a result, the seller decides not to sell, there is an option for him to sell land for long-term capital gain and lease improvements to buyer. This could add option to buy or provide option for 1031 exchange provision when like-kind is not available. Always check current law with tax advisor.

A, B, S, T

Figure 5-3, continued

61. Seller wants to avoid gain from installment sale, but needs cash. Have seller borrow against paper. Seller pays off loan from income, yet reports installment sale.

N

62. Buyer assigns additional collateral for release of mortgage from an installment sale. As long as seller does not discount note, a gain may be reported under the installment sale method. Procedure offers flexibility in development and negotiation possibilities.

Q

63. Collateral from installment sale need not be on property being sold.

N, Q

64. Seller may reduce ordinary income from interest by inverting the amortization schedule. Make heavy principal payments in early years and defer heavy interest payments to later years when seller may be in lower tax bracket. Check imputed interest rules with your tax advisor.

T

65. Dealer status is a problem for seller. Sell to a trust or corporation on terms acceptable to seller. This results in an installment sale for seller. Corporation then enters into joint venture or dealer activity. This one has risk; see tax advisor.

T, Q

66. "Starker-Type Delayed Exchange"—This is a delayed or nonsimultaneous exchange. See tax advisor before using a Starker Trust Exchange. However, if you are going to pay tax anyway, consider Starker; it may be a good alternative.

S

67. Partnerships may be structured with different tax benefits and different cash flow distribution. See your tax advisor. Can make dead-locked negotiations move.

A, B, E, T

68. Seller keeps out-lot surplus, building and/or part interest in property. He may be generous in allocation of basis between what he sells and what he keeps. See tax advisor.

C, T

69. Contact a foreign bank mortgage broker in New York, Chicago, Houston. When big money is needed (five million and up) guarantees to foreign trust banks and pension funds are made for a fee by a domestic bank or life insurance company.

K

70. Good developers or buyers want property, however, liquidity to buy is not available. Go to seller or buyer's bank. Buyer borrows and deposits cash in escrow with lending bank. Escrow is in favor of seller so seller is in constructive receipt of cash, but agrees to leave it in escrow as collateral to bank.
    Interest earned on escrow goes to seller, interest on loan paid by buyer. Bank holds cash in escrow as security in event of default and buyer is on note for default to seller and bank.

D, K

Figure 5-3, continued

71. IRC Section 38: Property with investment tax credit recapture—you want to sell before minimum holding period expires. Solution is to not sell Section 38 property but lease it until minimum holding period has expired. Build an option to sell into transaction at end of minimum holding period. Another option is to sell Section 38 property at book value. Consult tax advisor for new tax law effect.

T

72. Net investment interest limitation—buy Section 1221 property (net investment property, vacant land) in a corporate form to avoid limitations of individuals under net investment limitation (corporations are not subject to investment interest rules). Individuals are subject to limitations on interest deductions accruing from ownership of certain investment property.

T

73. Due-on-sale clause:

- Go to bank and ask policy on specific loan. You might be able to negotiate a fair, acceptable deal. Remember, negotiate; banks do not want to sue the mortgagor.
- Wraparound first mortgage—let seller take risk for increase in interest or acceleration. Theory is, higher price is function of better loan term.
- Sell contract for deed. This is harder to trace and subject to hard legal discussions and close inspection of due-on-sale language. Get legal advise on contract laws.
- Check language. Many older mortgages have clauses that say buyer *must* assume the loan. Lender, under such language, has no right to raise interest. Get bank's approval of assumption letter which usually includes higher interest range, then have your attorney send thank you note to bank for approval of assumption, but inform them that they have no right to increase interest. Seek legal counsel.
- Have a well-respected, informed, strong attorney discuss the bank's interpretation of due-on-sale clause saying that he will see them in court if something cannot be worked out.
- Take the risk. Some buyers and sellers are willing to take property subject to a loan with a valid due-on-sale provision. If parties find risk acceptable, property may be conveyed subject to valid due-on-sale provision. Consult attorney.

L

74. Subordination:

- Get additional collateral from buyer.
- Buyer gives substitute collateral.
- Buyer gives letter of credit for subordination.
- Seller gets enough consideration to release sufficient funds for first phase of project.
- Only subordinate to top amount of loan.
- Get additional guarantee from strong people or corporation. Buyer pays fee for guarantees.
- Give seller a participation interest in project.
- Pay more for subordination and property.
- Limit amount of subordination and make certain funds go for improving subordinated property.

M

75. Make two offers, one offer with soft terms and the second offer all cash, giving seller

Figure 5-3, continued

the option of getting his total purchase price with terms or getting something less with a cash offer.

A

76. Attorney problem—deal killing: If the attorney objects to a particular transaction, ask about the significance of the objection and the likelihood of such a problem occurring. Try not to argue with an attorney in the presence of a client. Ask, "Have you ever personally seen a problem similar to what you [the attorney] are describing?" Try to dilute the problem. Is the objection worth the client losing the transaction?

Y

77. The secret hand shake between attorneys or advisors can move mountains. Have your attorney or CPA call the advisor who is causing problems. People of the same professions respect each other and each other's comments.

Y

78. You need to offer additional collateral for an obligation loan. You could give a second mortgage on other property that the buyer owns, even though there may be considerable equity that you would not want subject to a second mortgage for a small amount. The "twist" mortgagor could give an option that the second mortgagee would take a third mortgage position if a certain sales price or market value was reached in the sale of the existing owned property. This makes it possible to make a sale without paying off a small second.

G

79. When there is a problem with a potential loan and the borrower wishes to keep the property, the lender could request a trade of collateral and then a foreclosure on a new property which lender would then acquire.

F

80. FHA 231 refinance program includes rehabbing apartments. This can enable the rehabber to get cash out as well as rehab apartments. Be sure to check all current FHA financing.

D

81. Raise price, lower down payment, and get second mortgage from credit union or other lender; in other words, "You name the price, I will name the terms."

A, D, K

82. Do not pay off certain encumbrances that will cloud the title at closing—this will reduce the amount of cash required to close. For example, a tax lien property could be taken subject to the taxes with the current new buyer understanding that he will have to pay the tax lien at some time in the future.

A, D, I

83. If landlease is a problem with buyer:
   • Buy out landlease and refinance.
   • Offer an interest in the transaction to landowner to sell landlease.
   • Move lease to another property; give adjustment to terms of former lease.
   • Exchange landlease into other like-kind 1031 (if like-kind property is another landlease, must be 30 years or more term).
   • Sell the property to landlease owner.

X

Figure 5-3, continued

84. Pre-sales deposits make deals. A substantial deposit equal to, for example, 25 percent of the total purchase price placed in escrow usually meets the construction lender requirements ensuring that a proposed purchaser will close a purchase upon completion of a prearranged agreement to buy within the proposed project. This enables the developer to get more upfront money than a lender would advance under a percentage of cost mortgage commitment. This gives you the ability to sell all-cash on projects to be built and to cash out of cost.

Sales Price, Office Condo $100,000
Pre-sales Deposit, Escrow $ 25,000

Construction Cost $ 60,000
Normal Loan Amount $ 50,000
Because of Escrow $ 60,000 Loan

H, R

85. Wraparound mortgage—example: $500,000 property, $100,000 down. There is a $100,000 first mortgage at eight percent interest. A new mortgage is written subject to the existing first mortgage and wraps around it in the amount of $400,000. This is sometimes referred to as an all-inclusive mortgage or deed of trust.

Be flexible on the terms and conditions of the wrap mortgage as long as you cover the first mortgage. You can match cash flows.

A, E, K

86. A sale buy-back is a good method of giving either additional profit to a lender or creating an additional profit center for lender. It also creates profits outside of restrictions placed on loans. Developer or seller sells property to lending institution and immediately buys it back on paper sometimes with release clauses. Developer gets cash from sale to build or convert. Lender gets equity position and immediate profit. Works well in tight money markets or where lender needs window dressing profit to offset a loss.

K, R

87. Real Estate Owned (REO)—Look at bank's balance sheet for REO properties. All classified assets must be sold. The bank will extend credit based on REO property as for no other loan. Ask for what you want because you will solve their problem also.

K

88. Use a negative pledge which is an agreement with your lender not to pledge or sell assets on financial statement.

K

89. Many banks will make you loans if their bank stock can be sold at the right price. Make sure you do not violate state or federal law, however.

K

90. Contingent price sale—make price a function of future performance of the property. Price or mortgage payments can also be a function of future income.

A

91. Phase down payment split—place part of down payment in escrow for future improvements or spread out down payment over time.

G

Figure 5-3, continued

92. Purchase a remainder interest. If seller wants to live on property for life, purchase his remainder interest or his right to property. Upon his death, you get property. Variation is to leave homestead in remainder trust, purchase all other property associated with homestead (for instance, all acreage other than farmhouse on 1000-acre farm), and take right of first refusal on homestead itself.

Z

93. Backwork mortgage or reverse amortization produces negative cash flow during the first few years. If normal amortization creates any shortfall in the interest carried or principal amortized, it may be accrued and added to principal. An alternative would be any combination of amortization that reduces cash flow in early years.

B, E, X

94. Buy properties from corporations and lending institutions that want earnings on financial statement. This helps corporations generate earnings. Approach real estate service corporation or company. Buy a percentage of real estate assets (perhaps 75 percent) or buy any combination of percentage interests in given properties. Require that company give and guarantee a return on investment satisfactory to an investor on a pretax basis (before depreciation). On all cash flow generated over the guarantees, the company would receive a percentage return related to its percent of ownership. Any additional cash flow is split either 50–50 or any other agreed upon combination, above an adequate return on invested capital. Investor gets solid ten percent return on capital invested. The company gets capital for growth and a gain from sale. Terms will also help achieve higher price on disposition sale. Depreciation is eliminated from statement because the depreciable assets are no longer owned by the corporation; all the upside over guarantees are split per agreement.

A, E, K

95. Seller should master-lease property back to guarantee cash flow. This lowers the risk and should increase sales price.

B, E

96. If personal liability is a problem:
    - Limit liability to top ten percent (or any other percentage) of loan.
    - Give additional guarantees; do not use personal guarantees or endorsements.
    - Have co-signer give personal guarantee for a fee.
    - Show benefits of getting property back after down payment.
    - Show the financial and legal problems of getting a deficiency judgment against buyer when no loss after foreclosure is reasonable.
    - Have one general partner guarantee notes. (Note: See your tax advisor. Techniques will effect depreciable basis.)
    - Guarantee terms of note and mortgage so if a default occurs, you meet terms, not lump sum. Make certain you are given notice in event of default.
    - Only guarantee for specific period, not forever.

W

97. Prelease to a credit tenant and finance investment based on lease.

F, K

98. Lease when you cannot buy.
    - Option either after death or every 50 years.
    - Obtain right of first refusal.

V

Figure 5-3, continued

99. Sale-leaseback—sell property. Seller leases back property from buyer. See your tax advisor to avoid treatment as a loan rather than the intended sale.

O

100. Raise cash. Sell only a portion of a long-term note. For example, the holder of a $50,000 note payable at $717.00 per month, with the last payment due in ten years, wants cash, but also needs some income. Total sale of the note will trigger recognition of all gain.

D

101. When you buy property, the note may be discounted. Add the following clause, "Payor has the first right to purchase this note or match the price offered if the note is offered in the future for sale or exchange."

A, B

102. Sell property at a loss and lease the land. Seller can sell lower value improvements at a loss and hold land on a lease. Buyer can allocate entire purchase price to improvements while deducting lease payments.

G, H, O, P, V, X

103. Use a lease to gain access to property before closing.

O

104. Options.
    • Offer letter of credit instead of cash when you think you will close.
    • Continuing option—payments on the option in regular periodic amounts of, for example, $50,000 each year voids all up-front option money.
    • Increase option payment, price or both. Increase option amount annually. Also, increase price after each option exercise date.
    • Apply option money against purchase price.
    • Use sweat equity or effort option. Option holder will set up plans for development, manage property or secure leases or buyers.
    • Deed other property as option money. Land or improvements may be free and clear or subject to mortgage, stocks, bonds, diamonds, boats, cars, etc.
    • Discount sale; buy back option. Sell at a discount, have option to buy back.
    • Option for a 1031 exchange.
    • Use option as collateral.
    • Brokers should option property when necessary to provide access to a listed property or to close a sale.
    Option hints.
    a. Option money is tax deferred until option is exercised or terminated.
    b. Optionor (seller) has use of property and income until exercised.
    c. Lease option gives use of property plus control.

Z

105. Seller buy back provision—if selling is a real problem because of a high price or a risky market or if the buyer is just uneasy and wants downside protection, you could have seller agree to buy back property within *limited period of time* if buyer elects to have him do so.

B, C, E, R

106. Lease with a forced purchase lease. Seller agrees to a lease, but wants a sale. He agrees to lease as long as a specific performance clause is in the lease to force the lessee to buy at a specific time.

P

Some Marketing Thoughts

- If the seller is motivated to sell, the property will be sold (not always by the listing agent, however).
- One man's lemon is another man's lemonade.
- There are no standardized marketing plans. All plans require constant creative input and modification.
- Do not rely on any one single program (the sign may not work).
- There is no right way or wrong way to market real estate as long as it is ethical. "Whatever works," should be your attitude.
- Learn the subtleties of owner and buyer education processes and make them part of your marketing plan.
- A plan without a schedule is paperwork without an end.
- Burn-out is a mental frame of mind not a marketing status.

The best approach to this complicated subject is to write down what you have read. Without looking, write out the steps in your marketing plan. What will you do differently as a result of Chapters 3–5?

Appendix to Chapter 5:
Putting the "Meeting of the Minds" on Paper

"Failures are divided in two classes. Those who thought and never did and those who did and never thought." Anonymous

All too often a well-taken listing is marketed with laser accuracy only to fail at the agreement stage. The pain of finding the perfect transaction structure only to drop the ball at the contract stage is a failure common in commercial-investment real estate. The task of reducing a concept or "meeting of the minds" to paper is formidable.

Complicated transactions demand team work. The CCIM program[1] is built on a philosophy of teamwork. A professional CCIM must focus on using the best real estate attorneys and tax counselors in the market. But often the time factor in negotiations requires that the broker, not the attorney, draw up, or commit to writing, the intent of the parties. It is essential that the professional commercial-investment broker understand the economics, the legal ramifications and the tax impact of various transaction structures as well as the techniques that exist for the buying and selling of real estate. This study module was designed to assist the commercial-investment broker in developing his ability to negotiate, write letters of intent and, where not in conflict with state law, prepare contracts. There is a wide variety of approaches available for dealing with specific problems. An examination of specific provisions of contract language may assist the reader in developing approaches for transaction structures and the actual contract. Book Two contains a chapter that gives many examples of these provisions. Here, only the fundamental guidelines are presented.

This appendix is not intended to be a legal thesis. In fact, no attempt has been made to develop an extensive series of alternative forms or sample

---

1. The CCIM (Certified Commercial Investment Member) certification was established in 1968. The CCIM designation is awarded only to those who have completed a series of intensive courses offered through the Institute, demonstrated the ability to apply the techniques taught in the courses to actual transactions in the marketplace and passed a rigorous comprehensive examination.

clauses. The language is suggested as a foundation for each broker's personal contract writing file or notebook. Look for and maintain a contract writing notebook or file that includes examples of the best language you observe.

Letter of Intent

For those brokers who, by state law, cannot write any form of contract and for all brokers who develop transactions too difficult to commit to writing in a formal contractual form, the author recommends the *letter of intent* approach.

The letter of intent is not meant to be a contract, but is a nonbinding memorandum of the intent of the parties. The letter of intent can be an excellent vehicle to use in getting a buyer committed to an offer and mentally involved in the acquisition of a property. Letters of intent are also useful when the contract itself will be very detailed and involve many issues of less importance than the initial transaction structures of price and terms.

A series of formal contract offers may be impossible or untimely or too expensive for the purpose of making a simple offer to determine the attitudes of the parties to the transaction. There are many people who will not execute a contract without all the "t's" crossed and full approval by an attorney. However, many of these same people will, with little hesitation, make an offer in the form of a letter of intent. The letter of intent allows people to negotiate in plain language without expensive legal counsel and without the threat of a contractual agreement. Most motivated, sincere buyers and sellers who sign letters of intent will eventually reach formal contract agreement. Those who are not motivated and sincere would not have reached a finalized formal contract no matter what time or expense was involved in the negotiations.

The Importance of Language

To fast-track negotiations and reach formal contract status, the broker must develop language which is clear, concise and accurately describes the intent of the parties. But beware! A contract may result from a letter of intent. Precautions must be taken to avoid this.

A contract is an exchange of promises. In deciding whether a contract exists, the court examines the statement made by each side. If the person to whom the promise is made reasonably believes that no strings are attached, then a contract exists.

As noted in the legal encyclopedia *Corpus Juris Secondum*, "preliminary negotiations do not constitute a contract, and an agreement to enter into a contract is of no effect unless all the terms and conditions of the contract are agreed on and nothing is left to future negotiations." A carefully worded disclaimer should be set forth in the letter to the effect that no contract, liability, or obligation is intended until a formal contract is signed.

The following is an example of a letter of intent which accurately describes the intent of the parties.

LETTER OF INTENT TO PURCHASE

The following shall serve as a letter of intent between JIM BUYER, President of World Builders, hereinafter referred to as "World", and THE ORANGE COMPANY, INC., hereinafter referred to as "Orange Company", regarding the terms and conditions by which World is willing to acquire the property legally described in attached Exhibit A.

TERMS AND CONDITIONS

1. Purchase price of TWENTY-ONE THOUSAND DOLLARS ($21,000) per acre for 11.1 acres, more or less. Total price to be determined by a land survey to be made at World's expense.

2. FIVE THOUSAND DOLLARS ($5,000) shall be held in escrow by Real Estate, Inc., REALTORS®, as an earnest money deposit by World.

3. World agrees to make an additional FIVE THOUSAND DOLLARS ($5,000) earnest money deposit on or before September 1, 1983.

4. Transfer of title shall be on or before December 1, 1983, if all terms and conditions of this agreement have been met. Balance of purchase price shall be due upon transfer of title.

5. Orange Company, at its expense, shall deliver title to World by good and sufficient Warranty Deed. Orange Company, at its expense, shall deliver a title insurance commitment to World within sixty (60) days after execution of formal contract showing good and insurable title of real estate being conveyed. After transfer of title, Orange Company shall deliver a final title insurance policy on the subject property in the amount of the full purchase price.

6. Orange Company agrees to cooperate fully with World's efforts to obtain building permits for a multi-family residential development. All application for permits and required documents shall be obtained at World's expense.

7. The formal contract on subject property shall be in the form of an Exchange Agreement. World agrees to assist Orange in acquiring like-kind property and facilitating a 1031 Tax Deferred Exchange for the benefit of the Orange Company. Orange Company to pay all costs associated with World assisting in the exchange. If Orange Company has been unable to locate an acceptable like-kind property for exchange by March 6, 1984, World may require a straight sale of the subject property as follows:
World shall pay the balance of the full purchase price in cash at closing. Closing shall be on or before December 20, 1983.

8. The obligations of World under the formal contract are conditioned upon (a) the proper zoning and land use designation to permit con-

struction of a multi-family residential development under Largo's RM 14.5 zoning, (b) the issuance of appropriate building permits by the City of Largo, (c) the granting of all curb cut permits and other access, ingress and egress permits which World may deem necessary for operation of said development, (d) the issuance of all permits, licenses and approval by all public authorities which are required in order for World to carry on its business on the premises, and (e) the soil and subsurface of the subject property in their present condition conforming to World requirements for construction of the proposed improvements. Orange Company hereby agrees to cooperate fully with World in securing aforesaid permits and approval and hereby grants to World the right to make application for them in the name of the Orange Company if necessary. In the event World has not effected the fulfillment of all the conditions contained herein within one hundred twenty (120) days from date of execution of the formal contract, said contract shall terminate without any liability on the part of any party and earnest money shall be refunded to World.

9. The obligations of World under the formal contract are conditioned upon utility services of sufficient capacity for proposed multi-family residential development (including electricity, water and telephone) being available for World's use without World having to incur costs and expenses for obtaining such availability. The exception to this condition is sanitary sewer which all parties acknowledge is available only on the west side of Ridge Road, and World shall assume the responsibility and cost for a "jack and bore" procedure under Ridge Road to gain access to said sewer. World also shall assume the cost of constructing a sewer lift station and force main, if required, to gain access to said sewer. For the purposes of this paragraph, said utilities shall be deemed available to the premises if they are available for use by World within one hundred feet (100') of any of the boundaries of subject property.

10. The obligation of World under the formal contract shall be conditioned upon Buyer obtaining a commitment for financing the acquisition and development of subject property. Said commitment acceptable to World shall be obtained within forty-five (45) days after execution of a formal contract.

The undersigned agree that the above shall serve as a letter of intent for the proposed purchase of property described in Exhibit A. In the event a formal contract is not entered into and agreed by July 1, 1983, this Letter of Intent shall become null and void and of no further force and effect. A binding agreement can only be reached by execution of a formal contract reviewed by attorneys for both parties.

Agreed to this ____ day of _____, 19____.

_____
JIM BUYER, President of WORLD BUILDERS

_____
THE ORANGE COMPANY, INC.

Ensuring Accuracy

A simple but necessary step in finalizing the copy for both letters of intent and contracts is checking to ensure that all elements have been included and that all provisions have been covered. Two convenient checklists are discussed here: the contract checklist and the red flag checklist.

Figure 5-4

CONTRACT CHECKLIST

____ Date of contract
____ Name of seller
____ Name of buyer
____ Escrow agent
____ Legal description
____ Address of property being conveyed
____ Personal property inventory
____ Purchase price

METHODS OF PAYMENT

____ Deposit
____ Deposit increase in special clauses
____ If contract contingent or default, does contract direct escrow payment
____ Subject to mortgage or ____ terms stated in special clauses
____ Assumption of mortgage or ____ terms stated in special clauses
____ Purchase money mortgage or ____ terms stated in special clauses
____ Other—define and qualify
____ Balance to close
____ Math adds to purchase price

FINANCING

____ Is contract conditioned on financing
____ Number of days to finance
____ Terms—interest rate ____
        Amount _____ Years ____

TITLE EVIDENCE

____ ____ Days to deliver
____ ____ Responsible for costs and delivery
____ Abstract given
____ Title commitment given
____ ____ Time to cure defects

TIME FOR ACCEPTANCE AND CONTRACT EFFECTIVE DATE

_____ is closing date
(Definite Yes or No)

ZONING

____ Is zoning defined?
____ Is intended use defined?
____ Is zoning an intended contingency (escrow disbursement)?
____ Occupancy/possession defined?
____ Assignability ____ Buyer may ____ May not
____ Brokerage fee defined—Deposit in event of default
____ All riders or addendum shall recite in contract:
"Addendum attached to and made a part of that certain Contract for Sale and Purchase dated _____, 19____, between _____, Buyer, _____, Seller, _____, Realtor(s).

Contract Checklist

The contract checklist is a simple inventory of salient terms to be covered in the letter of intent or contract. A contract checklist may be developed similar to Figure 5-4 by making a simple inventory of the existing state approved form contract. Most states develop a form contract for simplistic residential transactions in conjunction with the real estate commission and bar association. All contracts should be checked for missing elements. A contract checklist avoids mistakes and offers benchmarks for drafting contracts or letters of intent.

Another checklist should be developed by the commercial broker to cover those areas addressed in his own standard form that may not be addressed in a contract prepared by another broker or an attorney of the opposite party (this may occur especially in the small print on the back of a form contract). When reviewing contracts not prepared on your standard form, be certain to check for salient and important variables that may not be included because your own normal form isn't being used.

Red Flag Checklist

The Red Flag Checklist, Figure 5-5, should be scanned and reviewed whenever you are preparing a formal letter of intent or contract. Red flags are intended to alert the broker to the various areas of importance in almost all transactions. For example, a contract should contain an absolute outside closing date. Closing dates are often dropped when there are numerous contingencies in the contract. You will make certain there is an outside closing date when you check the Red Flag Checklist. Red flags are also intended to alert you to common and important areas in drafting. A continuous effort to add to the red flag list will enhance your drafting and reduce your liabilities.

Tips on Contract Language

This section is meant to be an introduction to contract language. A complete treatment of the subject as well as extensive examples may be found in Book Two. In fact, the desired language can be found by looking through the table of contents included with Chapter 2 of Book Two for the type of language needed and then turning to the suggested page. This will identify the actual language that fits the written agreement. In addition, it can be readily adapted to the specific situation and objectives.

Use caution that you do not become sloppy in your use of the English language when writing letters of intent and contracts. Small touches to your agreement language dress up and enhance your contract or letter of intent. Work to develop an ear for the lingo of the law world. Every statement does not have to begin with a "whereas" or "therefore," but certain phrases and terms offer credibility to your work while others will serve only to reduce its effectiveness.

Building trust is an important part of negotiations. Professional contract drafting and language can help build trust and confidence. "Releases shall be made in a continguous fashion from north to south," can also be stated, "Releases shall be made next to each other starting from north to south." Clearly, the first example is more concise and efficient and professional

Figure 5-5

RED FLAGS—ALL CONTRACTS

____ NO TAX ADVICE

Purchaser acknowledges that he has not received or relied upon any statements or representations by Realty World, Inc., or its representatives regarding the effect of this transaction upon Purchaser's tax liability or the transaction's potential tax effects.

____ BROKER ACTING AS PRINCIPAL

Seller acknowledges Buyer is a licensed real estate broker buying for his own account and potential profit.

____ DEPOSIT AS LIQUIDATED DAMAGES

IS IT THE INTENT THAT THE LIMIT OF DAMAGES IS THE EARNEST MONEY DEPOSIT? IF SO:

In the event of default by the Buyer, the earnest money deposit referred to herein shall be the full liquidated damages available to Seller.

____ RIGHT OF FIRST REFUSAL (Avoids Two Contracts, Same Property)

MAKE CERTAIN THAT SELLER HAS NOT GRANTED A RIGHT OF FIRST REFUSAL OPTION TO A THIRD PARTY:

Seller warrants he has not contracted with or granted a right of first refusal to any third party for the sale or lease of the subject property.

____ MORTGAGE

____ The note and mortgage may be prepaid at any time without penalty.
____ The sole security for the note shall be the subject property and the Seller/ Mortgagee shall not be entitled to a deficiency judgment.

____ PROPERTY SOLD IN "AS IS" CONDITION

Property to be conveyed in an "as is" condition.

____ LUMP SUM PRICE

The representations of the Seller as to acreage are approximate and believed to be correct; however, no variance in acreage conveyed shall adjust the sales price.

Figure 5-5, continued

___ CORPORATIONS OR PARTNERSHIPS AS BUYER OR SELLER

1. Establish validity of entity.
2. Authority of agent executing contract.

___ ESTATE DEEDING

Standard Exception "X" [in author's contracts] is hereby modified to provide that the conveyance shall be by Personal Representative Deed and Bill of Sale rather than a Statutory Warranty Deed.

___ DELETE TERMITE CLAUSE ON LAND AND FOR BUILDING(S) WHERE LAND IS VALUE

Termite clause in standard contracts should be deleted.

___ RELEASE

Use caution to make certain that, if you are making releases, they cannot be made indiscriminately on the tract unless so desired. Specifically, the most valuable property should not be released first, which would leave the Seller with the less valuable property. This is especially true where there is a uniform release price (i.e. 125 percent of the value per acre). Make certain all releases are contiguous (if that is intent) and that in order to obtain the release you must have accrued interest paid.

___ CLOSING DATE

When contingency used or requirements to close may extend closing date, make certain that absolute outside closing date is defined.

___ 1031 INTENDED

Seller agrees to assist purchaser in facilitating a tax-deferred exchange in accordance with the Internal Revenue Code, Section 1031.

___ LEASE RECEIPT AND ACKNOWLEDGMENT

Buyer acknowledges receipt of copies of existing leases prior to signing the contract and agrees to take title subject to the existing leases. Seller agrees to assign said leases to Buyer at closing. All parties agree that no new leases or extensions of existing leases shall be executed by Seller without Buyer's written permission. Prior to closing, Seller shall provide Buyer with an estoppel letter from all tenants verifying the terms and conditions of the existing leases and that there are no unfulfilled obligations by Seller under the terms of said leases.

sounding. It would reinforce the fact that you know what you're doing. Another example would be the use of effective legal terminology.

Use as few words as are necessary to complete a sentence accurately. However, use as much language as is necessary to complete the thought process. Many times a simple explanation of a process is enhanced by including an actual example within the explanation. This also will enhance the clarity of your drafting.

Figure 5-6

MISCELLANEOUS TERMS COVERED BY MOST FORMS

IF NOT USING A COMPANY CONTRACT, CHECK FOLLOWING STANDARDS.

_____ Time to cure title defects

_____ Existing mortgages-estopple statement provided by Seller

_____ Purchase money mortgage form and terms

_____ Survey paid for by Buyer or Seller

_____ Termites

_____ Ingress/Egress warranty by Seller

_____ Leases
   1. Title subject to existing leases
   2. Seller to obtain Buyer's approval before signing new leases

_____ Liens-Seller to provide affidavit of no liens

_____ Place of closing

_____ Time of closing

_____ Documents for closing
   Seller: deed, lien affidavit, assignment of leases
   Buyer: closing statement, mortgage, mortgage note, financing statements

_____ Expenses:
   Seller: state surtax, documentary stamps, intangible tax on mortgage, cost of record corrective instruments
   Buyer: documentary stamps on notes or purchase money mortgage and notes

_____ Proration of taxes (real & personal)

_____ Special assessments liens

_____ Personal property inspection, repair

_____ Risk of loss—by whom, until when

_____ Maintenance during contract period

_____ Proceeds of sale and closing procedure
   Will funds be disbursed at closing or will closing be in escrow?

_____ Escrow-Escrow agent duties defined

_____ Attorneys fees in the event of litigation

_____ Default-Is the deposit intended to be liquidated damages or do Seller and Buyer have specific rights in default?

_____ Prorations and insurance-taxes, rent, interest, insurance (as of date of closing?)

_____ Conveyance: Seller to convey title by statutory warranty deed

_____ All clauses and agreements in contract?

_____ All riders or addendums shall recite contract:
   Addendum attached to and made a part of that certain Contract for Sale and Purchase dated _____, 19___, among _____, Buyer, _____, Seller, _____, Broker(s).

Figure 5-6 is another checklist. This one will help you check language in contracts that your own company has not prepared. When preparing both letters of intent and contracts, it is very important to use every possible tool to ensure accuracy. Figure 5-6 is one more control to make use of.

A common mistake in drafting contracts is not "closing the loop." For instance, if you state that a contract becomes null and void if a certain event does not occur, then you should clearly define what happens to the deposits. An example, "If commercial zoning is not approved by the appropriate governmental agency by December of 1983, the contract shall be null and void." The question is, what about the deposit? The language in the contract should go on to state ". . . and the earnest money deposit shall be returned to the purchaser." Simply closing all loopholes will avoid conflicts in the event of defaults in contingency contracts. Many commercial-investment contracts have contingencies for review of books and inspection of properties. The handling of deposits in these situations must be clear.

A word of caution: the suggestions contained in this chapter are designed to present information for educational purposes. It is not to be regarded as providing opinion or advice for any individual case. This information is not intended to render legal, accounting or other professional service or advice. The appropriate professional should be consulted for any services or advice required.

In conclusion, if you hold yourself out as an expert and then write a bad contract or damage someone else, expect to pay the price. The study of contracts and contract language is as important as getting to closing. Knowledge of both your limitations and state laws will enhance your abilities as a negotiator and as a broker.

6

Exchanging as a
Problem Solver

W hat commercial-investment real estate marketing text would be complete without a discussion of exchanging? *Webster's New Collegiate Dictionary* defines an exchange as "an act of giving or taking one thing in return for another, a trade." All transactions are exchanges of one form or another. An all-cash real estate transaction is an exchange of cash for real property. Selling a property for cash and a mortgage is an exchange of two types of property—cash and mortgage for real property. Personal property for real property is another type of exchange.[1] The most important variables in an exchange are adequate motivation of the parties, adequate time to complete the exchange and adequate cash for the transaction expenses, including commission, attorney's fees and CPA expenses.

Exchanging is important because it is a method of marketing property that is not limited just to tax deferral. There are those who debate the future effectiveness of exchanges given the lower tax rates on long term capital gains and the new anti-churning rules affected by the 1981 Economic Recovery Tax Act. But, exchanging is still a way to solve problems.

Much emphasis has been put on the tax ramifications of Internal Revenue Code, Section 1031, Tax Deferred Exchange. Although many exchanges have been completed in the past primarily due to tax deferral, many have also been consummated for non-tax reasons. And, many more exchanges in the future will take place for other reasons. The future of exchanging is assured because it is a way of matching up the needs and wants of parties which results in transactions in which everyone involved in the exchange wins—the transactions result in win-win situations.

---

1. The REALTORS NATIONAL MARKETING INSTITUTE® offers an excellent six day course, which includes a discussion of exchanging, CI 103, "Advanced Real Estate Taxation and Marketing Tools for Investment Real Estate." For those who have an interest in pursuing the in depth ramifications of exchanging, it is highly recommended that they become involved in the CCIM program.

Non-Tax Reasons for Exchanging

Other motivations for exchanging, include:

• Changing markets and trends that may reduce the perceived potential income associated with the property. For example, a developer holds an inventory of vacant lots. Due to poor market conditions, he may be willing to exchange the lots for waterfront condominiums. This is an example of an exchange in which the developer would not qualify for gain deferral because the lots are other dealer property or inventory which does not qualify under Section 1031 of the Internal Revenue Code.

• Many times exchanges are effective ways to achieve desired or perceived market values that could not be achieved in an outright sale. If, for instance, you have a warehouse with a $500,000 listing price and little seller price flexibility. You also have a taker for the property, but he is not willing to pay the price. It is often possible for the taker to offer a portion of the purchase price in other like-kind or even unlike kind property which does not have an absolute value. This illustrates another motivation for exchanging properties, not totally born out of a desire for a tax deferral.

• An exchange is often a catalyst to a larger transaction in which an investor would like to divest himself of a smaller property in conjunction with acquiring a larger property.

• Exchanges can be initiated in an effort to reduce debt; this may create a taxable event.

• Exchanges are sometimes ideal when there is no need for cash and the exchange party simply wants to become involved in a satisfying transaction. Pride of ownership is a strong motivation that exchanging can sometimes satisfy.

• An absentee landlord may desire a property nearby to permit more frequent inspections and more enjoyment of the property.

• Individuals with vacation homes which may not qualify for 1031 may desire to exchange vacation homes for reasons other than tax deferral.

• Adjustments to the scope and size of an investment portfolio will motivate investors to alter their positions in properties through exchange.

• Exchanging a large property for a group of smaller properties to diversify risk is often a strategy used by knowledgeable exchangors.

• Conversely, exchanging smaller properties for one larger property is often done to decrease or consolidate management or to realize the economy of scale.

• A dealer with excess inventory in a down market will exchange inventory for almost any other commodity that he perceives as more marketable.

• Changing investment locations because of safety, diversity and trends will motivate parties to consider an exchange of property.

• An exchange leaseback (exchanging a property and then leasing it back) of commercial premises, frees or unlocks capital and equity for a new investment; this is often a strong motivating force. Proceed with caution, checking regulations for the effect of 1981 Economic Recovery Act.

• An exchange is an excellent method for dissolving a partnership. When exchanging partnership interest, consult a qualified tax counsel.

• Many times an exchange can be facilitated between people who just do not want what they own.

The list of motivations for exchanging of property is almost endless and only limited to the imagination of the commercial broker. An eye toward exchanging for reasons other than just tax deferral will open a world of opportunity to the commercial broker.

Tax Deferred Exchanges

The all important tax deferral concept of exchanging is still valid especially in cases where depreciable basis may not be a factor. A taxpayer who is exchanging vacant land for a larger tract of vacant land and is interested in preserving equity by deferring the gains, will often desire a 1031 tax deferred exchange. Older taxpayers may seek out the 1031 exchange when the holding period may exceed their lifetime and offer stepped up basis after death. Ultimate tax deferral at death may be a motivation to exchange for certain older taxpayers. A complete discussion of the 1031 tax deferral concept is beyond the scope of this text and the emphasis is on marketing and not on tax deferral.[2] However we will briefly examine the general concept of tax deferral. Assume a sale nets the owner $100,000, creating a tax liability of $20,000. If the owner exchanges his property for a qualifying like-kind property and complies with the rules of Section 1031, the entire tax may be deferred. An outright sale would reduce the equity by $20,000, leaving the investor only $80,000 to invest. Given the opportunity to invest the proceeds in an investment with an after tax return of ten percent on the equity invested, the following after tax cash flows to the investor would be realized.

1031 Exchange $100,000 × 10% = $10,000
Outright Sale $80,000 × 10% = $8,000

The exchange preserves most of the equity and may produce a greater after tax cash flow. This simple example is intended to show the effect of exchanging on the preservation of capital.

Qualifying for a Tax Deferred Exchange

Under Section 1031, there are three basic criteria needed for an exchange to take place.

1. Both properties in the exchange must be held for productive use in the *taxpayer's trade or business* or as an *investment*.

2. The property acquired must be like-kind, as defined under 1031, with the property surrendered.

3. The properties must actually be exchanged.

To qualify, it is essential that the properties be exchanged as opposed to being sold. A sale is deemed to be the transfer in consideration of a concrete

---

2. For a thorough discussion of exchanging, see *Real Estate Exchanges*, by Mark Lee Levine, CCIM, CRB, CRS (Chicago: REALTORS NATIONAL MARKETING INSTITUTE®, 1981).

price expressed in terms of money; an exchange is defined as a transfer of property in consideration of a reciprocal transfer of other property without the intervention of a specific amount of cash.

The taxpayer's *intent* as to the use of the property is the key to whether or not it qualifies. If the intent is to hold the property acquired in the exchange primarily for the production of income, for use in trade or business or for investment, the property qualifies as a 1031 property.

Property held primarily for resale, such as dealer property or inventory, does not qualify for a 1031 exchange. However, it is important that it is understood that dealer property can be involved in an exchange and that it can be used in a 1031 tax deferred exchange. It may not be tax deferred for the dealer; it may be tax deferred for the acquiring property holder if this person is acquiring the property for use in his trade or business or for investment.

For example, if a dealer/developer in waterfront condominiums were to exchange his interest, any gain he realized would be taxed as regular income. The property would not qualify for a 1031 deferral. However, this condominium property, which is dealer property in the hands of the developer, could be exchanged with Party B who owns a vacant tract of investment land. This exchange would qualify for tax deferral because the Property B is exchanging is held for investment. The property he is acquiring, the condo, will be used as a rental property and therefore qualifies under 1031 as like-kind. If the tax deferral nature of the transaction is not a concern, then the status of dealer property should not be a problem except in the case where we are trying to avoid gain through tax deferral provisions of 1031.

Under 1031, certain properties do not qualify for nonrecognition of gain. Properties that are specifically excepted by the Code include:

- Stock in trade or inventory held primarily for resale
- Stocks and bonds
- Notes
- Choses (personal property) in action
- Certificates of trust or beneficial interest
- Other securities or evidence of indebtedness or interest

It is not uncommon for a commercial broker to be asked to discuss what does and does not qualify for tax deferral. A knowledge of the items that are excepted by the Code as defined above should be part of all qualified brokers' working knowledge. In addition, a working knowledge of the qualifications for a 1031 tax deferred exchange and the like-kind concept is needed.

The Like-Kind Concept

The nature or character (real versus personal) of the property, not the grade or the quality (improved versus unimproved) is important. Real property for real property and personal property for personal property both qualify under Section 1031, if the properties have been held for trade or business or for investment. For example, a bulldozer used in trade or business could be exchanged for a dragline used in trade or business.

One variable that does not effect the like-kind test is improved versus unimproved. For instance, if we exchange a shopping center for a vacant tract of land, the properties would qualify as like-kind properites on that issue. The location is not important; however, the use of both must be trade, business or investment.[3] The following illustrates how this concept of like-kind qualifies properties for exchanging.

Investment Property	⟷	Investment Property
IRC S.1221[4]	⋈	IRC S.1221
Trade & Business Property	⟷	Trade & Business Property
IRC S.1231[5]		IRC S.1231

To further clarify this concept, here are some examples. The first example is of an exchange that *does* qualify under Section 1031:

• Unimproved land held for investment, S. 1221 Property, not principally held for sale in Texas for a shopping center in Florida, S. 1231 Property.

Examples of exchanges that *do not* qualify are:

• Land held for investment exchanged for diamonds held for investment, (not real property for real property, therefore not qualifying like-kind property).
• Shopping center exchanged for tax-free municipal bonds.

Analyzing Exchanges

The above discussion of tax deferred exchanges is intended to give a brief overview of some of the ramifications of the language used in exchanging. For our purposes, which stress marketing real estate, no further discussion will be given to the tax deferred nature of the exchange; more emphasis will be put on balancing the transaction and analyzing the motivations of the parties.

To analyze the exchange, three basic figures are needed:

1. the fair market value (or the agreed value) of the properties that are being exchanged,
2. the existing encumbrances or mortgages on the properties,
3. the equity being exchanged, calculated from the foregoing variables.

The Concept of Equity

There is a test known as the in-out test. An owner will not close if he does not get out of an exchange the equity equal to what he brought into the exchange. If you go to closing with $300,000 in cash, you are not going to walk away from the closing table with less than $300,000 worth of equity. The same concept holds if an owner has an apartment project worth

---

3. This concept of like-kind properties is discussed in great detail in several of the books listed in the Bibliography and also in the Institute's CI 103 course.

4. This refers to Internal Revenue Code, Section 1221, which defines capital assets as any land that is not held for sale during the ordinary course of business or used in trade or business.

5. Internal Revenue Code, Section 1231 deals with property involved in trade and business.

$1,000,000 subject to a $700,000 mortgage. He is not going to close an exchange of those properties unless he gets out at least $300,000 worth of equity.

The concept of equity is important to understand in balancing transactions. For example, consider owners of like-kind properties with the following information:

Figure 6-1

Equitable Exchange	A	B
Market Value	$200,000.	$300,000.
Mortgage	150,000.	250,000.
Equity	$50,000.	$50,000.

Figure 6-2

Inequitable Exchange	A	B
Market Value	$200,000.	$300,000.
Mortgage	150,000.	200,000.
Equity	$50,000.	$100,000.

In Figure 6-1, Party A and Party B both have $50,000 in equity; they would be satisfied, based on equities, with the exchange. (No consideration has been given to the tax effect associated with this exchange.) In Figure 6-2, Party A has $50,000 in equity and Party B has $100,000 in equity. The transaction is unbalanced. When this is the case, it will not close until equities are balanced. Transactions that do not balance need to have equity added to the exchange to even out the equity being brought into the exchange. In this case, B brought in $100,000 in equity and in order to close, B must receive $100,000 in equity. In this example, $50,000 in equity could be added by A by several different means, including cash, paper or other unlike kind property known as boot. It is not uncommon for the sophisticated exchangor to include personal property or property of unlike kind in balancing the equities of the transaction resulting in a partially or totally taxable exchange. Equity is increased by adding assets, reducing debt or eliminating debt. On the other side, equity is reduced by increasing debt through refinancing or taking away assets. The value is reduced or increased by adding or subtracting assets. *Each party must get out of an exchange the same amount of equity he puts into it.* If the in-out test shows equal amounts, the transaction is economically balanced; you should proceed to communicate the benefits of the exchange to the parties.

For Exchange Only

Listing a property for exchange only is a strategy that can result in many successful closings. The listing for exchange only scenario is commonplace when a property owner does not want to sell for all cash, but does want to divest the property. A common transaction would include some or all of the following events:

1. Broker lists Property A for exchange only.

2. The broker then markets the property on the open market as if it was for sale, lease, exchange, joint venture, build to suit or whatever a taker would like to do with the property.

Figure 6-3

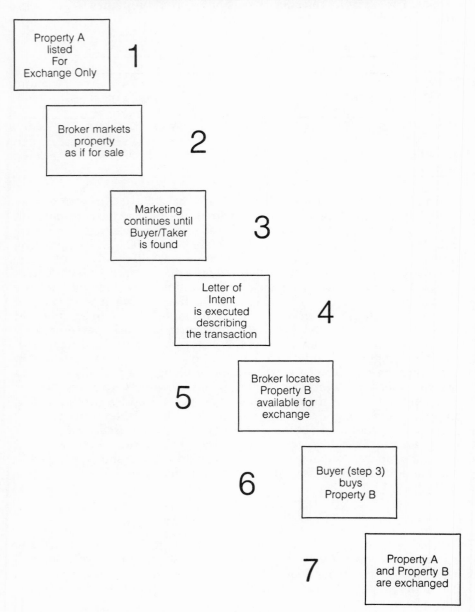

TRANSACTION STEPS IN A LISTING FOR EXCHANGE ONLY

Property A
listed
For
Exchange Only

1

Broker markets
property
as if for sale

2

Marketing
continues until
Buyer/Taker
is found

3

Letter of
Intent
is executed
describing
the transaction

4

Broker locates
Property B
available for
exchange

5

Buyer (step 3)
buys
Property B

6

Property A
and Property B
are exchanged

7

Seller has Property B; Buyer has Property A; Owner has cash; Broker gets paid.

3. When a buyer shows an interest in Property A but has no like-kind property to exchange, the broker still commits the exchange proposal to writing in a letter of intent.

4. The broker writes the letter of intent subject to the CPA's or attorney's approval and subject to finding Property A's seller an acceptable like-kind property and facilitating an acceptable exchange.

5. The broker finds a property that A would like to acquire. The owner of this property wants cash only.

6. The next step in the scenario is for the parties to go to contract. As stated, Mr. Owner wants cash only. Buyer's agent writes the contracts subject to a simultaneous closing of both properties. In other words, Seller A exchanges his property for Mr. Owner's property who in turn sells it to Mr. Buyer for cash. This type of exchange is typically referred to as a two-way exchange with a cash-out. It is not terribly complicated and does not involve substantial expertise. Figure 6-3, page 106, illustrates the flow of this type of transaction.

Balancing a Two-Way Transaction with a Cash-Out

Again, the most important aspect of this type of exchange is the balancing of equities. The following is an example of how this balancing works. Assume the following information: our client, A, wants to exchange his property valued at $300,000 for Mr. Owner's (B) property. Mr. Buyer (C) wants Property A and Mr. Owner wants cash only.

Figure 6-4

Two-Way Transaction with a Cash-Out

	A	B	C
Market Value	$300,000	$100,000	
Mortgage	225,000	0	0
Equity	75,000	100,000	$100,000 cash

Givens:
1. Client A wants exchange only and will take Owner B's property.
2. Buyer C wants Property A.
3. Owner B wants cash, only.

The solution then is for Mr. Buyer to buy Mr. Owner's property and exchange with Client A.

The following three diagrams illustrate how this transaction would be balanced.

Seller B	Market Value	Buyer C
$100,000	Market Value	
–0–	Mortgage	
$100,000	Equity	$100,000 Cash

BALANCED

Now that Buyer C owns Property B, he must exchange it with Client A.

Client A	Market Value	Buyer C
$300,000	Market Value	$100,000
$225,000	Mortgage	-0-
$ 75,000	Equity	$100,000

UNBALANCED

As our client only had $75,000 in equity, he must come up with an "evener" of $25,000 in either cash or other property in order to acquire the $100,000 property. The balanced exchange is diagramed as follows:

	Client A	Market Value	Buyer C
Cash Evener $25,000 +	$300,000	Market Value	$100,000
	$225,000	Mortgage	
	$100,000	Equity	$100,000

BALANCED

Balancing Complex Transactions

When cash is required for transaction costs and commissions, exchanges become somewhat more complicated. However, the basic concept of balancing exchanges is the same in that it requires an awareness of the balancing of equity concept. Here is an example of balancing equities in a more complicated two-way exchange.

Step One—Inventory Properties

First, take an inventory of the properties to determine the net equity.

Figure 6-5

	INVENTORY	
	A	B
Market Value	$224,000	$500,000
Existing Loan	152,500	175,000
Equity-Gross	71,500	325,000
Cash In	25,000	0
Less Commission	(14,000)	(24,000)
Less Transaction Cost	(2,500)	(4,000)
Net Equity	$ 80,000	$297,000

Must Get out What Is Put In

Once net equities are determined, there is a basis on which to determine what the clients will demand in equity in order to close the transaction.

Step Two—Determine Cash

Cash is almost always a problem in exchanging like-kind property. By determining the amount of cash that will become available through new financing and combining that with the cash both parties bring to the transaction, the amount of cash available for the transaction can be determined.

Some $316,700 is available in the transaction both from the net loan proceeds from refinancing of the two properties and from A's contribution of $25,000 in cash. After we pay the transaction costs for both A and B, we have $272,200 cash available to balance the transaction.

If the properties are exchanged, A would receive $80,000 in equity and, in fact, A contributed $80,000 in equity. It is assumed that A would be satisfied and close the transaction. B is receiving only $24,800 in property equity but brought $297,000 to the closing table. Unless B receives $272,000 in equity out of the transaction, B will not close. Figure 6-6 shows that $272,200 is available to be used in the transaction. If this amount is added to B's equity, it would result in his taking out $297,000, the same amount he put in. Then, both A and B will close. Figure 6-7 illustrates this procedure. In addition, the details of this transaction are worked out on page 112 using an exchange worksheet from REALTORS NATIONAL MARKETING IN-STITUTE.®

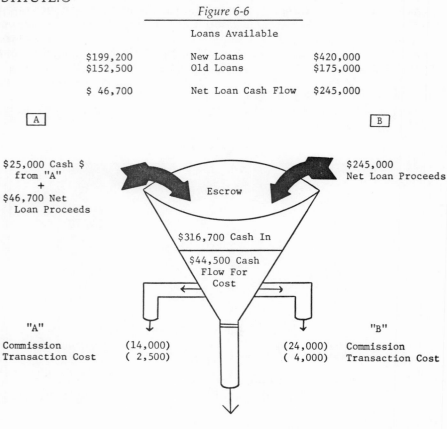

Figure 6-6

	Loans Available	
$199,200	New Loans	$420,000
$152,500	Old Loans	$175,000
$ 46,700	Net Loan Cash Flow	$245,000

A

$25,000 Cash $
from "A"
+
$46,700 Net
Loan Proceeds

Escrow

B

$245,000
Net Loan Proceeds

$316,700 Cash In

$44,500 Cash
Flow For
Cost

"A"

Commission   (14,000)
Transaction Cost   (2,500)

"B"

(24,000) Commission
(4,000) Transaction Cost

$272,200 Cash Available For Transaction

Figure 6-7

Exchange Properties		
	A Gets	B Gets
Market Value	$500,000.	$224,000
Mortgage	420,000.	199,200
Equity	$80,000	24,800
Cash		+272,200
Net Equity Out	80,000	297,000
Equals		
Original Equity In	80,000.	297,000

In reality, exchanges may be viewed simplistically. Two-way exchanges are popular in down economies or buyers' markets but most exchanges will not be two-way exchanges. Many will involve two-way exchanges with a third party cashing-out one of the property owners. If the exchange is totally for tax deferral purposes and the tax impact is less than $5,000, in the author's judgment, an exchange may be overly cumbersome and the outright sale option may be more realistic. An important reality when exchanging properties is that the tax impact must be understood, therefore, competent tax advisors must be consulted. Many times, the tax payer's basis in the new property received in the exchange will differ from that of the basis in a property acquired in an outright purchase.

The Exchange Team

Often the idea for an exchange is germinated in the minds of other members of the marketing team. It may come from the attorney, CPA or the broker himself. An exchange can be consummated without the other members of the team, but it has a higher probability of consummation and tax audit success when all members of the team work in concert.

Typical team problems to watch out for are:

1. Perhaps the attorney says, "My client should not sign the sales contract subject to finding a like-kind property for a 1031 exchange." Supply the counsellor with a copy of a case referred to as James Alderson, et al vs. Commissioner, 317 F2d 790 (1963).

2. Open conflicts and criticism or surprises might come up in front of the client. A marketing team should meet before the client meets with the team to avoid conflicts and embarrassment that would lower the credibility of all.

3. A conflict in communication may occur within the team. If you, as a broker are in conflict with the attorney, have your personal attorney or tax consultant communicate with the attorney. Attorneys sometimes respect input from other attorneys.

4. Because the closing of an exchange can be very complicated, problems can occur at closing. To avoid this, exchange closing statements should be checked by all members of the team at least 24 hours before closing. It is very difficult to cram an exchange into a standard residential closing form that cannot be adapted easily to the exchange concept. Remember that exchange closing statements are not sales contracts and it is easier to impress the auditors if they are always referred to as exchanges as opposed to sales, especially when we are trying to facilitate a 1031 tax deferred exchange.

Some Helpful Hints

The objective in an exchange should be to satisfy the client, not to satisfy your own ego. Form your team and solve your client's problems. There are several well known exchanging secrets that have been passed on that really have no author. These hints are offered to create food for thought.

• Real estate has no fixed measure of value.
• Separate, simultaneous closings reduce heartburn.

Exchange Recapitulation

Date _____

Property 1	Market Value 2	Existing Loans 3	Equity 4	Cash Gives (In) 5	Cash Gets (Out) 6	Paper Gives 7	Paper Gets 8	Comm. 9	Trans. Costs 10	Net Equity 11	New Loan 12	Old Loan 13	Net Loan Proceeds 14
A ADS	224,000	152,500	71,500	25,000				14,000	2,500	84,000	172,500	152,500	46,700
A G, ETS	500,000	424,000	51,000							51,000			
B HDS	500,000	175,000	325,000	-0-				24,000	4,000	297,000	424,000	175,000	249,000
B G, TS	224,000	172,000	24,000	272,000	272,000					297,000			
				25,000	272,000			35,000	6,500				41,700
				224,700	35,000			(33,000)	(1,500)				(27,200)
					6,500			-0-	-0-				-0-
				314,700	314,700								
				-0-									

Prepared by _____

- Never conduct a counselling session unless all parties (decision makers) are present.
- Never, never argue.
- Always explain the exchange concept to your client in terms of first, what he brings to the exchange, then, what he gets out of the exchange and last, and sometimes never, how he got there and how many deeds or contracts he will sign.
- Team members should be open and respect the importance of the others' role in the exchange.
- Balance the equities and wants, then worry about the taxes.
- Discuss nothing over the telephone, use it for making appointments only.

Murphy's Laws of Exchanging

- All exchanges will take longer to consummate than when they were first conceived.
- Absolutely no exchange is as easy as it appears on the surface.
- If someone can possibly mess up an exchange, they will.

7

Two Case
Studies

T he commercial-investment real estate broker's role is a finely tuned combination of skills focused in such a manner as to solve problems and consummate transactions for clients at a profit. Previous sections of this book have been devoted to a presentation of a marketing and management framework which can enhance marketing success. Much attention has been given to the business philosophies, listing and marketing techniques necessary to consummate successful transactions. The purpose of this section is to discuss and demonstrate the practical aspects of listing properties, planning your marketing efforts and then scheduling the marketing process.

Case Study A

A land transaction will be used for the first case study to avoid the complexities of more sophisticated transactions. The property profile for a land transaction is relatively simple and does not involve detailed schedules or diagrams.

The subject property is a 9.5-acre tract of land[1] in a C-3 zone which allows for most commercial activities and some light industrial activities such as warehousing, certain electronic plants and medical assembly activities. The property is well located on a major four lane highway in the center of an active industrial market. It is not contiguous to a strong residential market, but enjoys excellent visibility on a well-travelled east-west artery. It is just 300 feet west of a major north-south artery known as Starkey Road. There has been considerable industrial park development in the immediate area demonstrating demand for C-3 zoned property. In addition, there is active growth within a five-mile radius. The property is one of the few properties left with C-3 zoning in the immediate area. The initial listing contact resulted from a personal referral.

---

1. The author wishes to thank Warren J. Hughes, REALTOR®, president of U.S. Resico, Inc. and purchaser of the site, for his permission to use this property as a case study and for providing collateral information.

An important role of the overall marketing plan is to educate and inform the seller. A complete analysis was made of comparable sales and potential competitive properties in the marketplace and the market evaluation range (see page 121) was given to the seller. The seller accepted the market evaluation at $559,800 and signed the exclusive right of sale listing. The initial steps of the marketing plan included using the Target Market Generator (see pages 122–25) to develop a marketing plan. The marketing plan was developed and a budget was created.

It was essential to the seller that he receive at least $250,000 in cash which made the sale more difficult than if a minimum down payment had been required. The tract is on a well-travelled highway relatively close to an intersection, but is not actually on the intersection. There is a "median cut,"—one crossover—centrally located for the tract. A very congested highway makes for less than advantageous ingress and egress for most developments.

The property was priced at the top of the market for its size which dictated a user rather than a speculator for the acquisition. One of the first phases of any land marketing program would include contacting the contiguous property owners. Initial contacts with the contiguous property owners in this case resulted in a formal contract offer and acceptance within two weeks of the initial listing. This first contract put on the subject property ultimately failed to close due to the contiguous property owner failing to complete the terms of the contract. The marketing plan was reinstituted and a second contract was generated from an industrial developer who had been targeted. Ultimately, this contract also failed to be consummated as this developer desired to acquire the site only if he could acquire the contiguous property to the east. A third developer was targeted and offers were made involving exchanges of other property and cash.

Finally, the property was sold to a developer originally targeted for an office/warehouse project by including the sale of out parcels (parcels not included in the original tract but contiguous to it). It was ultimately necessary for the company, acting as the listing broker, to place contracts on the contiguous property in order to consummate a transaction on this property and provide ingress and egress to the four-lane highway to the east. This increased access made the property considerably more valuable and resulted in the ultimate sale.

The property profiles and flyers that were created for the subject property are included for reference. An example of an Active Listing Marketing Feedback report to the seller is also included (page 127). This was part of the overall education process necessary to consummate the transaction. A complete partitioning program, in which the tract was broken into smaller portions, was prepared for the seller in an effort to sell parcels smaller than the entire tract (page 128). It is evident from a study of the use of the marketing plans and forms that no one program should be relied upon, but all programs that have been developed in the plan should be continuously worked.

ULMERTON & STARKEY Road intersection approximately 341 feet west of Subject Property. Central Pinellas County, Florida "HOT SPOT"!

9.324 ACRES Rectangular parcel with 682.52 feet more or less on Ulmerton Road with a depth of 596.47 feet. Visual inspections and the tree survey show mostly pine trees and palmetos cover the entire area.

ZONED C-3 Commercial, Wholesale & Warehousing. C-3 allows all C-1 and C-2 uses. Most general commercial uses and various light manufacturing are allowed in this zoning classification. Land use is consistent with zoning.

HIGHEST & BEST USE The demand for real estate in the Ulmerton/Starkey Road market has been very strong in recent years. Zoning has played an important role in directing growth and the resulting land use. Few sites along Ulmerton Road offer the intensive quasi Commercial/Industrial uses and size that this site offers. At 9.3 acres, it is an excellent size for a major office/industrial research park with Commercial use fronting Ulmerton Road.

PRICED AT $559,000 Terms: Minimum cash $225,000. Seller will consider holding a purchase money mortgage for a short term at market interest rates. $59,953 per acre.

(This information is believed to be accurate, we are not responsible for misstatements of facts, errors or omissions, prior sale, changes of price or withdrawal from the market without notice.)

LOCATOR MAP

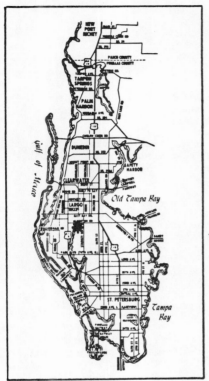

ULMERTON ROAD

9.5 ACRES
ZONED C-3

CENTRAL PINELLAS
"HOT SPOT"

- COUNTY

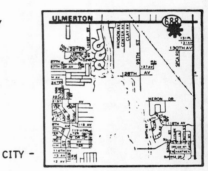

CITY -

SITE -

N

EAST BAY DRIVE

ALT 19

STARKEY ROAD

ULMERTON ROAD

Subject

(Not To Scale)

(This information is believed to be accurate, we are not responsible for misstatements of facts, errors or omissions, prior sale, changes of price or withdrawal from the market without notice.)

PROPERTY DESCRIPTION

PHYSICAL
DESCRIPTION: The Subject Property is rectangular shaped and consists
               of 9.324 acres with 682.52 feet more or less on Ulmerton
               Road with a depth of 596.47 feet.

               A topographic survey by Coast Engineering indicates
               a generally flat parcel with east elevations in the 17.5
               to 18 foot range with 17 feet to 17.5 feet on the western
               zone.

               Visual inspections and the tree survey show mostly pine
               trees and palmetos cover the entire area. Tree sizes
               range 8 to 12 inches in circumference on the tree survey.

LOCATION: The 9.324 acres is located approximately 341 feet west of
               the intersection of Starkey and Ulmerton Roads, Central
               Pinellas County, Florida. (See Locator Map).

INGRESS AND   The property has direct access off of Ulmerton Road.
EGRESS: There is a median break that provides westbound traffic
               access to the property.

ZONING: The current owner zoned the property from M-1, Light
               Manufacturing & Industry to C-3 Commercial, Wholesale and
               Warehousing on February 20, 1979. This zoning is
               compatible with the Comprehensive Land Use Plan. C-3
               allows all C-2 and C-1 uses. Most General Commercial
               uses and various Light Manufacturing are allowed in this
               zoning classification.

WATER: A twenty-four inch (24") Pinellas County water line is
               available along the south side of Ulmerton Road and may
               be tapped.

SEWER: The property is located within the Largo sanitary sewer
               service area, however, sanitary sewer is not on site. It
               is anticipated that elevated sand filter will be used, as
               is typical for the area and just approved for the
               contiguous property owner. There is a sanitary sewer
               within 800 feet of the southwest corner that can be
               accessed with a force main and lift station.

HIGHEST AND BEST USE OF PROPERTY: The demand for real estate in the Ulmerton/Starkey Road market has been very strong in recent years. Zoning has played an important role in directing growth and the resulting land use. Few sites along Ulmerton Road offer the intensive quasi Commercial/Industrial uses (C-3) and size that this site offers. At 9.3 acres, it is an excellent size for a major office/industrial research park with commercial use fronting Ulmerton Road.

TAXES: 1980: Assessed amount: $195,050.00
Amount due in November: $3,322.98

OWNER'S NAMES: J. A. Jones

LEGAL DESCRIPTION: Lots 2 and 3 Pinellas Groves in the Northeast 1/4 Section 11, Township 30 South, Range 16 East. Pinellas County, Florida.

PRICE: $559,000

TERMS: Minimum cash $225,000
Seller will consider holding a purchase money mortgage for a short term at market interest rates.

SPECIALIZED INFORMATION: Completed warehouse plans and engineering available including expired Department of Transportation driveway permits. Contact listing office.

FOR ADDITIONAL INFORMATION CONTACT: Real Estate, Inc.
1345 South Missouri Avenue
Clearwater, Florida 33516

This information is believed to be accurate, we are not responsible for misstatements of facts, errors or omissions, prior sale, changes of price or withdrawal from the market without notice.

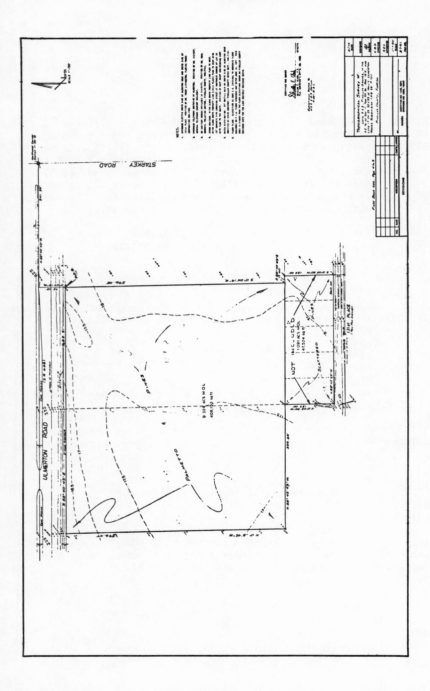

VALUE RANGE & MARKET EVALUATION

BUYER APPEAL: (How does subject appear in the eyes of objective buyers)

(1)	Location	20	%
(2)	Terms; financing	10	%
(3)	Under market price	10	%
(4)	Development potential (water, sewer, zoning, etc.)	10	%
(5)	Area market conditions/property appeal	20	%
	TOTAL RATING	70	%

MARKETING POSITION: (Evaluation of saleability)

(1)	Seller motivation (reason)		15	%
(2)	Time period sale must be completed		15	%
(3)	Seller will help finance	Yes _x_ No ____	15	%
(4)	Property listed at market value	Yes _x_ No ____	15	%
(5)	Seller will consider _alternatives_ - lease, exchange build-to-suit		15	%
	TOTAL RATING		75	%

In grading, list five items representing 100%. Each item represents a maximum unit of 20%. A yes can be 5, 10, 15 or 20%; a no is zero.

Assets/Benefits Location very good. Zoning allows good flexibility. Owners are aware of Development problems.

Negatives/Drawbacks No sewer. Cost of cross over. Large ditch on Frontage Road very congested. No access on Starkey. Not a corner.

Area Market Conditions Good growth in area. Leasing of C-3 warehouses somewhat slow. No comparable tract in immediate area on market.

Recommended Terms Look for a Section 1237 Sale with at least one partition to generate cash to pay off 1st mortgage, then offer owner financing on balance.

RANGE OF VALUE:

	(Terms)		
Top Listing Price		$559,800	$60,000 P/A
Probable Final Sale Price		$513,150	$55,000
Cash to Mortgage Sales Price		$447,840	$48,000

This recommended Listing Price is a measure of the top value Real Estate, Incorporated estimates the property should be offered. There is no absolute value for any one property. Our estimate is based on generally acceptable valuation techniques but is not intended to be a formal appraisal.

TARGET MARKET AND
MARKETING PLAN GENERATOR

Listing Code ___VF 8.03-A111___

Property ___9.5 ACRES - ULMERTON ROAD___

Date ___May, 1983___

1. PROPERTY CHARACTERISTICS (BASIC)

Zoning ___C-3___ APOD Owner statement ___n/a___

Land Use ___Industrial___

Size ___9.5 Acres___ APOD Broker's Forecast ___n/a___

Topography ___Pine trees, palmetto and flat___

Water ___Ulmerton Road frontage___ Specialized Information ___Cross-over on frontage.___

Sewer ___Not available on-site, however,___ Construction ___n/a___
___available within 800' of site - may require lift station.___

2. FINANCING

	Assumable Existing	Owner Pur. Mon.	New Institutional
Current Balance	200,000	yes	
Annual Interest Rate	New York - prime	12-13%	
Payment Am't. & Frequency	Interest only	mo.- quarterly	
Remaining Term		1 year balloon	
Assumption Provisions	Line of credit loar, No assumption	yes	
Prepayment Penalties		no	
Personal Endorsement	Yes	no	
Release Clauses	None	Possible	
Subordination Clauses	None	no	

___Best approach is to payoff first mortgage of approximately $200,000.___

___Provide approximately $50,000 cash to seller___

a) WHAT ALTERNATIVE FINANCING APPROACHES ARE AVAILABLE?

___Acquisition Development Loan. Possible to get.___

___Subordination from seller with letter of credit.___

b) WHAT IS THE LIKELY FINAL FINANCIAL STRUCTURE OR APPROACH THAT WILL BE USED TO CLOSE THE SALE?

___All cash at closing or $250,000 cash down; balance in one year. Possible to get subordination on purchase money mortgage portion.___

DEVELOP TARGET MARKET

1. How does the property relate to the market? Based on market price, property characteristics and financing, what are the best uses that will result in the highest price in Owner's time frame?

   Market dictates listing price, however, price dictates a user, not a speculative buyer. User must produce a product that can support the price. A mini-warehouse or office warehouse project could support asking price. The retail user of a shopping center is best suited to support price. Market not ideal commercial area.

2. What use "need" is most sought after based on Market Conditions that the property could meet?

   Office/Condo/Warehouse --- Retail possible.

   Look at bank site location.

   Warehouse showroom.

   Research/Office complex or park - study various divisions.

3. Describe and define size and scope of market for Subject Property. Local, State, Out Of State, World, Investment/User, etc.

   Best market is local developer based on size of product, however market offers good potential. Most likely target is a Tampa Bay industrial/commercial developer/user.

4. What use or user is missing or limited in the market?

   No apparent gaps in market, contiguous property owner has rental product available; office retail center in vicinity has product availability; office/warehouse; population driving pattern doesn't support strong retail location.

5. What are the benefits this property offers?

   Good central location; C-3 zoning with consistent land use.

   Negatives to deal with are: priced at top of market - cash required by seller. Access poor on heavily traveled property. Sewer not immediately available.

6. Define Highest & Best Use of Property.

   Shopping center or office/warehouse complex with sale of out parcels to free-standing retail or banks.

7. Given the above thought process, list in order of priority the potential target prospects, in general.

   Contiguous property owners

   Office/warehouse developer list

   Joe Greunete

   Shopping Center Developers

   Banks

   Restaurants

DEVELOPING MARKET PROGRAMS

(1) Marketing programs should be developed based on Time and Cost.

(2) Primary focus on Target Prospect/Market.

(3) Develop plan based on needs that property can satisfy.

(4) List ALL of various programs that logically should facilitate a sale.

(5) Develop Marketing Budget:

- What is estimated FEE?
- What is percentage probability of co-brokerage?
- What is total dollar to be expended in marketing?

Allocate to Programs:		
Gross Fee	$	59,000
Co-brokerage	$	29,500
In-house Salesperson	$	14,750
Company	$	14,750
Classified	$	300
Direct Mail	$	500
Signage	$	150
Engineering Other (special publications, etc.)	$	1,500

(6) Schedule Programs:

a) Highest probability first.

b) As schedule is developed, choose programs with highest probability that fall within Budget until allocated funds are exhausted.

LIST PROGRAMS BEST SUITED FOR PLAN — HIGHEST PROBABILITY VS. COST.

1. Personal contact/contiguous property
2. owners and developers
3. Direct mail
4. Broker programs
5. Newsletter featured listing
6. Have engineer design project
7. Specialized sign 4' x 6'
8. Branch bank contact program
9. Inventory past 2 yrs. C-3 sales
10. Market in Tampa/Industrial/Commercial
11. MLS Clearwater/St. Petersburg
12. Engineer site for development of
13. office/warehouse
14. Solve sewer problems
15. Hotsheet/flyer
16. Property profile
17. Setup property division
18. Acquire contiguous property to east
19.
20.
21.
22.
23.
24.
25.
26.
27.
28.
29.
30.
31.
32.
33.
34.
35.
36.
37.
38.
39.
40.

8. Based on needs that can be fulfilled by property, what prospects come to mind?

1	Mr. Mel	41	
2	Nibur	42	
3	Acquire	43	
4	Iley	44	
5	Paul Revere	45	
6	Island Construction	46	
7	Starkey Development Corp.	47	
8	Follow up on banks - calls	48	
9	Developer across street	49	
10	Mini-warehouse developers	50	
11	Blackman	51	
12	Rarydyre	52	
13	Individual with 1031 money	53	
14	Warren Dynamic	54	
15	A.Davis, Cen. Plaza Bank:ABA Indust. on Board	55	
16	Roger Park	56	
17	Berger	57	
18	Tall Pines Group; Gulf States Corp.	58	
19	Highrise complex developer on Rose-	59	
20	velt Blvd.	60	
21		61	
22		62	
23		63	
24		64	
25		65	
26		66	
27		67	
28		68	
29		69	
30		70	
31		71	
32		72	
33		73	
34		74	
35		75	
36		76	
37		77	
38		78	
39		79	
40		80	

$$\frac{4/14/83}{\text{AS OF (DATE)}}$$

Comparable properties that have sold in the last two years.

Loc.	Dimensions	Total Sq.Ft.	Zoning	Price $ Price Sq.Ft.	Date
(1)	47 Acres	2,047,320	C-3	$416,000/ .20	4/11/83
(2)	2.44 Acres	106,286	C-2	68,000/ .64	3/83
(3)	6.099 Acres	265,672	C-2	460,000/1.73	4/83
(4)	8.02 Acres	349,351	C-2	850,000/2.43	7/83
(5)	11.57 Acres	503,989	C-2	1,150,000/2.28	7/82

Comparable properties that are for sale.

Loc.	Dimensions	Total Sq.Ft.	Zoning	Price $ Price Sq.Ft.	Date
(7)	165x590 / 2.235 Ac.	97,350	C-2/M-1	$275,000/2.82	3/83
(8)	180x360 / 1.48 Ac.	64,800	C-3/LU.1	135,000/2.08	4/83
(9)	102x300 / .7 Ac.	30,600	C-2/Comm	85,000/2.78	4/83
(10)	100x295 / .677 Ac.	29,500	C-2/Comm	(Asking-under contract) 85,000/2.88	4/83
(11)	250x622 / 3.56 Ac.	155,509	C-2/Comm	400,000/2.57	4/83
(12)	420x700 / 6.74 Ac.	294,000	C-2/Comm	225,000/ .77	4/83

LISTING NAME_____9.5 ACRES_____   CODE_____

WEEK OF_____

DIRECT ACTION TAKEN TO MARKET PROPERTY
Direct mail - Banks (personal contact at most visible office), warehouses,
development businesses, contiguous property owners, produce property profiles
and two types of aerial briefs, broker program, in-house brainstorm and sale
programs.

OWNER CONTACTED BY (at least once a week) PHONE, IN PERSON, LETTER, ETC.

Contacts made bi-weekly.

PEOPLE CONTACTED AND HOW CONTACTED
See attached partial list.

WHY LISTING HAS NOT SOLD
Timing, missed on Joe Greunete by one month; have not matched the developer
in market; broker programs have not resulted in firm contract; in-house
program has developed most leads; contract failure with contiguous property
owner.

WHAT WOULD HELP SELL LISTING
More contacts; better distribution of new brochures; establish program for
property development; establish strong broker program; re-contact developer
list. Develop a program for partition of the property.

WHAT ADJUSTMENTS TO MARKET PLAN (SEE PROBLEM SOLVING PROCEDURE)
Best program is a stronger program with retail emphasis, developers - industrial
distribution warehouses.

                                        Salesman

Two Case Studies   127

PROPOSED SUBDIVISION MARKETING PLAN

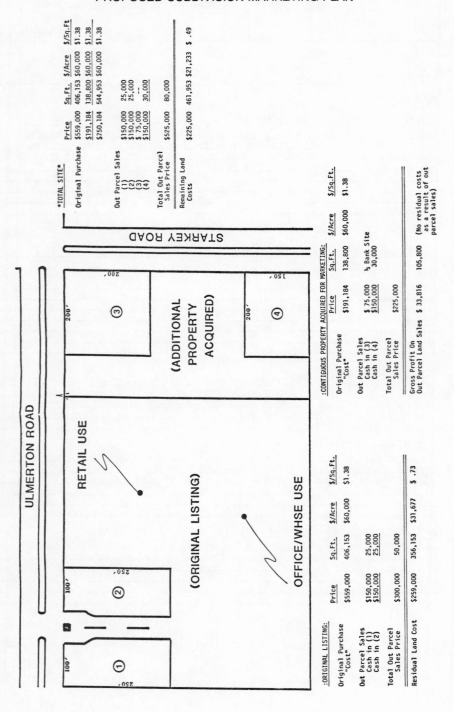

TOTAL SITE

	Price	Sq.Ft.	$/Acre	$/Sq.Ft.
Original Purchase	$559,000	406,153	$60,000	$1.38
	$191,184	138,800	$60,000	$1.38
	$750,184	544,953	$60,000	$1.38
Out Parcel Sales				
(1)	$150,000	25,000		
(2)	$150,000	25,000		
(3)	$ 75,000	--		
(4)	$150,000	30,000		
Total Out Parcel Sales Price	$525,000	80,000		
Remaining Land Costs	$225,000	461,953	21,233	$ .49

:ORIGINAL LISTING:

	Price	Sq.Ft.	$/Acre	$/Sq.Ft.
Original Purchase "Cost"	$559,000	406,153	$60,000	$1.38
Out Parcel Sales				
Cash in (1)	$150,000	25,000		
Cash in (2)	$150,000	25,000		
Total Out Parcel Sales Price	$300,000	50,000		
Residual Land Cost	$259,000	356,153	$31,677	$ .73

:CONTIGUOUS PROPERTY ACQUIRED FOR MARKETING:

	Price	Sq.Ft.	$/Acre	$/Sq.Ft.
Original Purchase "Cost"	$191,184	138,800	$60,000	$1.38
Out Parcel Sales				
Cash in (3)	$ 75,000	½ Bank Site 30,000		
Cash in (4)	$150,000			
Total Out Parcel Sales Price	$225,000			
Gross Profit On Out Parcel Land Sales	$ 33,816	105,800	(No residual costs as a result of out parcel sales)	

ULMERTON ROAD

STARKEY ROAD

RETAIL USE

OFFICE/WHSE USE

(ORIGINAL LISTING)

(ADDITIONAL PROPERTY ACQUIRED)

9.5 ACRES

MOST IMPORTANT ACTION

1. Contract with contiguous property owner.

2. Close review by Joe Greunete of Master Rentals rejected due to timing conflict with another project. In-house personal contact.

3. Reach Construction Co. - After careful review, chose different site (east of 49th St. on Ulmerton) based on numbers and access. Sign/switch from another sign on 49th St.

4. Golf Cart developer - Rejected size due to industrial neighborhood. Personal contact.

5. Jim Hayworth of Builder Corporation - still considering site with cash-out from public offering; would take 6 months to complete. Personal contact.

6. Shown to the Office Group, Tampa - next meeting scheduled Monday with architect, Bill Harrigan. Tampa. Personal contact.

7. Super SuperMarket - Presented to V.P. of Real Estate Acquisitions; would replace unit at Ulmerton and 19.

8. Close review by contiguous property owner again; rejected due to high interest rates.

9. Sylvia Hardawaf - Client is reviewing property; principal problem is accessing - will know in two weeks. Personal contact by company associate.

10. Banker-targeted direct mail completed.

11. Kingman - Wants 5 acres; is considering offer on just 5 acres.

12. Plastic Pens - 50,000 square feet plant; should know by Monday.

Case Study B

The second case study, which is rather complex, has been chosen to demonstrate techniques not normally observed in less complex marketing efforts. Forms and procedures and presentations have been graciously approved for publication by the parties to the transaction. The case study is of an actual sale closed in 1982. The principal corporation listing the property with Real Estate, Inc., who granted use of the internal information and use of corporate data, is gratefully and respectfully acknowledged. The owner of the building which was the subject of the listing and sale was Pioneer Federal Savings and Loan Association, Chairman of the Board, William Nodine. The purchasing corporation was Sterile Design, President Richard Isel. The other names referred to herein, including the name of the brokerage company, have been changed and are fictitious. As is evidenced in this case study, an important and key role was played by Joel L. Parker, REALTOR®, an independent contractor associated with Real Estate, Inc.

Description of Property Being Sold

The property to be sold was a freestanding, five story office building, the former home of a large regional savings and loan. The building is in a single tenant configuration and is on partially leased land. The sale included a freestanding, 5,000 square foot office building, a gas station and remote parking lots. The city in which it is located has experienced reasonable rental absorption, but over the last 12 months, because of the national recession, has experienced some declines in demand for new rental space.

The CCIM designated courses program places great emphasis on building a team and the CCIM's role in team coordination. A copy of the MAI appraisal of the subject property has been included (appendix to Chapter 7) with the permission of Warren J. Hunnicutt, Jr., MAI appraiser. The appraisal is included because it demonstrates the importance of the professional appraisal to the team and gives the reader an opportunity to view the property through the eyes of a professional, sophisticated appraiser.

The Exclusive Right of Sale Listing

The basis of the business philosophies contained throughout the text have focused on the necessity of an exclusive right of sale listing. This has been borne out by the level of intensity of marketing efforts required to consummate this particular sale. The actual exclusive right of sale resulted from the most basic listing technique known to most brokers—the cold call. The author observed in the local newspapers that Pioneer Federal was in the process of building a new headquarters and quite possibly would not need the existing building. A direct cold call telephone contact of the Chairman of the Board resulted in a lunch and subsequent discussion of marketing techniques. Subsequent to the initial contact with the Chairman of the Board and Senior Vice-President, we were requested to provide a listing proposal to the Board of Directors of the Federal. The following reflects our perception of the property early in the listing process. It should be noted that we were advised in our initial meetings that the Federal felt the value of the property was 3.3 million dollars. The following is our initial proposal letter:

August 18, 1981

Mr. Parker J. Stafford
Senior Vice-President
Pioneer Federal Savings and Loan
P.O. Box 4608
Clearwater, Florida 33518

Re: Pioneer Federal—Cleveland Street Properties

Dear Mr. Stafford:

At your request we have carefully reviewed plans and specifications, made a physical inspection, and have studied the MAI appraisal prepared by Warren J. Hunnicutt, Jr. for the above referenced property. The scope of our review has been limited to 1) listing value, and 2) market potential.

Listing value is the maximum listing price for which Real Estate, Inc. recommends the subject property be offered. The market potential is an estimate of the probability of a sale or satisfactory transaction structure within the listing term based on the listing price recommended.

Listing Value

Your appraiser, Warren J. Hunnicutt, Jr. made an exhaustive, professional and well thought-out appraisal of the subject properties. We believe that subject to reasonable adjustment for time (appraisal date January 15, 1981) that your appraiser's appraisal is accurate and clearly defensible given generally accepted appraisal techniques.

Real Estate, Inc. is a full-service, exclusively commercial-investment marketing company. We do not offer appraisal services for fee. We specialize in marketing.

Marketing is the sum total of all efforts used to identify and attract potential buyers that results in the consummation and orderly transfer of the subject property at the highest price, in a reasonable time frame, based on acceptable terms.

Our efforts are concentrated on creating desire and turning desire into need. We buy what we feel we need. We are sold on what we are persuaded we want and to the point of satisfying need.

Through translation and communication of the benefits of the subject property we are often able to obtain sales at prices not realized through the normal appraisal process. It is in this context that we developed our estimate of the listing value. The price you choose to sell your property at and the ultimate sale is more a function of the terms than the total dollars. This transaction offers flexibility as the Federal controls numerous variables, including but not limited to:

- Mortgage financing terms and conditions
- Leaseback terms and conditions
- Time period of executive space availability

- Partial or total sales
- Joint venture transactions
- Cash flow associated with the landlease
- Method of sale and transaction structure
- Type of prospect to be sold
- Confidentiality of sale

Specifically, the Federal has more influence on the price than does the market itself or the physical structure. It is in this context we judge marketability.

As previously stated the MAI appraisal is an excellent example of informed valuation techniques. Mr. Hunnicutt's methodology is based on sound principles, excellent research and experienced judgment. Our comments are intended to offer a marketing perspective and not in any way intended to negate the validity of the appraisal made by Mr. Hunnicutt.

On page five of your appraisal, a basic premise of the appraisal stated that, "We are of the opinion that an implicit assemblage value is not applicable to the appraised property due to the distinctive physical and economic division of the entire property." We would suggest there may exist a very real additional benefit associated with the assemblage of this tract as opposed to individual buildings being located on different comparable parcels. If we are able to identify the benefits through assemblage and communicate the same, a higher listing price would be suggested.

Investment value as defined in the appraisal is predicated upon certain defined parameters including but not limited to absorbtion rates (1;000 sq. ft. per month), operating expenses, holding periods and debt service. The investment market is one of our primary targets. In our judgment we may be able to show a higher absorbtion rate and lower operating expenses which may improve the investment value estimates. However, we are cognizant of a higher debt service potential which may offset these positive adjustments to the pro forma. We will be making extensive investment projections and testing sensitivity with our computer in an effort to communicate the best sales scenario possible, that is, of course, within professional, ethical and reasonable standards.

We do not in any way contest the validity of the appraisal. We, in fact, tempered our estimate by the very careful study that was completed. We do however feel that due to the numerous transaction structures that can be created and consummated, that a higher listing value is warranted.

There are certain variables that will make our marketing effort a formidable challenge at the higher than appraised listing price. These variables include:

1. an office building market that desires waterfront visibility,
2. the City of Tampa may face an overbuilt office market in 1982–83 with a negative ripple effect for the Clearwater market,
3. Orange Bank's new project which is in the advanced planning stage,
4. the current cost of money certainly plays a role in today's marketing plans,
5. a marketing plan that will be very limited in an effort to maintain a low profile locally,
6. the functional aspects of a five story building which is essentially designed for a single user, rather than a multi-tenant user, more typical of the market place,
7. marketing restricted to nonfinancial institutions.

The aforementioned are not insurmountable negatives but are realities to be faced with well thought-out sales techniques. After careful consideration of the marketability of this product we recommend that the properties be offered as a total assembled package.

We suggest that the leaseback terms be left flexible during the initial stages of our marketing effort.

Financing should be expected and a management decision made between ultimate top sales dollar and loan return. We will make a careful review of potential loan and transaction structures, including participation loans, partial and full joint ventures, partial and full sales, and other approaches that will maximize the Federal's return and wealth.

A top listing price of $3,199,000 is recommended. A probable final sales price of $3,000,000 to $3,050,000 should be expected. Our listing agreement calls for cash or terms acceptable to the Federal. The sale will be subject to successful negotiation of a leaseback of the executive space on a short term and the main first floor and drive-in facilities on a long term.

We have not attempted to develop a representative marketing plan or to recommend an advertising budget at this time. We have devoted our energies to establishing a listing value and discussing alternative marketing approaches in order to foster this higher than appraised value sales price.

We believe we are uniquely qualified in the Tampa Bay market to handle the sale of this property. In your immediate market we sold the South Building, the Heart Hotel, the Restaurant House, former Worth Building, leased to T.O.T., which has now been sold for what will be known as the Jones Bank Building. We have also recently consummated the sale to Kane Federal of the T-K Office Building. We sold the old high school property, the Law Office Building site, Square Office Building site, the Hope Office Building, Fort Harrison Office Building to the Plant Hospital, the current Doctor Office Building site and others. Current activities in the market include insight into the current office building market for downtown Clearwater. We are leasing agents for the Jones Bank Building, the second phase of Law Office Building, Dr. Smith Building, the Dr. Kite Office Building and numerous other office buildings throughout Clearwater. We have represented World Federal, Kane Federal, First Bank, State Bank, Plaza Bank, and Pine County in the acquisition and sale of real estate.

We have provided you a copy of our South Building sale and negotiations file. Please note it involves extensive sophisticated investment analysis in an effort to bring the parties together under acceptable terms and conditions.

We appreciate the time and candor you personally have offered in our initial stages of this marketing effort. It is extremely important to maintain this level of rapport if we are going to optimize our team effort. We look forward to beginning work immediately.

Sincerely,

Broker, CCIM

The proposal letter was delivered to the Federal and a formal presentation was made to the appropriate vice-president in charge of disposition of the property. While our highest recommended price was $3,199,000, we agreed to take the property as high as $3.3 million, consistent with the seller's expectations. It is often difficult to dispute a seller's perception of value early in the listing effort. In the author's opinion, when sincere motivation has been determined to be strong, it outweighs the initial listing price determination. As a result, the $3.3 million listing was consummated and the marketing effort began.

Our initial marketing program was rather basic and involved preparing initial property profiles and briefs with a full understanding of property characteristics. As is often the case, the first property profile is rather detailed and will eventually be scaled down. The copy of our first marketing plan and the first property profile is as follows.

LEE ARNOLD & ASSOCIATES, INC.
COMMERCIAL-INVESTMENT REAL ESTATE
REALTORS

TARGET MARKET AND
MARKETING PLAN GENERATOR

Listing Code _____

Property ____ Pioneer Federal _____

Date _____

1. PROPERTY CHARACTERISTICS (BASIC)

Zoning ____ DD _____ APOD Owner statement _____

Land Use ____ Conforms _____

Size ____ 54,000 Gross _____ APOD Broker's Forecast _____

Topography _____

Water ____ OK _____ Specialized Information _____

Sewer ____ OK _____ Construction _____

2. FINANCING

	Assumable Existing	Owner Pur. Mon.	New Institutional
Current Balance		2,000,000±	
Annual Interest Rate		13%-15%	
Payment Am't. & Frequency		Monthly	
Remaining Term		25-30	
Assumption Provisions			
Prepayment Penalties			
Personal Endorsement		Yes/Possibly No	
Release Clauses			
Subordination Clauses			
Balloon expected year 10			

a) WHAT ALTERNATIVE FINANCING APPROACHES ARE AVAILABLE?
Cash, participation financing, pension fund

b) WHAT IS THE LIKELY FINAL FINANCIAL STRUCTURE OR APPROACH THAT WILL BE USED TO CLOSE THE SALE?
Leaseback of at least 1 or 2 floors with 2-3 year lease

DEVELOP TARGET MARKET

1. How does the property relate to the market? Based on market price, property characteristics and financing, what are the best uses that will result in the highest price in Owner's time frame?

    Office use highest and best use/user property ideal

    In order to convert to multi-tenant need plans completed

2. What use "need" is most sought after based on Market Conditions that the property could meet?

    Office space – multi-tenant, not major floor user

    A 7,000 square foot user is rare in Clearwater

    2,000 – 3,000 square foot normal

3. Describe and define size and scope of market for Subject Property. Local. State. Out Of State. World. Investment/User. etc.

    Scope is national on full leaseback or soft terms

    Local user if sold noninvestment

4. What use or user is missing or limited in the market?

5. What are the benefits this property offers?

    Financial institution, 1st floor, largest quantity of prestigious

    space, immediate availability, 16,306 sq. ft. leaseback.

    Location, size, below replacement cost, main street, executive

    quality space, flexibility in sale/leaseback

6. Define Highest & Best Use of Property.

    Office space for main building, multi-tenant, gas station

    conversion to office or parking lots

7. Given the above thought process, list in order of priority the potential target prospects, in general.

    a) general user targets on mass media

    b) target investment buyer – look for transaction structure

        that results in a win-win transaction

DEVELOPING MARKET PROGRAMS

(1) Marketing programs should be developed based on Time and Cost.

(2) Primary focus on Target Prospect/Market.

(3) Develop plan based on needs that property can satisfy.

(4) List ALL of various programs that logically should facilitate a sale.

(5) Develop Marketing Budget:

- What is estimated FEE?
- What is percentage probability of co-brokerage?
- What is total dollar to be expended in marketing?

Allocate to Programs:		
Gross Fee	$	
Co-brokerage	$	
In-house Salesperson	$	
Company	$	
Classified	$	300
Direct Mail	$	500
Signage	$	
Other (special publications, etc.)	$	2,000

(6) Schedule Programs:
a) Highest probability first.
b) As schedule is developed, choose programs with highest probability that fall within Budget until allocated funds are exhausted.

LIST PROGRAMS BEST SUITED FOR PLAN — HIGHEST PROBABILITY VS. COST.

1 _____
2 Initial Plan: _____
3 Preparation of action file (staff)
4 Feature in monthly newsletter (staff)
5 Ad budget and plan (staff, LEA, JLP)
6 Prepare property profile (JLP)
7 Review appraisal (JLP, LEA)
8 Fla Power audit (JLP)
9 Study maintenance and A/C contract (JLP)
10 Obtain copies landlease (JLP)
11 Meet w/ facility systems operator (JLP,LEA)
12 Complete broker audit expense (JLP)
13 Prepare APOD (JLP)
14 Prepare absorption projections (JLP)
15 Competitive sales analysis (JLP)
16 Talk w/ key appraisers (JLP,LEA)
17 Confirm lease parameters (JLP, LEA)
18 Run computer projections (JLP, LEA)
19 Establish contact prospect list (JLP,LEA)
20 Review past wants for prospects (JLP,LEA)

21 _____
22 Contact major investors (LEA)
23 Establish target market (JLP, LEA)
24 Establish broker program — lunch
25 with top 10 commercial brokers,
26 cocktail party on site (JLP, LEA)
27 Contact CPM building managers (LEA)
28 _____
29 _____
30 _____
31 _____
32 _____
33 _____
34 _____
35 _____
36 _____
37 _____
38 _____
39 _____
40 _____

DOWNTOWN CLEARWATER
PRESTIGIOUS OFFICE COMPLEX

Pioneer Federal Savings & Loan Association offers for sale their original home office located on Cleveland Street. This outstanding office investment is enhanced by Pioneer Federal's financing the acquisition and leasing back major portions on a long term basis. Your personal viewing is recommended to fully appreciate the excellent use of space and interior appointments this property offers.

The Pioneer Federal complex includes three buildings totalling over 54,000 square feet of office space. This complex is supported by 3.8 acres of land which provides more than adequate parking. Offered at $3,300,000. Contact Joel Parker, af.hrs. 581-1596.

Property Profile

54,000 Square Foot Clearwater Office Complex

(This information is believed to be accurate. We are not responsible for misstatements of facts, errors or omissions, prior sale, changes of price or withdrawal from the market without notice.)

Pioneer Federal Savings and Loan Association
Cleveland Plaza
Clearwater, Florida 33516

Improvements

4 Buildings and Supporting Land

4 Buildings

1. 5 Story   —41,000 gross square feet main building
2. 2 Story   — 8,000 gross square feet attached to main building
3. 1 Story   — 5,000 gross square feet east building
4. Gas Station ——
                  54,000 Total Square Feet of Office

Supporting Land

2.53 Acres—Owned Fee Simple
1.27 Acres—landleased (74 years remaining)
3.8 Acres (M.O.L.) PERHAPS ROOM FOR MORE OFFICE SPACE!!

Purchase Price

$3,300,000

Terms

The Federal will finance the purchase with 20 percent down, balance over 30 years at market interest rate.

Leaseback

The Federal will lease back the ground floor and the second floor of the main building on a long-term basis.

1

PIONEER FEDERAL
SAVINGS AND LOAN ASSOCIATION

PINELLAS COUNTY, FLORIDA

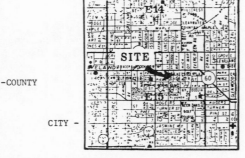

A PRESTIGIOUS OFFICE COMPLEX
IN DOWNTOWN CLEARWATER

-COUNTY

CITY -

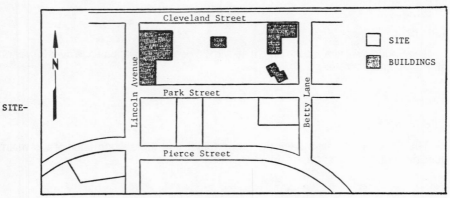

SITE-

SITE

BUILDINGS

(This information is believed to be accurate, we are not responsible
for misstatements of facts, errors or omissions, prior sale, changes
of price or withdrawal from the market without notice.)

2

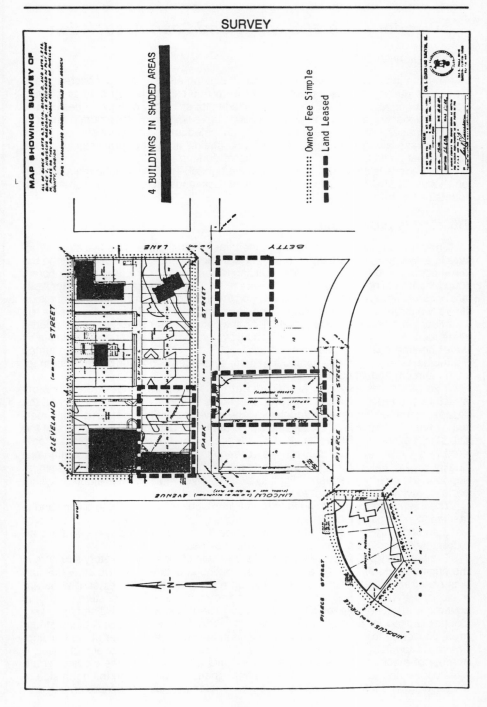

3

Pioneer Federal Savings and Loan Association

Site Improvement

The site improvements consist of asphalt parking and driveways, concrete walkways and curbing and landscaping. There are approximately 150 marked parking spaces. It appears the site is not fully utilized in its efficiency of parking design and layout. Excessive curbing and parking islands have limited the maximum number of parking spaces, although presenting an uncongested and scenic appearance. (Note: Green space along Park Street and service station area of approximately 20,000 square feet could be converted into additional parking.)

The Federal is attractively landscaped throughout. The fronts of the main building on Cleveland Street and Lincoln Avenue have lush landscaping, with two ornamental fountains on the north side.

Building Improvements

The main structure appears as a modern institutional office. This five story structure is a two phase development; the first two floors were built in 1963, with the top three floors being built in 1973. The building is constructed on a reinforced concrete foundation; framing is poured concrete with rebar to specifications. The exterior walls are concrete block with exterior face brick on the ground floor and cotico tile panels on floors two through five. The finished floor elevations vary from 12 to 13 feet for the top four floors and 16 feet for the ground floor; the floor structures are precast or poured reinforced concrete. Central air conditioning system is chilled water and heating is by water heating coils. The mechanical and electrical systems include a roof-mounted lightning protection system, central fire alarm system and communication system for both intercom and video tv screens.

Two passenger elevators are located at the southwest corner of the five story structure and are incorporated within the entrance lobby on the ground level and the reception area on levels two through five. The elevators are made by Otis. The emergency fire proof stairwells are located at the northeast and southeast corners of the five story building for all five levels. All walls are finished drywall and/or plaster, covered in a variety of vinyl or suede wall coverings. All floor covering is commercial quality wall-to-wall carpeting. All ceilings are dropped, acoustical tile on aluminum supports with various recessed lighting fixtures. Over the fifth floor atrium, skylight panels provide direct sunlight to floors three through five.

The interior space, including the ground floor/lobby areas, is of high quality and is fashionably appointed in contemporary design. Extensive utilization of fixed and/or freestanding partitions has been made. Overall, this layout and design offers an extremely attractive appearance for executive offices.

The two story building located immediately south of the main five story structure is the original Federal Savings and Loan Association structure. This two story building was constructed in the early 1950s. Built on a concrete slab, the exterior walls are masonry with a brick face along the west and southern sides. The eastern exterior is covered with cotico tile panels to provide a consistent look with the five story building. Copper is used for all roof flashings, rain gutters, and down spouts. A glass atrium area, converted to useful space, is recessed in the southwest corner of the building. The roof support system is steel beam with a flat, built-up tar and gravel roof cover. A number of mechanical systems are roof top mounted, including the elevator shaft. Main access to the two story structure is through the main lobby on the north side of the building. The interior space has been remodeled with fixed and freestanding par-

4

titioning and a number of built-in work spaces. All floors are carpeted with commercial grade wall-to-wall carpeting. The walls are covered in various wall coverings. The ceiling is acoustical tile. Lighting is generally recessed fluorescent fixtures. The third elevator, by Otis, is on the west side of the building and services the second floor.

The one story, freestanding building located at the northeast corner of the property actually consists of two freestanding buildings, although appearing to be a single building. These buildings are built on concrete slabs, and constructed of concrete block with brick along the north and western sides of the building. The roof is a flat, built-up tar and gravel roof. Each building has interior space of average office quality, including carpeting, partitioned walls, panelled walls and acoustical tile ceilings.

An older service station, built during the early 1960's, is located between the five story main building and the one story building at the northeast corner. The fuel tanks (14,000 gallon capacity) and pumps are in working order. This existing structure adds to the inefficiency of the overall site layout.

The drive-in banking facility is located at the southeast corner of the main block. Two expansive canopies extend north and south over the four drive-through lanes.

Service contracts on the air conditioning equipment, elevator and ground maintenance are available at Real Estate, Inc., REALTORS.®

Public Utilities

The office facility is serviced by all utilities. Electricity is provided by Florida Power Corporation, telephone services by General Telephone, water and sewer are provided by the City of Clearwater as is police and fire protection.

Zoning

The property falls in four different zoning categories. See page 12 for Zoning Map.

DD(EC)   Block B—Lots 1–22
CG   Block B—Lots 23–44, Block J—Lots 1–3
RM-12   Block D—Lots 1, 2, 3, 6, 7
RM-28   Block D—Lots 15, 16

Inventory

All items which are attached to the building shall remain except: vault doors, file cabinets, computer air conditioning equipment and telephone hardware.

Owner

Pioneer Federal Savings and Loan Association.

Price

$3,300,000

Terms

Down payment: 20 percent minimum required
Interest rate: The current quoted rates (adjusted annually)
Amortization: Thirty years
Balloon: Twenty years
Prepayment penalties: Three (3%) percent during first one-third of loan term.
                      Two (2%) percent during next one-third of loan term.
                      One (1%) percent during remaining one-third of loan term.

5

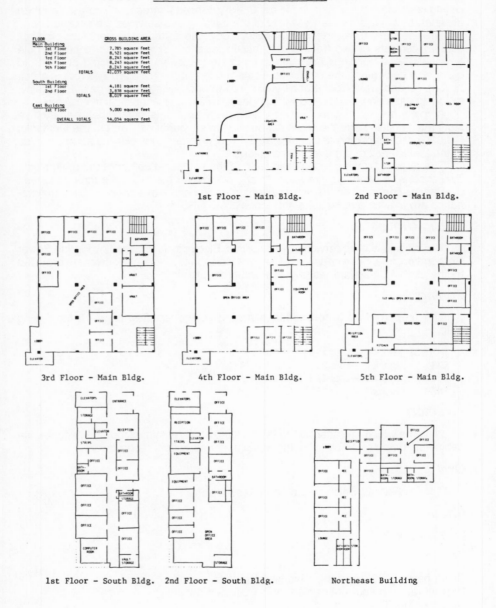

FLOOR	GROSS BUILDING AREA
Main Building	
1st Floor	7,785 square feet
2nd Floor	8,521 square feet
3rd Floor	8,243 square feet
4th Floor	8,243 square feet
5th Floor	8,243 square feet
TOTALS	41,035 square feet
South Building	
1st Floor	4,181 square feet
2nd Floor	3,838 square feet
TOTALS	8,019 square feet
East Building	
1st Floor	5,000 square feet
OVERALL TOTALS	54,054 square feet

1st Floor – Main Bldg.   2nd Floor – Main Bldg.

3rd Floor – Main Bldg.   4th Floor – Main Bldg.   5th Floor – Main Bldg.

1st Floor – South Bldg.   2nd Floor – South Bldg.   Northeast Building

6

Pioneer Federal Leaseback Parameters

The Federal Savings and Loan Association will lease back, on a long term basis, the first floor and second floor of the main building and the drive-through teller facilities.

The Federal projects vacating the following floors on the dates indicated:

Main Five Story Building

Floor 3—June, 1982
Floor 4—July, 1982
Floor 5—January, 1982
South Building—First Floor, May, 1982
                    Second Floor, May, 1982
East Building—April, 1982

Preliminary discussions with the Federal Savings and Loan Association have ascertained that the Federal will pay:

Net Rentable by Building Owner Managers Association (BOMA):

Main Building

Floor 1—$14 per square foot
Floor 2—$10 per square foot
Floor 3—$9 per square foot
Floor 4—$9 per square foot
Floor 5—$12 per square foot

South Building

Floor 1—$8.50 per square foot
Floor 2—$8.50 per square foot

East Building

$8.50 per square foot

Drive-In Facility

$30,000 per year

All lease amounts will be a gross amount with the building owner paying utilities, taxes (first year/base year), insurance, exterior maintenance, etc. The Federal Savings and Loan Association shall pay for janitorial service in the space they occupy.

The rent shall be increased based upon the Consumer Price Index not to exceed six percent.

All areas which shall be leased on a temporary basis shall be on a month-to-month lease at the option of the Federal Savings and Loan Association. The leased area which is needed on a long-term basis shall be leased for a minimum of ten years. In addition the Federal requires two five year renewal option periods.

7

1981 Expenses

Electric	$ 81,047
Water	7,460
Repairs & Maintenance	18,837
Custodial	31,000
Lawn	6,600
Taxes	40,195
Insurance	12,529
Total Operating Expenses	$197,668
Landlease	$ 9,600
Total Expenses	$207,268

1982 Expenses

Present custodial service is on a five day basis. We estimate a 25 percent savings when service is switched to a twice a week service.

Taxes for 1982 will increase to $62,985.

Insurance for 1982 will decrease to $9,600.

All other operating expense figures are projected to increase at five percent for a total potential 1982 expense figure of $225,076. However, three expense figures (electric, water and custodial) will be affected by occupancy. Therefore, the variable expense will be a pro rata share based upon estimated square footage occupied.

8

Landlease Summary

The two story building and certain parking lots are subject to the following lease terms and conditions.

Date: 01/01/56

Lessor: Lessor

Lessee: Federal Savings & Loan Association, Inc.

*Land included
in lease:*   Hibiscus Gardens, Block B: Lots 23, 24, 25, 26, 27, 28, 29, 30, 31
Hibiscus Gardens, Block D: Lots 1, 2, 3, 6, 7, part of 8, 15, 16

Term: 100 years (01/01/56–12/31/2055); 74 years remaining

Cancellation: After 12/31/80 Lessee may cancel after six (6) months notice

*All taxes &
assessments:* Payment by Lessee

Renegotiation: At end of each ten (10) year period, lease may be renegotiated to a fair level of payments. If the parties are in dispute then the renegotiations are subject to legal arbitration.

Improvements: All improvements on leased land are the property of the lessor upon termination or expiration of this lease.

Base rental: $800 per month

*Additional
rental:* $75 per million dollars of deposit for first $100,000,000.
$50 per million dollars of deposit for each $1,000,000 deposit in excess of $100,000,000 (only deposits at home office at this address are used for this calculation).
(This "additional rental" shall be paid by the savings and loan.)

9

Land Area Calculations

Land Owned Fee Simple

Block B:
Lots 1–22 and 32–44 (89,400 square feet m.o.l.)
Block J:
Lots 1–3 (20,820 square feet m.o.l.)
Totaling approximately *110,230 square feet.* (2.53 acres m.o.l.)

Land Leased from Lessor (See Lease Summary)

Block B:
Lots 23–31 (1980)
Block D:
Lots 1–3 (15,567 square feet m.o.l.) and 6, 7, 15, 16 (19,899 square feet m.o.l.)
Totaling approximately *55,266 square feet.* (1.27 acres m.o.l.)

Total Land Controlled

Owned Fee Simple: 110,120
Leased: 55,266
                                  165,386 square feet (3.8 acres m.o.l.)

Legal Description

Pioneer Federal's Fee Interest

Lots 1 through 22, 32 through 44, Block B, Hibiscus Gardens, as recorded in Plat Book 14, pages 55 through 59 of Public Records of Pinellas County, Florida.

Lots 1, 2 and 3, Block J, Hibiscus Gardens, according to the map or plat thereof as recorded in Plat Book 14, page 55 through 59 of the Public Records of Pinellas County, Florida.

Leased Parcels

That certain property in Hibiscus Gardens, Plat Book 14, pages 55 to 59, inclusive, Public Records of Pinellas County, Florida, described as follows:

"Lots 23, 24, 25, 26, 27, 28, 29, 30 and 31, Block 'B,' Lots 6, 7, 15 and 16, Block 'D;' and that portion of Lot 8, Block 'D' lying Easterly of a straight line described as follows:

"Begin at the Northwest corner of Lot 9, Block 'D', Hibiscus Gardens, according to the map or plat thereof as recorded in Plat Book 14, pages 55 to 59 inclusive, Public Records of Pinellas County, Florida, and run thence East along the North line of said Lot 9 and Lot 8, said Block 'D', a distance of 94.79 feet for the Point of Beginning of said line; run thence Southerly in a straight line parallel to the East line of Lincoln Avenue (also known as Floral Way), as said East line is established by resolution of the City Commission of the City of Clearwater adopted on March 4, 1957, a distance of 103.78 feet more or less to the South line of said Lot 8, and the end of said line; all in Hibiscus Gardens, according to the map or plat thereof as recorded in Plat Book 14, pages 55 to 59 inclusive, Public Records of Pinellas County, Florida."

Lots 1, 2, and 3, Block "D" Hibiscus Gardens, Plat Book 14, pages 55 to 59 inclusive, Pinellas County Records.

10

Assessments, Tax Rate and Taxes

For 1981, the property, both fee simple and landleased, was assessed for $3,036,130. Tax bills paid in November (or the date of receipt) receive a four percent discount, decreasing one percent per month until March, after which a penalty is assessed.

1981 Assessment

Parcel Number	Mills	Assessment	Tax
15-29-15-38574-002-0010 & 15-29-15-38574-002-0140 (Assembled Block "B")	20.791	$2,897,730	$60,245.83
15-29-15-28574-010-0010 (Remote southwesterly parking facility)	19.791	$ 31,730	$ 627.96
15-29-15-38574-004-0060 15-29-15-38574-004-0150 15-29-15-38574-004-0160 (Leased southerly parking facility)	19.791	$ 47,780	$ 945.59
15-29-15-38574-004-0010 15-29-15-38574-004-0030 (3 leased residential lots at southeast)	19.791	$ 58,890	$ 1,165.46
Total Assessments		$3,036,130	
1981 Taxes *			$62,984.84

---

*This figure represents an undiscounted tax amount which disregards time of payment.
NOTE: Figures do not include Lots 1, 2 and 3, Block "D," under lease.

11

12

Downtown Clearwater Office Space Study
by
Clearwater Downtown Development Board

Annual Absorption of Office Space 1976–80

In July, 1976, Gladstone Associates, economic consultants, surveyed office space in downtown Clearwater as part of the research that went into the *Plan for Downtown Clearwater,* (1977). In January, 1980, the Clearwater Downtown Development Board surveyed office space as part of its ongoing participation in the Annual Downtown Data System (ADDS). ADDS data is published annually by the International Downtown Executives Association. A comparison of major downtown office buildings indicates that in three and one-half years, 132,400 square feet has been absorbed in existing buildings.

In addition, new construction added 38,700 square feet of office space from July, 1976 to January, 1980. Taken together, absorption of existing and new office space totaled 171,100 square feet over the three and one-half year period or an average of 48,885 square feet per year.

Need for Office Space Through 1982

The office space absorption rate from July, 1976, through January, 1980, was 48,885 square feet per year. The pre-1976 office space absorption rate was 35,000 square feet per year.[1] By January, 1980, class A and B office space had been almost fully occupied, except for odds and ends in the 1100 Building, and major new prospects for first-class downtown office space simply had nowhere to go.

The need for new office space in 1980 was predicted three years earlier in the Downtown Plan.[2] The Plan projected absorption rates of 30,000 to 50,000 square feet per year. Actual experience proved to be on the high end of that projection. The Plan projected that new office space necessary between 1980 and 1982 would total 95,000 square feet.[3] In view of the actual absorption rates being on the high end of projections, the projection of a need for 95,000 square feet can be considered conservative. Actual absorption rates are about 20 percent above the projected 40,000 square feet per year. Increasing the estimated need of 95,000 square feet by 20 percent results in an estimated need of 114,000 square feet through 1982.

During 1980, two office projects have broken ground. The Colony, Ltd. on Cleveland Street is a mixed retail and office building and will have 7,000 square feet of office space. Chestnut Court on Chestnut Street will be an office condominium and will have 7,840 square feet of marketable space. Subtracting these two developments from the estimated need of 114,000 square feet yields a net estimated need of 99,160 square feet through 1982.

During the three and one-half years from July, 1976 to January 1980, 171,000 square feet of office space was absorbed in downtown buildings. *This averages 48,885 square feet per year and could probably have been higher* if available space in attractive buildings such as the Bank of Clearwater had not become completely depleted.

The projected office space absorption rate contained in the *Downtown Plan* (1977) was "between 30,000 and 50,000 square feet per year," and has proven to be accurate. A continuation of this rate demonstrates *a need for 99,160 square feet of new office space between now and 1982.*

---

1. Source of pre-1976 rate is the *Plan for Downtown Clearwater* (1977), pg. 29
2. Ibid. pg. 39
3. Ibid. pg. 71

13

Recapitulation of Office Building Rental Rates and Space Availability

As of 10/81

Building Name	Location	Net Useable Space	Currently Available	Lease Rate
Arbor Ofc. Center	1321 US 19 S	71,000	10,000	$12.00
Arbor Shoreline	1306 US 19 S	134,785	70,000	$13–$16
The Colony	421 Cleveland	10,000	850	$10.00
1100 Building	1100 Cleveland	135,000	8,500 top 8,500— Window	$10–$11 Top $8.00 lower
Sentinel Square	300 S. Dowlan	54,000	3,000	$9.00
Belcher Plaza	50 S. Belcher	95,000	1,600	$9.50
Bank of Clearwater	600 Cleveland	137,575	1,200	$12.00
Causeway Office Center				$9.25
Barnett Bank Building (Leased only to Bank)				
Coachman Building (Substandard Space)				$5.50
Times Building (Leased only to Times)				

Study Completed by Real Estate, Inc., Leasing Department

Driving Time from Property—Distance Study

	Miles	Time
Site to: U.S. Highway 19	4	10 Minutes
Clearwater Beach	2.2	5 Minutes
Waterfront	3 Blocks	1 Minutes
Tampa International Airport	15	20 Minutes
Downtown St. Petersburg	20	30–40 Minutes

(Times subject to time of day, time of year and month taken)

14

Response to the Marketing Plan

We made numerous contacts of targets with whom we had familiarity and knew were capable of acquiring the property. We were having considerable amount of difficulty in bringing any of the parties to either a letter of intent or formal contract offer. We felt as though part of the problem associated with the marketing effort was our failure to properly communicate the benefits and possibly a failure to accurately interpret and estimate both potential revenues and operating expenses. A detailed item by item review of the operating statistics indicated that there were several items contained in the operating expenses which, in fact, should not have been directly expensed to the subject property. Some of these expenses included full-time maintenance personnel which also maintained other properties, certain personnel supplies including high quality personal supplies—coffee, doughnuts and miscellaneous products—not normally contained in operating expenses. We also soon learned that the Federal did an exceptional job maintaining its property and, for example, would maintain five day janitorial service rather than three day service. We were also questioning the power consumption of the building and requested that the Federal fund a full energy audit. A copy of the energy audit has not been included in this case study. The study, prepared by Florida Power Corporation, indicates that the building itself was being operated efficiently and within acceptable energy saving standards.

After numerous contacts and rejections, it became clear that our most important objective would be to inform the Board of Directors of the Federal as to our marketing efforts. After 60 days of serious marketing efforts on the property, we were certain that we had a serious price problem as well as terms which were not acceptable in the current market. The following is a report of marketing activities. This report is intended to inform the seller and to justify an offering price at near the MAI appraised value. We, in effect, devoted our entire attention for several weeks to informing and providing additional information to our client as we felt it was the highest priority on our marketing plan. It should be clear from the tone of our report that one of our main objectives was to better enhance our ability to translate the benefits and the economies of the property to potential buyers. As you read this report, try to envision the importance of each step of the presentation and its effect on the perceptions of the client.

January 13, 1982

William E. Nodine, President and Chairman of the Board
Parker J. Stafford, Senior Vice-President
Pioneer Federal Savings and Loan Association
Clearwater, Florida 33516

Dear Gentlemen:

The following report has been prepared for you in an effort to give you additional information on the status of our marketing efforts. It is important that you and your

Board are given positive, constructive feedback on our marketing efforts. This report is intended to both inform and to discuss with you some of the problems we have encountered in marketing your property. It is not a simple verbalization of our marketing efforts. It is a very in-depth financial and physical review of your property. A considerable amount of man hours has gone into this particular study with two specific goals in mind. The first goal, of course, is to better enhance our ability to translate the benefits and the economics of the property to a potential buyer. The second, and equally as important, objective is to give you additional information upon which to make your decisions relative to the property. It is important that we not underestimate your impact as sellers in our marketing process.

Please study the recommendations and give us whatever information and direction you can as early as possible. We look forward to making a formal presentation of this study to both of you once you have had an opportunity to read it over and to digest its contents. After you have studied the information herein, we would appreciate a formal meeting to discuss the ramifications of the presentation.

Sincerely,

Broker, CCIM

B/sbd

Marketing Report

When a prospect is contacted and an initial interest sparked, based on primary sales data, it is necessary to supply in-depth financial projections and information.

The information requested to make a final decision consistently evolved around the following:
1. Income projection
2. Expense projection
3. Absorption rates
4. Building modifications and expense
5. Financing and financial structure
6. Federal leaseback parameters
7. Landlease status

The most important variable, income projection, is the most difficult to project and sell. The net useable in the building is a nebulous, if not, fluctuating number based on ultimate use—multi- or single tenant user. It is a high risk assumption to assume all single tenant users for each floor.

The building, while meeting the needs of the Federal in an effective and efficient manner, is quite inefficient for multi-tenant users with as high as a 15 percent load factor of inefficiency percentage on some floors. (See Schedule A for net useable square footage assumptions.)

The current economic condition makes the risk associated with the absorption of the space higher, with the estimate of future income even more difficult to project.

The uncertainty associated with the cash flow has resulted in an apprehension by some well-targeted prospects to ever spend the necessary time to make a qualified bid. By mid-December, we had made enough presentations to qualified prospects to realize that we would continue to market to qualified targeted prospects who would reject this project based on economics and risk factors. We have several prime prospects, including one prospect who could bring as much as one million in cash to closing from the sale of another property, 1031 tax deferred. The prospect's statement to us was clear and definitive, "We will buy the property, if we can make it work financially."

Working financially, of course, is a very subjective statement, but there are parameters, as discussed in your MAI appraisal, which tend to dictate what does make investment value in today's marketplace.

A study of the economics of the income, the buildings' inefficiencies with vast amounts of net useable loss to equipment rooms, elevator shafts and atrium effects, dictated a lower than acceptable efficiency factor or a higher load factor than is normally found in modern office buildings. The building's inefficiencies are not as critical as two other important variables on the income side.

The big unknown is the absorption rate. With the vast amount of space coming on line at one time upon the vacating by the Federal, there are many skeptics in the marketplace who say that the space will not be absorbed by more than 1,000 square feet per month. This is consistent with your MAI appraiser's estimates. Our estimates indicated an absorption rate as high as 1,500 square feet a month during the first year and 3,000 square feet during the second year, giving us approximately an 18 month absorption rate as opposed to a 24 month absorption rate in the MAI appraisal. It was also our expectation we would lease the top floor "as is" or with minor modifications and the small one story 5,000 square foot building within the first six months of the lease-up efforts. It was necessary to make certain estimates as to absorption which we have done in Schedule B.

The second and equally important variable is the cost associated with converting the building to multi-tenant space. The Clearwater market has not experienced large tenant users, but instead is made of many smaller tenant users in multi-tenant space in the 1,500 to 3,000 square foot range. Typically, a 2,000 square foot user would be a better example of the average size space demanded. Therefore, a multi-tenant building or a modification of the existing building is necessary in order to make a careful estimate of absorption rate. With this in mind, we must face substantial building modification capital expenditures, as well as down time associated with construction efforts in order to meet these future leasehold improvement requirements.

The unknowns associated with absorption rates, net useable space and conversion costs are substantial and a deterrent to our marketing efforts. At the close of this report, we will have several suggestions in order to mitigate, if not eliminate, some of the negatives associated with the unknowns described above.

Assumptions to Derive Net Operating Income

In order to arrive at our net operating income, a key factor in an orderly financial analysis, it is necessary to estimate the operating expenses. It took several weeks to pin down what we felt were reasonable operating expenses for the structure. We, with the assistance of Parker Stafford and Bill Wright, made in-depth studies of the operating expenses. The operating expenses associated with the Federal's main structure were considerably higher than those typically realized in the Tampa Bay market.

We made comparisons to generally accepted operating statistics compiled by the Institute of Real Estate Management and presented in Management's Annual Experience Exchange. We also have, through our management company, feedback on local operating expenses. The Federal was running consistently higher, which led us to believe that there were certain expenses incorporated within the operating statement that might not be associated with a typical owner. After careful study, we were able to remove expenses not associated with typical investment ownership. However, we did find that the Federal was running $.30 to $.50 a square foot higher than we would have normally expected for similar space. Obviously, the higher our operating expenses, the lower our net operating income and it is the net operating income which is the basis of the concept of investment value. It is also a major cash flow benefit that we sell when we are out in the marketplace presenting your property. Expense projection can be reviewed on Schedule C.

The income associated with this property is an unknown until such time as the space is offered in the marketplace. It is one thing to estimate $9.00 a square foot gross rental and it is another to obtain that rental. In today's marketplace, new space in downtown Clearwater is experiencing some resistance at rentals in the $11.00 range. We are seeing a resistance on the part of existing tenants to move out of space which will see marginal increases in rent from, say, the $8.50–$9.50 range into new lease-hold space in the $11.00 range. The absolute rental value of this space is an unknown and increases the risk associated with the acquisition. We have rental income from the Federal at $14.00 a square foot and $10.00 a square foot projected for the first and second floors. We have $30,000 associated with the drive-in facilities. However, both of the rentals are predicated on certain pass-throughs or caps associated with first year operating expenses and/or varying financing terms. There is considerable amount of skepticism by our targeted investors over the amount of rent we will be able to generate out of the building as opposed to, say, a new or existing prime, glass walled, steel structured building. All rental income assumptions can be reviewed on Schedule D, a summary of D(1), D(2), and D(3).

It is obvious that to sell through the difficulties associated with net operating income projections, we must have considerable amounts of information or an excellent financial structure going into the sales presentation. The main benefit we have when we sell this type of property is potential future profits. The more uncertainty we have associated with both the income and the operating expenses, the less certainty we have of projecting future profits. As the profit potential decreases or is subject to higher risk, the sale becomes more difficult and less probable.

The Financial Structure

The net operating income projection as described above and the problems associated with it, are only half of the total financial formula necessary to make a sale on the subject property. The second variable and the other half of the equation revolves around the financial structure or the potential financing available either from the Federal or from outside sources.

To finance the subject property outside of the Federal has been one of the alternatives we have examined. For the most part, we are looking somewhere in the neighborhood of a 16½ percent rate with certain limitations on funding based on absorption. There is potential pension fund financing available; however, the risk associated with the absorption rate has negated the acceptance at this time. The obvious target for financing is the existing Seller, in this case, the Federal. As you will note in our property profile, our current suggested financing from the Federal is as follows:

Down Payment:	20 percent ($660,000)
Interest Rate:	The current quoted rates (adjusted annually)
Amortization:	30 years
Balloon:	20 years
Prepayment Penalties:	Three percent (3%) during first one-third of loan term.
	Two percent (2%) during next one-third of loan term.
	One percent (1%) during remaining one-third of loan term.

This suggested financing is similar to financing available in the open market and has not generated positive excitement by potential prospects. In today's market, the transactions which we are closing are predicated either on acceptable, flexible financing or a sales price which offers a reasonable up-side profit. Today, financing at market rates is the same as a cash sale. If one is to generate a return based on current market financing, it is the same as an outright cash sale. Therefore, with the current financing, we should be offering the very closest to the bone sales price acceptable to the Federal.

If the Federal is not willing to offer more flexible financing to a potential buyer, then we would suggest a cash sale approach to the sales price.

Another important stumbling block has been the acceptability or lack of acceptability of the existing landlease. There is a great deal of apprehension on the part of potential buyers over the increase in rental associated with the 1985 negotiation of the landlease. In less than four years, a potential buyer could be faced with substantial increases in nonoperating expenses associated with the landlease renegotiations. This, of course, is an unacceptable, uncontrolled contingency to most potential buyers. Therefore, we believe that it is necessary that the landlease element of this sale be faced immediately.

Alternatives to Problems and Potential Solutions

Investment Base Concept

The obvious decision point for the Federal is to attempt to sell the property at the $3.3 million price range under somewhat rigid financing terms and not realize a sale within the time frame scheduled. If the property has not sold by March or April, the pressure from the Board for results will increase. We are confident that the delay in our recommendations will only mitigate the validity of any future recommendations made by Real Estate, Inc.

In any investment, whether deemed a user property such as the subject property or a strict investment property, an owner makes the decision daily either to sell or hold the asset. If a sale is not consummated due to price or terms then, in effect, the Federal has decided to hold on to the subject property.

The determination between a soft terms or flexible terms sale as opposed to a hold must be faced in today's challenging market. We have suggested several alternatives, including increasing the size of the entire marketing package we are currently selling. This would include the addition of several other alternative properties owned by the Federal which the Federal would lease back or which currently have multi-tenant space leased to third parties which would spread the risk of the subject property. We must either spread the risk or lower the risk associated with the acquisition of the home office facility. This can easily be done with increasing the size of the package as well as opening up an entire market (larger asset buyer) for the property. The $3 million range is low for many pension funds as is evidenced by the responses in the first international contacts we made.

Net Useable Area Totals

- Main Building/Floor 1   7,160 square feet
- Main Building/Floor 2   6,507 square feet
- Main Building/Floor 3   6,600 square feet
- Main Building/Floor 4   5,979 square feet
- Main Building/Floor 5   6,870 square feet
- South Building/Floor 1   4,259 square feet
- South Building/Floor 2   4,571 square feet
- N.E. Building/Floor 1   <u>5,000 square feet</u>
  Total Net Useable   46,946 square feet

Net Useable Area is measured as the interior dimension of each floor, less elements of the building which penetrate through the floor or are not available to tenant access (items excepted: stairs, atrium, ducts, and elevators).

What the Federal is selling is a special user or single tenant, five story building. We are not selling a clean, leased-up strict income investment. We have two broad potential markets:

- the user market (large user) and
- the investor—investment market.

The "user market" marketing approach is logical and requires a good bit of timing. Examples of contacts made are those with the City of Clearwater, Franklin Telephone, Bob Smith of XYZ Bank, S. Jones of Western and Life Insurance Company. Also quasi-users such as Joe Developer, Sam Developer and XYZ Group. A sale to a user will typically carry a higher ultimate sales price. Selling to the user market takes more time and requires timing. In periods of low economic activity, large users will be slow to take on the added space necessary to sell the building. Our market for the building would seem to be best targeted in the investment sector; however, 40 percent of our efforts will go to the user market.

Approximately 60 percent of the effort is being directed toward the "investor-investment market," a market that demands answers to the hard numbers and risk questions.

The following information has been prepared to assist the Federal in its decision making and also to assist potential buyers in making projections. The bottom line on the Net Operating Income before landlease payments and construction is projected to be as follows:

EOY (1) 1982	$169,530	
EOY (2) 1983	$222,538	
EOY (3) 1984	$236,486	
EOY (4) 1985	$248,310	
EOY (5) 1986	$260,725	
	See attached Schedule D	

These are pre-tax cash flows before landlease payments, construction costs and debt service.

The Net Operating Income is the basis of the buyer projection. Net Operating Income also plays a role in a lending institution's coverage ratio.

Would the Federal Make This Loan Arm's Length?

If we assume that the Federal makes an arm's length loan to a potential buyer on this property, what coverage ratio would you expect? Many lenders would ask at least 1.2 percent coverage of debt service by the Net Operating Income.

The average Net Operating Income over the next five years is estimated to be $227,517. The maximum cash flow available to service debt with a 1.2 percent desired coverage ratio is $189,598. The maximum principal that would be suggested at various interest rates using a 25 year amortization is as follows:

Average Monthly Cash Flow Available for Debt Service $15,799
Assume 1.2% Coverage

Interest Rate	Principal Amount of Loan
9%	$1,882,735
10%	$1,738,729
11%	$1,612,043
12%	$1,500,141
13%	$1,400,900
14%	$1,312,540
15%	$1,233,562
16%	$1,162,703

From the Federal's perspective, with a 1.2 percent coverage ratio, the maximum loan at nine percent interest would be $1,882,735; at 16 percent interest it would be $1,162,703.

Let's assume for discussion, a loan is granted to the investor in the amount of $1,500,000, cash flow after debt service at 12 percent interest, 25 year amortization (assume a five year balloon):

Average NOI $227,517
Debt Service   (189,598)
                $ 37,919 Pre-Tax Cash Flow

NOTE: No capital expenditures for improvements

What reaction would be expected if the lender was to look to a normal financial structure for loan security or protection? From a lender's perspective, the asset has risk because the absorption rates are at question and cash flow is subject to substantial variation. An important question would be, "What about the additional cost to complete or modify the building for multi-tenant users?"

The lender could demand and receive a bona fide bid by a respected contractor and some assurance that the borrower had the resources to make the necessary improvements.

Remodel to Multi-Tenant Space

We were successful in getting Mr. Roe, an England-based investor, very interested in the property. He has worked very closely with Bob Tom of Tom Construction. Tom Construction is a contractor of national prominence and much experience. Mr. Roe has purchased, for S.W. Properties, an international partnership, hundreds of thousands of square feet of office buildings. The estimate to convert to multi-tenant space based on Mr. Roe's instructions ran $20 per square foot. Attempts to close off the atrium to improve net rentable area seem infeasible.

The cost to remodel the space will run between a low of $15 per square foot and a high of over $20 per square foot. The estimate of cost is only an estimate until full architectural plans are completed.

However, for the purposes of our lender scenerio, let's estimate the cost at a low of $18 per square foot for the Main Building and $10 per square foot for the South Building.

	Gross	Cost	Total
Main Building/Floor 3	7,765	$18	$139,770
Main Building/Floor 4	7,765	$18	$139,770
South Building/Floor 1	5,194	$10	$ 51,940
South Building/Floor 2	5,194	$10	$ 51,940
Projected Total Cost to Convert to Multi-Tenant			$383,420

The Federal, as lender, would look to the borrower to fund at least $383,420 in conversion remodeling cost in addition to the required down payment.

Let's look at the loan from the Board of Directors' perspective. Remember, this is an arm's length loan the Federal does not have to make. It is just an application or loan portfolio investment opportunity.

1. Cash flows to cover debt service
   Averaging five year NOI $227,517
   Required coverage ratio   1.2%
2. Cost to convert to multi-tenant
   $383,420

3. At 15 percent, what will the Federal loan—$1,233,562, maximum, assuming the developer can give acceptable guarantees of the $383,420 conversion cost required to lease multi-tenant.

A difficult loan, at best.

If we put the shoe on the other foot and tell the Buyer to make a similar study, what we find is:

1. Average NOI $227,517, assuming the Seller agreed to a purchase money mortgage of 12 percent, 25 year amortization, 15 year balloon

2. With 1.2 percent coverage the investor could borrow $1,500,000 of the purchase price

3. $1,500,000 loan leaves cash flow, pre-tax, of $37,919

4. $37,919 total average, pre-tax cash flow after debt service on the $1,500,000 loan

At this point, the investor has enough information to make a preliminary go, no go decision on the property.

Asking price	$3,300,000
Potential loan	1,500,000
Equity required	$1,800,000
Equity required	$1,800,000
Construction money required	383,420
Total cash	$2,183,420
Total cash flow pre-tax to offer	
a pre-tax return	$ 37,919

$$\frac{37,919}{2,183,420} \text{ at } 1.7367\% \text{ pre-tax return}$$

$$\% \text{ Capital Investment } \frac{2,183,420}{3,300,000} = 66\%$$

For a 1.73 percent pre-tax return, the investor has $2,183,420 cash investment or 66 percent. At this phase, we have lost a few investors. We have reached the point known as "TOO FAR APART."

Art and Science

Art says most investors and developers are optimists. Science says they are optimists only to a point.

We sell many properties that have had equally dismal initial or holding period numbers. But to own, at negative cash flows, the "tax losses" approach only works if the reversion or sale at the end of the holding period makes sense.

Projection of future reversions or sales price is guess work at best. The typical thought process follows this scenario: Where am I today on purchase price compared to the market? How much buyer appeal (future) does the property have? Can I expect unusual or good market performance?

How do I compare to the market?

See attached appraisal update (Schedule E). The cost per square foot is in the range of $36 to $57 per square foot on net useable space.

Building asking price $3,300,000 ÷ 46,946 useable
                                    $70.29 per square foot of land & bldg.

MAI appraisal $2,615,000
                                $55.70 per square foot

Asking price is 26 percent over appraisal and 40 percent over today's market place.

The upside through growth due to acquisition price is nonexistent to the buyer.

How much buyer appeal does property have?
No windows, high operating expenses, one major tenant first two floors that restricts other types of tenants and building name.

Can we expect an unusual or good market performance?
Not foreseeable with any degree of certainty. Last major project in 1978, City Bank. Lot of talk, but no certain growth. Not booming like Tampa market.

Thought Process of Buyers

The building is priced substantially over the market at $3,300,000; the project does not have great buyer appeal; and the market is questionable at best. The total sale based on a reversion is difficult, if not, impossible at current structure.

From the information we have developed, we (the Federal and Real Estate, Inc.) have a very real problem. There is a buyer for the Federal, but the current financial structure would indicate the sale is not going to occur as structured or within a reasonable (acceptable) time frame. To continue to present the building as dictated by the financial structure, price and terms, would not seem prudent. We must not lose or burn out the best targets with an unreasonable structure and allow the building to become tainted as an unreasonable product.

Alternatives

We must either reduce the risk or increase the up-side potential. Reducing the risk can be directly controlled by the Federal.

Methods to Reduce Risk
1. Lease back project on a master lease.
2. Adjust terms on mortgage to follow cash flows or be contingent upon building performance.
3. Federal gives buyer an option to sell back property if lease-up cannot be effected (this option requires that buyer have strength and monies invested in project as in conversion cost).
4. Federal can vacate the entire building and allow a lease to another financial institution. We have talked to Bob Tom, who is buying the Cleveland Plaza, about a build-to-suit for the Federal on the Cleveland Street parking lot of Cleveland Plaza. He is receptive to the idea. Or, we could build to suit on the east side of the property where the appraisal building is.
5. Sell only the improvements and lease back land on a long-term basis. This approach lowers purchase price, leaves no depreciable assets on books. Allows greater flexibility than a normal mortgage from the Federal might. This would allow the Federal to, in effect, wrap around the landlease.
6. The Federal could joint venture the project with an investor. This profit structure has many forms.
7. A formula to get the depreciative assets off the books, preserve cash flows and have a potential of the future up-side benefits is to sell 75 percent interest and give a purchase money mortgage that has a 25 percent participation clause. For example, after debt service on first mortgage, cash flow next ten percent to investor before depreciation. The Federal gets next ten percent cash flow and all additional cash flows (from combined resales) split 50/50 with the Federal.

- Gives Federal positive future cash flow, gets property off books and Federal can experience positives of sale.
- This formula reduces risk to Buyer; also, partnership can have a disproportionate allocation of loss provision with agreement. Federal statement looks better without depreciation losses.

8. Minimal down payment with cost to convert being escrowed as down payment.
9. Allow buyer to borrow construction money from outside source and put new first mortgage on the property. Federal takes a second.
10. Write mortgage to track cash flows. Interest not paid is made part of principal, reverse amortization or negative amortization.
11. Federal puts up cash to convert Building A, begins lease, immediately shows track record.

There are numerous transaction structure variations that can be and have been suggested. These 11 structures are intended to solicit information and thought from the Federal management.

Methods to Increase Profit Potential

The other approach, rather than adjusting risk, is to increase upside profit potentials to buyer. At some point, the risk is rationalized when the upside profit potential warrants the buyer's risk. The price we are selling at, as has been previously demonstrated, lacks a motivating upside potential. Our first approach is to go "real world" on the asking price for the total property.

	Net Useable	Price Per Sq. Ft.	Total
Main Building			
Floors 1–5	33,116 sq.ft.	$50.00	$1,655,800
South Building	8,830 sq.ft.	$47.00	415,010
N/E Building	5,000 sq.ft.	$50.00	250,000
			$2,320,810
Excess Land			120,000
			$2,440,000
+ 10% for error and negotiations			240,000
Range of Value		$2,440,000 to	$2,684,000

The property should be presented at:

Main Building and South Building (including excess parking) at $54.00 per square foot (41,946 square feet)	$2,277,000
Northeast Building at $55.00 per square foot (5,000 square feet)	275,000
Excess land	120,000
Gas Station	150,000
	$2,822,000
Discount for total purchase	$2,684,000

Pricing assumes that Federal works out a purchase at Federal cost of landlease.

Suggestions on Landlease

Exchange landlease lessor—1031 tax deferred—into other like-kind acceptable property. Create a similar landlease income that Federal would guarantee. For example, exchange landlease lessor into land under part of the new facility (built by Pioneer Federal) and lease it from him with similar income or cash flows. Remove the problem from the existing property. Allow new lease structure.

Another alternative is to buy the lease in an outright sale.

Still another alternative is to exchange "paper" first mortgages, held in the Federal portfolio, for the landlease to give Lessor a similar cash flow, with underlying security. The Federal could assign the notes with recourse in the event of a default and as an added "kicker" could agree to service the mortgage at no cost to Lessor. The exchange of paper for the landlease would not be tax deferred for Lessor.

The landlease is a deterrent to the sale that must be faced. Buyers will buy subject to a landlease, but the price must reflect that the land is not included in the purchase price. We are asking prices as if lease obligation is not included—$50–$55 per square foot. If the lease was minimal or very low and was for most of the property, it could work as an incentive. However, an open-end pricing of future increases and only on part of the property adds uncertainty to a transaction.

Most buyers are unfamiliar with landlease valuation and tend to discount any upside. "I do not own the land and I have their obligations, yet I am paying as if I do own land." That response is hard to sell through.

We *must* address the landlease.

How Does the Pricing Look to a Buyer?

The newly proposed asking price increases buyer appeal, but this is still a difficult sale.

$2,600,000	Final sales price
520,000	20% down payment
2,080,000	12% interest, 25 years, 10 year balloon

Payment—$ 21,907 per month
$262,884 per annum

N	$		
0	903,420*		
	NOI	*Debt Service*	*Pre-tax Cash Flows*
1	169,530	(262,884)	(93,354)
2	222,538	(262,884)	(40,346)
3	236,486	(262,884)	(26,398)
4	248,310	(262,884)	(14,574)
5	260,725	(262,884)	(2,159)

*Down payment $520,000, Construction cost $383,420 = $903,420

An investor must look at the following pre-tax cash flow:

N	$	
0	(903,420)	PV 15%
1	(93,354)	(81,177)
2	(40,346)	(30,507)
3	(26,398)	(17,357)
4	(14,578)	(8,335)
5	(2,159)	(1,073)

The true initial investment with a cost of capital of 15 percent (line loan rate) using financial management rate of return techniques, is the present value of future negative cash flows at 15 percent. The true initial investment is $1,041,869 pre-tax.

It is obvious that the light at the end of the tunnel is the future sales price and the tax benefits of ownership. The following computer analysis (pages 174–78) gives insight into the tax benefits of ownership.

Summary

Real Estate, Inc. has spent untold hours in research analysis and presentation of the subject property. Our report is based on valid "in the trenches" feedback that has been carefully analyzed. We have an obligation to the Federal's Board of Directors to advise them of the market as we see it.

1. We must market the property at a real world competitive, comparable price.
2. We recommend open minds as to the financial structure. We recommend that tentative Board approval be requested for a participation loan approach, that the landlease with lessor be addressed and the problem solved.
3. We recommend that permission be granted to open up the marketing—to allow a more visible marketing program.
4. We should begin pre-leasing the project, which would include an advertising budget from the Federal and a leasing sign.
5. Architectural plans for conversion to multi-tenant floors 3 and 4 with South Building should be initiated.

The Federal has no different investment posture than any investor. Each day an investor owns a property, he makes the conscious or unconscious decision to sell, hold, lease, etc. The investor sets the price and terms and controls the sale or nonsale.

A conscious decision to sell has been made by the Federal. However, a conscious decision on price and terms also has been set; this deters saleability. The Federal has a nonearning asset. The *investment base* in the asset is deemed to be, by definition, *the after-tax cash flow from an arm's length sale.*

Let's assume, for discussion purposes, that "investment base" after-tax should approximate $2,000,000. (May be higher or lower based on adjusted basis in property and final sales price.)

If we agree that the after-tax cash flow from an all cash sale is approximately $2,000,000, then the Federal has an investment base of $2,000,000. The decision to sell or not to sell is based on the opportunity cost of the $2,000,000. Does the $2,000,000 have a better return potential in the subject property or is there an opportunity of higher return?

Not to sell would suggest that the Federal is equipped and prepared to deal with the following benefits and obligations of long-term ownership:

1. $2,000,000 cash investment (investment base concept)
2. Future cash obligation for construction $383,000
3. Lease up risk
4. Delusion of management time
5. NOI cash flow similar to our projection

N	$
0	2,000,000 + 383,000
1	169,530
2	222,538
3	236,486
4	248,310
5	260,725

The tax loss is not a benefit to the Federal; in fact, it is a detriment on the financial statement. Real Estate Owned—"REO"—does not enhance typical corporate operating statements.

5 year average NOI	$ 227,517
Investment	$2,383,000

The optimum solution, most likely, is a combination of lower price or terms/participation sale. Simultaneously, the Federal should move the plans toward multi-tenant conversion.

There is always room to say that our projections are off because of absorption, construction costs, interest rates, adjusted basis or whatever. Any variable may be adjusted; however, the effect in the decision making process is minimal. We encourage deep thought by management, including challenges to our assumptions. If we have missed a significant point, we will adjust and pursue the proper approach.

The analysis we have completed is based on ten years of marketing and owning, not just appraising, similar types of property. We sold and closed the ABC Building in 90 days from exclusive right of sale listing execution. The ABC Building had been on the market over five years.

We hestitate when we take a listing to make strong recommendations with cursory knowledge and information on the subject property. After 60 days, we know the property and the specific market well enough to handle most buyer problems. When we cannot adjust through the buyer problems, we must adjust through the seller. Six months from now is too late to try to readjust the marketing plan. Your Board wants results and the program suggested here is structured to get results within an acceptable time period.

SCHEDULE A
Net Useable Square Footage

MAIN BUILDING/FLOOR 1   7,680 gross square feet less 520 square feet of stairs equal 7,160 square feet of net useable area. Leased to Federal.

MAIN BUILDING/FLOOR 2   7,920 gross square feet less 1,413 square feet of stairs and elevator shafts equal 6,507 square feet of net useable area. Leased to Federal.

MAIN BUILDING/FLOOR 3   7,765 gross square feet less 1,165 square feet of stairs and atrium less an additional *(new halls)* five percent load factor equals 6,600 square feet of net useable area. New multi-tenant space.

MAIN BUILDING/FLOOR 4   7,765 gross square feet less 1,433 square feet of stairs and atrium, less an additional *(new halls)* five percent load factor equals 5,979 square feet of useable area. New multi-tenant space.

MAIN BUILDING/FLOOR 5   7,765 gross square feet less 895 square feet of stairs, atrium and duct equal 6,870 square feet of net useable area. Leased as is, single tenant.

SOUTH BUILDING/FLOOR 1   5,194 gross square feet less 660 square feet of stairs and elevator, less an additional *(new halls)* five percent load factor equals 4,259 square feet of net useable area. New multi-tenant space.

SOUTH BUILDING/FLOOR 2   5,194 gross square feet less 344 square feet of stairs and elevator, less an additional *(new halls)* five percent load factor equals 4,571 square feet of net useable area. New multi-tenant space.

N.E. BUILDING   5,000 gross square feet on a gross lease basis equals 5,000 square feet of net useable area.

SCHEDULE B

Occupancy Projections

Main Building/Floor 1

The Federal Savings and Loan Association shall lease this entire floor on a long-term basis.

Main Building/Floor 2

The Federal Savings and Loan Association shall lease this entire floor on a long-term basis.

Main Building/Floor 3

The Federal Savings and Loan Association shall lease entire floor until 5/1/82 at which point leasing agents shall begin to lease all vacant space at the projected rate of 1,500 square feet per month during 1982.

Main Building/Floor 4

The Federal Savings and Loan Association shall lease entire floor until 6/1/82 at which point the entire floor will be vacant. This vacancy is projected to continue until the third floor is 100 percent occupied (9/82) and the leasing of Floor 4 is projected to begin on the basis of 1,500 square feet per month during 1982. The leasing is projected to increase to 3,000 square feet per month beginning 1/1/83 until the entire floor is 100 percent leased in 1/83.

Main Building/Floor 5

This floor is projected to be vacant beginning 1/1/82 for six months until 7/1/82 at which point a tenant is projected to be leasing the entire floor.

South Building/Floor 1

The Federal Savings and Loan Association shall lease entire floor until 5/1/82 at which point the entire floor will be vacant. This vacancy is projected to continue until the third and fourth floors are 100 percent occupied (1/1/83) and the leasing of Floor 1—South Building is projected to continue at 3,000 square feet per month until 100 percent occupied during 2/83.

South Building/Floor 2

The Federal Savings and Loan Association shall lease entire floor until 5/1/82 at which point the entire floor will be vacant. This vacancy is projected to continue until Floor 1—South Building has been 100 percent occupied during 2/83. This floor is projected to lease on the basis of 3,000 square feet per month beginning 2/83 until 100 percent occupied during 4/83.

N.E. Building/Floor 1

This building is projected to be vacant 1/1/82 for four months until 5/82 at which point a tenant will be found to lease the entire building.

Drive-in Facility

The Federal Savings and Loan Association shall lease back this entire facility on a long-term basis.

SCHEDULE C

1981 Expenses

Electric	$ 81,047
Water	7,460
Repairs & Maintenance	18,837
Custodial	31,000
Lawn	6,600
Taxes	40,195
Insurance	12,529
Total Operating Expenses	$197,668
Landlease	$ 9,600
Total Expenses	$207,268

1982 Expenses

Present custodial service is on a five day basis. We estimate a 25 percent savings when service is switched to a twice weekly service. Taxes for 1982 will increase to $62,985. Insurance for 1982 will decrease to $9,600.

All other operating expense figures are projected to increase at five percent for a total potential 1982 expense figure of $225,076. However, three expense figures (electric, water and custodial) will be affected by occupancy. Therefore, the variable expense will be a pro rata share based upon the square footage occupied. When the variable and fixed expense figures are calculated and a management fee of four percent on gross income is added, the total 1982 expenses are projected to be $203,078.

1983 Expenses

The 1983 expenses are projected proportionately to the square footage occupied under the aforementioned schedule. In addition, all operating expenses are projected to increase five percent over 1982 operating expense figures and a four percent management fee is added. Therefore, total operating expenses for 1983 are projected to be $252,733.

1984 Expenses

For 1984 expenses we assumed 100 percent occupancy with an increase of five percent over 1983 operating expenses and a four percent management fee. Therefore, total operating expenses are projected to be $267,811.

1985 Expenses

1985 total expenses with aforementioned assumptions, are projected to be $281,203.

1986 Expenses

1986 total expenses with aforementioned assumptions, are projected to be $295,263.

SCHEDULE D

NET OPERATING INCOME

	Square Footage	1982 Gross Scheduled Income	1983 Gross Scheduled Income	1984 Gross Scheduled Income	1985 Gross Scheduled Income	1986 Gross Scheduled Income
Main Building/Floor 1	7,160	at $14 = $100,240	(+5%) $105,252	(+5%) $110,515	(+5%) $116,041	$121,843
Main Building/Floor 2	6,507	at $10 = $ 65,070	(+5%) $ 68,324	(+5%) $ 71,740	(+5%) $ 75,327	$ 79,093
Main Building/Floor 3	6,600	at $ 9 = $ 59,400	(0) $ 59,400	(+5%) $ 62,370	(+5%) $ 65,489	$ 68,763
Main Building/Floor 4	5,979	at $ 9 = $ 53,811	(0) $ 53,811	(+5%) $ 56,502	(+5%) $ 59,327	$ 62,293
Main Building/Floor 5	6,870	at $12 = $ 82,440	(0) $ 82,440	(+5%) $ 86,562	(+5%) $ 90,890	$ 95,435
South Building/Floor 1	4,259	at $8.50 = $ 36,202	(0) $ 36,202	(+5%) $ 38,012	(+5%) $ 39,913	$ 41,909
South Building/Floor 2	4,571	at $8.50 = $ 38,854	(0) $ 38,854	(0) $ 38,854	(+5%) $ 40,797	$ 42,837
N.E. Building/Floor 1	5,000	at $8.50 = $ 42,500	(0) $ 42,500	(+5%) $ 44,625	(+5%) $ 46,856	$ 49,199
Drive-In	*	= $ 30,000	(+5%) $ 31,500	(+5%) $ 33,075	(+5%) $ 34,729	$ 36,465
GROSS SCHEDULED INCOME AT 100% OCCUPANCY		$508,517	$518,283	$542,255	$569,369	$597,837
- VACANCY FACTORS (FROM OCCUPANCY ASSUMPTIONS AND VACANCY FACTORS OF 7% FROM E.O.Y. 1983)		- 135,909	- 43,012	- 37,958	- 39,856	- 41,849
PROJECTED GROSS INCOME		$372,608	$475,271	$504,297	$529,513	$555,988
- EXPENSES		- 203,078	- 252,733	- 267,811	- 281,203	295,263
NET OPERATING INCOME		$169,530	$222,538	$236,486	$248,310	$260,725

E.O.Y 1 (1982) – PROJECTED GROSS INCOME

	January	February	March	April	May	June	July	August	September	October	November	December	
Main Building/Floor													
(1)	8353	8353	8353	8353	8353	8353	8353	8353	8353	8353	8353	8353	
(2)	5423	5423	5423	5423	5423	5423	5423	5423	5423	5423	5423	5423	
(3)	4950	4950	4950	4950	1125	2250	3375	4500	4950	4950	4950	4950	
(4)	4484	4484	4484	4484	4484	-0-	-0-	-0-	675	1800	2925	4050	
(5)	-0-	-0-	-0-	-0-	-0-	-0-	6870	6870	6870	6870	6870	6870	
South Building/Floor													
(1)	3017	3017	3017	3017	-0-	-0-	-0-	-0-	-0-	-0-	-0-	-0-	
(2)	3238	3238	3238	3238	-0-	-0-	-0-	-0-	-0-	-0-	-0-	-0-	
N.E. Building/Floor 1	-0-	-0-	-0-	-0-	3542	3542	3542	3542	3542	3542	3542	3542	
Drive-In	2500	2500	2500	2500	2500	2500	2500	2500	2500	2500	2500	2500	
SCHEDULED INCOME	31965	31965	31965	31965	25427	22068	30063	31188	32213	33438	34563	35688	= 372,608
Net Sq. Ft. Occupied													
Main Building 1	7160	7160	7160	7160	7160	7160	7160	7160	7160	7160	7160	7160	
2	6507	6507	6507	6507	6507	6507	6507	6507	6507	6507	6507	6507	
3	6600	6600	6600	6600	1500	3000	4500	6000	6600	6600	6600	6600	
4	5979	5979	5979	5979	5979	-0-	-0-	-0-	900	2400	3900	5400	
5	-0-	-0-	-0-	-0-	-0-	-0-	6870	6870	6870	6870	6870	6870	
South Building 1	4259	4259	4259	4259	-0-	-0-	-0-	-0-	-0-	-0-	-0-	-0-	
2	4571	4571	4571	4571	-0-	-0-	-0-	-0-	-0-	-0-	-0-	-0-	
N.E. Building 1	-0-	-0-	-0-	-0-	5000	5000	5000	5000	5000	5000	5000	5000	
TOTALS	35076	35076	35076	35076	20167	21667	30037	31537	33037	34537	36037	37537	
Variable Exp. (.206/sq.ft.) =	7225.5	7225.5	7225.5	7225.5	4154.5	4463.5	6187.5	6496.5	6805.5	7114.5	7423.5	7732.5	
+ Fixed Exp.	9074.5	9074.5	9074.5	9074.5	9074.5	9074.5	9074.5	9074.5	9074.5	9074.5	9074.5	9074.5	
Operating Expenses + 4% of Gross Income for Management	16300	16300	16300	16300	13229	13558	15262	15571	15880	16189	16498	16807	= 188,174
													−14,904
TOTAL OPERATING EXPENSES													203,078

E.O.Y 2 (1983) - PROJECTED GROSS INCOME

	January	February	March	April	May	June	July	August	September	October	November	December	
Main Building/Floor													
(1)	8771	8771	8771	8771	8771	8771	8771	8771	8771	8771	8771	8771	
(2)	5694	5694	5694	5694	5694	5694	5694	5694	5694	5694	5694	5694	
(3)	4950	4950	4950	4950	4950	4950	4950	4950	4950	4950	4950	4950	
(4)	4484	4484	4484	4484	4484	4484	4484	4484	4484	4484	4484	4484	
(5)	6870	6870	6870	6870	6870	6870	6870	6870	6870	6870	6870	6870	
South Building/Floor													
(1)	1714	3017	3017	3017	3107	3107	3017	3017	3017	3017	3017	3017	
(2)	-0-	822	2947	3238	3238	3238	3238	3238	3238	3238	3238	3238	
N.E. Building/Floor 1	3542	3542	3542	3542	3542	3542	3542	3542	3542	3542	3542	3542	
Drive-In	2625	2625	2625	2625	2625	2625	2625	2625	2625	2625	2625	2625	
Scheduled Income - 7% Vacancy Factor	38650	40775	42900	43191	43191	43191	43191	43191	43191	43191	43191	43191	= 511,044 -35,773
PROJECTED GROSS INCOME													475,271
Net Sq. Ft. Occupied													
Main Building 1	7160	7160	7160	7160	7160	7160	7160	7160	7160	7160	7160	7160	
2	6507	6507	6507	6507	6507	6507	6507	6507	6507	6507	6507	6507	
3	6600	6600	6600	6600	6600	6600	6600	6600	6600	6600	6600	6600	
4	5979	5979	5979	5979	5979	5979	5979	5979	5979	5979	5979	5979	
5	6870	6870	6870	6870	6870	6870	6870	6870	6870	6870	6870	6870	
South Building 1	2420	4259	4259	4259	4259	4259	4259	4259	4259	4259	4259	4259	
2	-0-	1160	4160	4571	4571	4571	4571	4571	4571	4571	4571	4571	
N.E. Building 1	5000	5000	5000	5000	5000	5000	5000	5000	5000	5000	5000	5000	
TOTALS	40536	43535	46535	46946	46946	46946	46946	46946	46946	46946	46946	46946	
Variable Exp. (.21655/M) = + Fixed Exp. (9.488)	8778 9488	9428 9488	10077 9488	10166 9488									
Operating Expenses - 4% of Projected Gross Income for Management	18266	18916	19565	19654	19654	19654	19654	19654	19654	19654	19654	19654	= 233,722 -19,011
TOTAL OPERATING EXPENSES													214,711

SCHEDULE D(3)

E.O.Y. 3 (1984) - PROJECTED GROSS INCOME

	January	February	March	April	May	June	July	August	September	October	November	December	
Main Building/Floor													
(1)	9210	9210	9210	9210	9210	9210	9210	9210	9210	9210	9210	9210	
(2)	5978	5978	5978	5978	5978	5978	5978	5978	5978	5978	5978	5978	
(3)	5198	5198	5198	5198	5198	5198	5198	5198	5198	5198	5198	5198	
(4)	4708	4708	4708	4708	4708	4708	4708	4708	4708	4708	4708	4708	
(5)	7213	7213	7213	7213	7213	7213	7213	7213	7213	7213	7213	7213	
South Building/Floor													
(1)	3168	3168	3168	3168	3168	3168	3168	3168	3168	3168	3168	3168	
(2)	3238	3238	3238	3238	3238	3238	3238	3238	3238	3238	3238	3238	
N.E. Building/Floor 1	3719	3719	3719	3719	3719	3719	3719	3719	3719	3719	3719	3719	
Drive-In	2756	2756	2756	2756	2756	2756	2756	2756	2756	2756	2756	2756	
Scheduled Income	44771	44771	44771	44771	44771	44771	44771	44771	44771	44771	44771	44771	= 542,255
- 4% Vacancy Factor													-37,958
PROJECTED GROSS INCOME													504,269

Net Sq. Ft. Occupied

Main Building 1
                2
                3
                4
                5

South Building 1
                2

N.E. Building 1

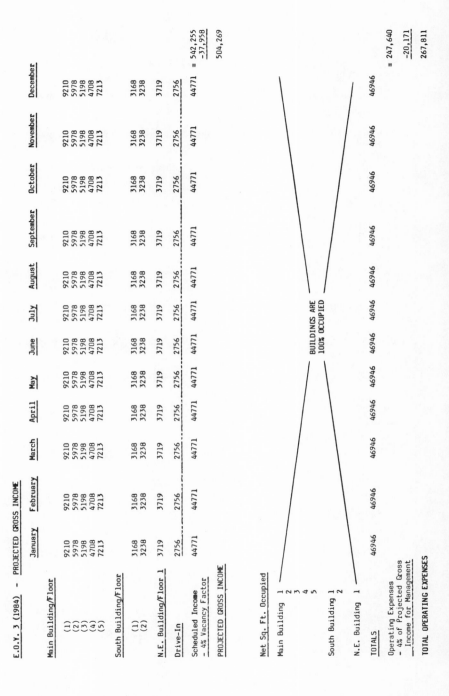

BUILDINGS ARE 100% OCCUPIED

	January	February	March	April	May	June	July	August	September	October	November	December	
TOTALS	46946	46946	46946	46946	46946	46946	46946	46946	46946	46946	46946	46946	
Operating Expenses													= 247,640
- 4% of Projected Gross Income for Management													-20,171
TOTAL OPERATING EXPENSES													267,811

SCHEDULE D(4)

Projected Rental Rates and Increases per Floor

MAIN BUILDING/FLOOR 1 $14 per sq. ft. Leased to the Federal. (increase at five percent per annum beginning 1/1/83)

MAIN BUILDING/FLOOR 2 $10 per sq. ft. Leased to the Federal. (increase at five percent per annum beginning 1/1/83)

MAIN BUILDING/FLOOR 3 $9 per sq. ft. (increase at five percent per annum beginning 1/1/84)

MAIN BUILDING/FLOOR 4 $9 per sq. ft. (increase at five percent per annum beginning 1/1/84)

MAIN BUILDING/FLOOR 5 $12 per sq. ft. (increase at five percent per annum beginning 1/1/84)

SOUTH BUILDING/FLOOR 1 $8.50 per sq. ft. (increase at five percent per annum beginning 1/1/84)

SOUTH BUILDING/FLOOR 2 $8.50 per sq. ft. (increase at five percent per annum beginning 1/1/85)

N.E. BUILDING/FLOOR 1 $8.50 per sq. ft. (increase at five percent per annum beginning 1/1/84)

DRIVE-IN $30,000 per annum—Leased to the Federal (increase at five percent per annum beginning 1/1/83)

SCHEDULE E

Appraisal Update

Description	Date	Location	Building Area Sq. Ft. Net	Sales Price	$/Sq. Ft. Net
Gateway Executive Center	6/80	4th St.	32,915	$1,300,000 (90% Leased)	$39.50
Bay West	5/81	4th St.	30,382	$1,100,000 (85% Leased)	$36.00
Belcher Plaza	7/81	Belcher Rd.	110,000	$6,300,000	$57.27
Bay Park Executive Center		U.S. 19	60,846	$2,175,000 (96% Leased)	$35.75

Pioneer Federal Savings And Loan Association Computer Runs

The computer investment analysis is intended to offer information to prospective buyers on estimated cash flows and returns based on the following information.

$2,600,000 Asking Price

Purchase Price: $2,600,000
Investor with otherwise taxable income of $200,000
Five year ownership period
Initial investment of $660,000 cash
Capital improvements—remodeling $383,420
Loan: $2,080,000
  12 percent interest
  25 year amortization
  12 payments per year
Net Operating Income based on assumptions (Schedule E):
Depreciation: Straight line
    90 percent depreciable basis
    15 year life (ACRS 1981)
Reversion at end of five years, capitalize N.O.I. at five percent
Landlease: $9,600 per year

$3,300,000 Asking Price

The following computer investment analysis is intended to offer information to prospective buyers and sellers on estimated cash flows and return on listed price and terms:

Assumptions:
 Purchase Price: $3,300,000
 Investor with other taxable income of $200,000
 Five year ownership period
 Initial investment $660,000 cash
 Capital investment—remodeling $383,420
 Loan: $2,640,000
    16.5 percent interest
    25 year amortization
    12 payments per year
 Net Operating Income based on assumptions (Schedule E):
 Depreciation: Straight Line
     90 percent Depreciable Basis
     15 Year Life (ACRS 1981)
 Reversion end of five years capitalize
 NOI at five percent
 Landlease: $9,600 per year

```
        PROPERTY CATALOG ID NUMBER      7
  681.  PROPERTY IDENTIFICATION         CLEARWATER FED 2.6
  682.  ANALYSIS PREPARED BY            L ARNOLD & ASS.

  173.  INVESTMENT BASE, 1. PROJECTION  903420          5 YEARS
  352.  ANY EXCESS CARRYOVER            0
  198.  RESIDENTIAL RENTAL              0
  356.  AGE OF IMPROVEMENTS AT BOY-1    20
  164.  YEAR 1 OF PROJECTION            1982

    2.  NUMBER OF LOANS                 1

        STARTS                PMTS  INTEREST    PAYMENT  BALLOONS    LOAN
  LOAN    BOY    AMOUNT  TERM  /YR     RATE      AMOUNT      EOY     TYPE
  1       1    2080000  25.00  12    12.000   21907.06              100

  174.01 NOI 1, BEGINNING YEAR         169530          1
  174.02 NOI 2, BEGINNING YEAR         222538          2
  174.03 NOI 3, BEGINNING YEAR         236486          3
  174.04 NOI 4, BEGINNING YEAR         248310          4
  174.05 NOI 5, BEGINNING YEAR         260725          5
  191.  NOI 5 APPREC FACTOR            5%

  197.  NUMBER OF DEP/AMORT/ACRS ITEMS  1

  197.01 ITEM 1 AMOUNT, LIFE           2685078        15 YEARS
         YEAR TO START, METHOD         1              1
         TYPE, S/L REVERSION           1              0
         SALVAGE VALUE                 0

  163.  FUTURE NON-DEP CAP ADDNS        0

  346.  NON-OPERATING EXPENSES          1
  346.01 EXPENSE 1 AMT, YEAR           9600            5

? 357.  FUNDED RESERVES                 0

  368.  PERCENTAGE OF OWNERSHIP         100
  340.  OTI CONSTANT(1) OR CHANGES(2)   1
  342.  REPORTING METHOD                2
  341.  CONSTANT OTI AMOUNT             200000

  370.  FMRR SAFE RATE, 371. REINV RATE 10%            15%
  372.  MIN REINV AMT, 171. CASH PORTION 30000         20%

  192.  EOY SALE PRICE CALC METHOD      1
  169.  CAP RATE, 170. MIN SALE PRICE   8%             2600000

  194.  CALC BASIS(1) OR GIVEN(2)       1

  345.  COSTS OF DISPOSITION            7%

  373.  OUTPUT FORMAT, 374. YEAR OPTION 3              1
```

◆◆

```
CASH FLOW ANALYSIS: CLEARWATER FED 2.6                        01/27/82.

◆◆01◆◆ LOAN INFORMATION

        STARTS           SCHED PMTS   INTEREST      PAYMENT   BALLOONS     LOAN
LOAN     BOY    AMOUNT    PMTS  /YR       RATE        AMOUNT        EOY     TYPE
 1        1    2080000    300   12      12.000      21907.06               100

$INVESTMENT BASE              903420              %OWNERSHIP            100.00

◆◆◆◆◆◆◆◆◆◆◆◆◆◆◆◆◆◆◆◆◆◆◆◆◆◆  EOY 1       EOY 2       EOY 3      EOY 4      EOY 5
                           1982        1983        1984       1985       1986

$LOAN 1                  2065959     2050138     2032311    2012223    1989586
=TOTAL LOAN BALANCES     2065959     2050138   203231LPP    2012223    1989586

(PRINCIPAL PAYMENTS)       14041       15821       17827      20088      22636

◆◆02◆◆ TAXABLE INCOME

$NET OPERATING INCOME     169530      222538      236486     248310     260725
-REG DEPREC/RECOVERY      179005      179005      179005     179005     179005
-NON-OP EXPENSES            9600        9600        9600       9600       9600
-DEDUCTIBLE INTEREST      248844      247064      245057     242796     240249
=TOTAL TAXABLE INCOME    -267919     -213131     -197176    -183091    -168129

◆◆03◆◆ CASH FLOWS
?
$NET OPERATING INCOME     169530      222538      236486     248310     260725
-NON-OP EXPENSES            9600        9600        9600       9600       9600
-PRINCIPAL & INTEREST     262885      262885      262885     262885     262885
=PRE-TAX CASH FLOW       -102955      -49947      -35999     -24175     -11760
-INCOME TAX               -89149      -85702      -82782     -80579     -76802
=AFT-TAX CASH FLOW        -13806       35755       46783      56404      65043

◆◆12◆◆ ANALYSIS OF EOY 5 SALE PROCEEDS

 ADJUSTED BASIS:          EXCESS DEPRECIATION:      SALE TAXES/PROCEEDS:
$ORIG BASIS   2983420    $DEPR TAKEN     895026    $ON RECAPT              0
+CAP ADDNS          0    -DEP&SEC 179    895026    +ON CAP GAIN      211554
+SALE COSTS    239541    =EXCESS DEPR         0    +ON TAX PREF           0
=SUB TOTAL    3222961    +DSALOWD S/L         0    +ITC RECAPT            0
-DEPR TAKEN    895026    =TOT RECAPT          0    =TOTAL TAXES      211554
-PART SALES         0                             $SALE PRICE      3422016
-TOT AMORT          0     GAIN:                    -SALE COSTS      239541
+AMORT ADDNS        0    $SALE PRICE    3422016    -LOAN(S)        1989586
=AB AT SALE   2327935    -AB AT SALE    2327935    =PR-TX PRCDS    1192888
                         =TOTAL GAIN    1094081    -TOTAL TAXES     211554
                         -TOT RECAPT          0    +RES BALANCE          0
AFT-TAX IRR      5.54    =CAP GAIN      1094081    =AF-TX PRCDS     981334
AFT-TAX FMRR     6.03

TIME: 17.00.49.
```

INVESTMENT ANALYSIS FROM INVESTOR WITH $1,000,000
OTHERWISE TAXABLE INCOME

●●●

```
CASH FLOW ANALYSIS: CFS 2.6 1000M                          01/27/82.

♦♦01♦♦ LOAN INFORMATION

        STARTS         SCHED PMTS   INTEREST    PAYMENT  BALLOONS    LOAN
LOAN    BOY    AMOUNT  PMTS  /YR       RATE      AMOUNT       EOY    TYPE
1       1    2080000   300   12      12.000    21907.06              100

$INVESTMENT BASE          903420              %OWNERSHIP          100.00

♦♦♦♦♦♦♦♦♦♦♦♦♦♦♦♦♦♦♦♦♦♦♦♦  EOY 1     EOY 2     EOY 3     EOY 4     EOY 5
                          1982      1983      1984      1985      1986

$LOAN 1                  2065959   2050138   2032311   2012223   1989586
=TOTAL LOAN BALANCES     2065959   2050138   2032311   2012223   1989586

(PRINCIPAL PAYMENTS)       14041     15821     17827     20088     22636

Y♦♦02♦♦ TAXABLE INCOME

$NET OPERATING INCOME     169530    222538    236486    248310    260725
-REG DEPREC/RECOVERY      179005    179005    179005    179005    179005
-NON-OP EXPENSES            9600      9600      9600      9600      9600
-DEDUCTIBLE INTEREST      248844    247064    245057    242796    240249
=TOTAL TAXABLE INCOME    -267919   -213131   -197176   -183091   -168129

♦♦03♦♦ CASH FLOWS

$NET OPERATING INCOME     169530    222538    236486    248310    260725
-NON-OP EXPENSES            9600      9600      9600      9600      9600
-PRINCIPAL & INTEREST     262885    262885    262885    262885    262885
=PRE-TAX CASH FLOW       -102955    -49947    -35999    -24175    -11760
-INCOME TAX              -133960   -106565    -98588    -91546    -84064
=AFT-TAX CASH FLOW         31005     56619     62590     67371     72305

♦♦12♦♦ ANALYSIS OF EOY 5 SALE PROCEEDS

 ADJUSTED BASIS:          EXCESS DEPRECIATION:      SALE TAXES/PROCEEDS:
$ORIG BASIS    2983420   $DEPR TAKEN    895026    $ON RECAPT          -0
+CAP ADDNS           0   -DEP&SEC 179   895026    +ON CAP GAIN    218816
+SALE COSTS     239541   =EXCESS DEPR        0    +ON TAX PREF         0
=SUB TOTAL     3222961   +DSALOWD S/L        0    +ITC RECAPT          0
-DEPR TAKEN     895026   =TOT RECAPT         0    =TOTAL TAXES    218816
ZPART SALES          0                            $SALE PRICE    3422016
-TOT AMORT           0    GAIN:                    -SALE COSTS     239541
+AMORT ADDNS         0   $SALE PRICE    3422016    -LOAN(S)       1989586
=AB AT SALE    2327935   -AB AT SALE    2327935    =PR-TX PRCDS   1192888
                         =TOTAL GAIN    1094081    -TOTAL TAXES    218816
                         -TOT RECAPT         0    +RES BALANCE         0
                         =CAP GAIN      1094081    =AF-TX PRCDS    974072

AFT-TAX IRR       7.61
AFT-TAX FMRR      8.32
```

INPUT INFORMATION

```
WHAT PROPERTY ID NUMBER(ENTER ZERO FOR CATALOG)      ? 6 CLEARWATER FED 3.3
DO YOU WISH TO REVIEW PREVIOUS INPUT(1 OR 0)      ? 1

        PROPERTY CATALOG ID NUMBER          6
681. PROPERTY IDENTIFICATION                CLEARWATER FED 3.3


173. INVESTMENT BASE, 1. PROJECTION      1043420      5 YEARS
352. ANY EXCESS CARRYOVER                0
198. RESIDENTIAL RENTAL                  0
356. AGE OF IMPROVEMENTS AT BOY-1        20
164. YEAR 1 OF PROJECTION                1982

  2. NUMBER OF LOANS                      1

       STARTS                    PMTS  INTEREST    PAYMENT  BALLOONS     LOAN
LOAN    BOY     AMOUNT    TERM    /YR    RATE      AMOUNT        EOY     TYPE
 1       1    2640000   25.00    12   16.500    36913.66                 100
~
174.01 NOI 1, BEGINNING YEAR             169530       1
174.02 NOI 2, BEGINNING YEAR             222538       2
174.03 NOI 3, BEGINNING YEAR             236486       3
174.04 NOI 4, BEGINNING YEAR             248310       4
174.05 NOI 5, BEGINNING YEAR             260725       5
191. NOI 5 APPREC FACTOR                 5%

197. NUMBER OF DEP/AMORT/ACRS ITEMS      1

S 197.01 ITEM 1 AMOUNT, LIFE             3315078      15 YEARS
         YEAR TO START, METHOD           1            1
         TYPE, S/L REVERSION             1            0
         SALVAGE VALUE                   0

163. FUTURE NON-DEP CAP ADDNS            0

346. NON-OPERATING EXPENSES              1
346.01 EXPENSE 1 AMT, YEAR               9600         5

357. FUNDED RESERVES                     0

368. PERCENTAGE OF OWNERSHIP             100
340. OTI CONSTANT(1) OR CHANGES(2)       1
342. REPORTING METHOD                    2
341. CONSTANT OTI AMOUNT                 200000

370. FMRR SAFE RATE, 371. REINV RATE     10%          15%
372. MIN REINV AMT, 171. CASH PORTION    30000        20%

192. EOY SALE PRICE CALC METHOD          1
169. CAP RATE, 170. MIN SALE PRICE       8%           3300000

194. CALC BASIS(1) OR GIVEN(2)           1

345. COSTS OF DISPOSITION                7%
```

CASH FLOW ANALYSIS
$3,300,000 ASKING PRICE

```
CASH FLOW ANALYSIS: CLEARWATER FED                              01/12/82.

◆◆01◆◆ LOAN INFORMATION

        STARTS            SCHED PMTS   INTEREST      PAYMENT  BALLOONS    LOAN
LOAN    BOY     AMOUNT    PMTS  /YR      RATE         AMOUNT       EOY    TYPE
  1       1    2640000     300   12     16.500      36913.66              100

$INVESTMENT BASE           1043420                 %OWNERSHIP           100.00

◆◆◆◆◆◆◆◆◆◆◆◆◆◆◆◆◆◆◆◆◆◆◆◆◆◆◆  EOY 1       EOY 2      EOY 3      EOY 4      EOY 5
                             1982        1983       1984       1985       1986

$LOAN 1                    2632053     2622691    2611661    2598668    2583361
=TOTAL LOAN BALANCES       2632053     2622691    2611661    2598668    2583361

(PRINCIPAL PAYMENTS)          7947        9362      11029      12993      15307

◆◆02◆◆ TAXABLE INCOME

$NET OPERATING INCOME       169530      222538     236486     248310     260725
-REG DEPREC/RECOVERY        221005      221005     221005     221005     221005
-NON-OP EXPENSES                 0           0          0          0       9600
-DEDUCTIBLE INTEREST        435017      433602     431935     429971     427657
=TOTAL TAXABLE INCOME      -486492     -432069    -416454    -402666    -397537

◆◆03◆◆ CASH FLOWS

$NET OPERATING INCOME       169530      222538     236486     248310     260725
-NON-OP EXPENSES                 0           0          0          0       9600
-PRINCIPAL & INTEREST       442964      442964     442964     442964     442964
=PRE-TAX CASH FLOW         -273434     -220426    -206478    -194654    -191839
-INCOME TAX                 -89149      -85702     -83100     -83100     -83100
=AFT-TAX CASH FLOW         -184285     -134724    -123378    -111554    -108739

◆◆12◆◆ ANALYSIS OF EOY 5 SALE PROCEEDS

 ADJUSTED BASIS:            EXCESS DEPRECIATION:      SALE TAXES/PROCEEDS:
$ORIG BASIS    3683420    $DEPR TAKEN   1105026    $ON RECAPT             0
+CAP ADDNS           0    -DEP&SEC 179  1105026    +ON CAP GAIN       73309
+SALE COSTS     239541    =EXCESS DEPR        0    +ON TAX PREF           0
=SUB TOTAL     3922961    +DSALOWD S/L        0    +ITC RECAPT            0
-DEPR TAKEN    1105026    =TOT RECAPT         0    =TOTAL TAXES       73309
-PART SALES          0                             $SALE PRICE      3422016
-TOT AMORT           0     GAIN:                    -SALE COSTS      239541
+AMORT ADDNS         0    $SALE PRICE   3422016    -LOAN(S)         2583361
=AB AT SALE    2817935    -AB AT SALE   2817935    =PR-TX PRCDS      599114
                          =TOTAL GAIN    604081    -TOTAL TAXES       73309
                          -TOT RECAPT         0    +RES BALANCE           0
AFT-TAX IRR     -29.37    =CAP GAIN      604081    =AF-TX PRCDS      525805
AFT-TAX FMRR    -22.49
```

A Potential Buyer

After having completed the rather extensive market status report to the seller, it is clear that we put a great deal of emphasis on the importance of presenting better information to the seller. Within five days of delivering this formal report to the Federal, a price reduction to $2.7 million dollars was authorized. Within two weeks of this authorization, a formal contract was executed with a third party on the following terms and conditions through the assistance of a co-broker in our local market. This co-brokerage relationship resulted from a presentation made by associate, Joel Parker, at a local Board of REALTORS® commercial-investment meeting.

Terms and Conditions of Contract

- Purchase Price: $2,650,000
- Escrow Deposit: $ 250,000
  Initial deposit of $100,000 in the form of a personal note to be replaced by $250,000, in cash, ten (10) days after acceptance of Contract.
- Cash at Closing $2,400,000
- Buyer to take assignment of landlease. Pioneer Federal to pay any and all increases or additional landlease rental related to savings account deposits.
- Long-term Leaseback: Pioneer Federal to lease back Floors 1 and 2 and drive-in facilities on long-term basis. Lease to be for a term of ten years with three renewal options of five years each, commencement of term to be date of closing. Common use of parking, lobby, elevators and common area.
- Minimum Annual Base Rent:
  Floor 1—6,865 net rentable sq.ft. × $14.00 = $96,110
  Floor 2—6,426 net rentable sq.ft. × $10.00 = $64,260
  Drive-In Facilities—Minimum Base Rent   = $30,000
  All base rents prorated and payable monthly. Commencing at second lease year, annual base rental shall be adjusted in accordance with Consumer Price Index. Said increase shall not exceed six percent per annum.
- Short-term Leaseback: Pioneer Federal to lease back Floor 1 of the South Wing for a period of one (1) year and Floor 2 of the South Wing for a period of two (2) years. Common use of parking, lobby, elevators and common area.
  Minimum Annual Base Rent:
  Floor 1—2,893 net rentable sq.ft. × $7.00 = $20,251
  Floor 2—2,921 net rentable sq.ft. × $7.00 = $20,447

As is sometimes the case, the purchaser did not fulfill his obligations and the contract was not closed. The purchaser failed to make the increased escrow deposit required under the contract. This contract was terminated and it was necessary for the marketing team to gear up the marketing effort. We lost approximately one month attempting to consummate this contract, entered into almost immediately after the price reduction. As the exclusive right of sale listing agreement was due to expire in approximately 30 days, we felt that even though our marketing plans had not resulted in a new contract, we were moving in the right direction. We also felt it was important that we keep the seller informed of our marketing efforts and therefore made a formal marketing report on May 14, 1982, to the Board of Directors. This marketing report contains specific information on our marketing plan as well as problems we were attempting to solve.

May 14, 1982

Mr. Harlan Merhige, President
Pioneer Service Corporation
5770 Roosevelt Blvd.
Clearwater, Florida 33520

Dear Harlan:

Please allow this letter to serve as a written report to you and your Board regarding the status of our marketing on the downtown Pioneer Federal building.

We lost considerable amount of marketing momentum when the Buyer failed to close on the contract. At the time we were under contract, we were poised with several interested parties, one of which was interested in leasing at least two of the floors of the building. That particular prospect, because he was unable to obtain the top floor, went to Tampa and leased space.

We have attached a copy of our April 25th marketing plan and program for your inspection. We have been following the marketing plan very closely through the month of May and as we approach mid-May, we have realized reasonable success in our marketing efforts. We have modified our package down to a seven to eight page presentation in an effort to avoid confusion and to enhance our distribution of information on the property. We have had numerous meetings with architects and contracted with Right Architects in Tampa, a firm with a history of successful renovations in the North. Our major problem has been dealing with multi-tenant conversion of floors three and four. The load factor or the unuseable space on these two floors is unacceptable for modern buildings. With the atrium, we have almost 26 percent space which cannot be rented. The architectural plans are intended to mitigate the risk associated with conversion of the building to multi-tenant. Few potential purchasers have shown any interest in attempting to lease the building on a single floor basis. It is generally agreed that the fifth floor will be leased to a single tenant without major modifications. We, in fact, have an excellent prospect for the top floor at this time which was germinated by one of our marketing programs. Obviously, if we can find a user, the building will sell immediately. There is little question that the building is of interest in the investment market; however, there is a great deal of apprehension over the absorption rate of the unleased space. On Thursday we received the plans for conversion. We are not satisfied with the architect's proposed renovations of those two floors and plan to have at least one other architect give us a proposal prior to finalizing any recommendations to the Federal.

One of our marketing programs is to begin leasing the space to outside tenants. We have hesitated to do this as long as we have had good active potential buyers working on the property. At this time, we have several very strong prime prospects working one of whom, we believe, will make some form of an offer. We are using numerous marketing programs described in our list of programs in the marketing plan. Not surprisingly, our advertising media blitz has not resulted in the types of prospects we had hoped for. However, our personal contact with property owners who have similar buildings in the Tampa Bay area is resulting in good, qualified prospect traffic for the building. We have shown the building almost every day for the last three weeks; today, we are scheduled to show the building three times. This building is only shown to prospects who have been qualified, have been given information on the building and wish to proceed with a personal inspection. We are not showing the building to unqualified prospects. We are continuing to press hard on our broker program with personal contacts, direct mail and a telephone campaign. We have good, active interaction with brokers in Tampa and several of the local Clearwater commercial brokers who have all been through the building and shown interest. We are getting play on the national market from our broker program as well as some of our media advertising, but in most cases the national market has been penetrated by personal contact by a member of this firm.

Currently, the most exciting interest we have is from Joe Developer in Tampa, a well-known office building owner and renovator. He has brought in his New York partners and we have now had three meetings on the building with this group. R. Nelson, out of Tampa, is also a very qualified prospect with office building interest. Mr. Nelson has been in the building twice and is working with his partner, John Kite, to decide if they are going to proceed with the acquisition. John Kite is the Chairman of the Board of the First Bank. Mr. Nelson would like the entire building to be a First Bank facility. Both of these prospects are targeted and qualified and have been on the property several times and are asking very detailed and specific questions. We are having a second meeting with the Joe Smith Foundation this afternoon in an effort to clarify for them the benefits to the Foundation of acquiring the building and utilizing the space necessary for their future growth. We have good, strong, positive responses from that Foundation. They are also, obviously, qualified to acquire the building. We had a third meeting with Mr. Broker and he has had several discussions with his partners relative to acquisition of the building and we are now working with a client who would lease the top floor. It obviously makes the entire transaction fall into place if we can find a single tenant user for one or more of the floors. You will note that we have featured the Pioneer Federal again on our monthly newsletter which is targeted to over 1,000 investors in the immediate market. This is in an effort to re-expose it as so many people felt the property was under contract and sold. We have made an attempt to work the Tampa market and we have made serious presentations to Al Time, office builder, Jim Washington of the Poe Group and Bob Jones of the Jones Realty Corporation. One of our strongest prospects is the Real Estate Company of New York who recently reviewed the property. We had a lengthy lunch discussing the ramifications of lease-up.

Without any doubt, our major marketing problem is the lease potential of the property and the absorption time it will take to fill the building.

We have made contact with numerous prospects on a direct, personalized basis, a few of whom include the following: Another attempt has been made to rekindle the interest of the City of Clearwater; Bill Rue and Bill Cook, both CPA's, for referrals and potential personal use; John Kite and Paul Row, investors in St. Petersburg who built The Square; Bob Roads of A.B. Roads Co. of Tampa. We worked with and have shown the building to Dime Corporation and personally visited with Mr. Rink on the site; Don Deer, a broker in Tampa, who has been through the building three times and has shown it twice; Bob Wood of Orlando, a well-known commercial broker who is known throughout the State to have had several sale-leasebacks with Federals, has received a package and has presented it to his clients; Gary Hope, a Tampa broker, has also presented it several times and had a very positive client flying in to look at the property at the time we went to contract. We have not been able to rekindle that individual client. We have gone back to the School Board on three different occasions in the last 30 days trying to generate interest for the School Board needs. Frank Krer of the Corporate Real Estate Trust has had the property presented to him twice in the last 30 days to solve his personal problems with the property. Roger Rick in Pinellas Park, who is an up and coming investor/syndicator, is scheduled to see the property today. George Broker has received a package on the property and a personal presentation and has a client he is working with. Scott Little of the Beach Newspaper was presented the building but has no interest. Dennis Pope of J. Real Estate, a management company in Tampa, has made a personal inspection of the property and has presented it to his clients. We have worked with Sam Casela numerous times trying to get some referrals or interest out of the Downtown Development Board with little result from the Board at this time. We have scheduled appointments with Barry Pert of State Life Insurance Company. They have a real need for the property and they are a good potential prospect for the property. We have had several discussions with Roger Heart of Wisconsin, a national syndicator, and he has made a personal inspection of the property. Jim Dine of the Committee of 100 has been presented the property several times in an effort to keep his interest and referrals currently in mind. We have again presented the property to Bob Parks to try and see if there would be any interest out of the Bank and potential of moving the Federal to a freestanding pad on the adjacent shopping center at Cleveland Plaza. Bob Parks is not interested in proceeding on this theory. However, we do feel that another bank might be. We have had several discussions with Hal Wake and a national leasing company currently working in Tampa. Mike Stone, office building owner in Tampa, has been given the information and has not responded. Harry Hughes, Brothers Development in Tampa and office building developer and owner, has been given the package and is considering the proposal. Miami broker Tony Smith has been given a package for a client he was researching in the Tampa market. Lee Forest of Tampa is not buying properties at this time and has rejected the proposal. We have made a verbal presentation to Al Mann and we are looking for further contact with Al in the coming week.

My personal working list goes on and on, and there have been numerous presentations which we have not represented to you here due to the volume and time. Of course, none of Joel Parker's personal presentations or presentations made by other members of our firm are included in this as we are just attempting to give you a feel for the type of activity we have been creating since the expiration of the contract [contract to purchase property].

The main thrust of our program for the next two to three weeks will be to continue the personal contact to targeted prospects and our current active buyers. We do need, though, to prepare for changes in our marketing program if we do not have a contract in three weeks. We would like to prepare a leasing sign and install it on the front of the property in an effort to generate prospects for the building. We have studied four or five different leases in the market which are currently being used and are competitive to your space. We would expect to make a recommendation within two weeks on the format to follow in leasing your building. I had lunch yesterday with Dave Lee of the First Bank, the only space downtown that competes with your property, and obtained a copy of his lease and a current vacancy report. We will supply you with four or five competitive leases in the marketplace for your consideration. We will recommend a particular format based on our expectations of the lease-up of the building. It will be necessary, if we go in to a multi-tenant leasing program on floors three and four, to make some very difficult decisions and expend capital for renovations. We have been avoiding this in an effort to sell the property to a user or investor who will make those difficult space utilization decisions. We would like to have the Federal allocate funds for additional architectural work and redesign floors three and four. We would also like the Federal to consider matching our marketing fund of $5,000 so that we can expand our advertising on a more national basis and enhance the property's exposure to the marketplace. We will be scheduling a meeting with you in the next two weeks in an effort to present the next 30 day marketing plan.

We look forward to your comments on this report.

Sincerely,

Broker, CCIM

TARGET MARKET AND
MARKETING PLAN GENERATOR

Listing Code ___4/25/82___

Property ___Pioneer Federal___

Date _____

1. PROPERTY CHARACTERISTICS (BASIC)

Zoning __DD__	APOD Owner statement	__none__
Land Use __Conforms__		
Size __54,000 gross__	APOD Broker's Forecast	__Completed__
Topography _____		
Water __OK__	Specialized Information	__See Federal presentation__
Sewer __OK__	Construction	__Some modification required__

2. FINANCING

	Assumable Existing	Owner Pur. Mon.	New Institutional
Current Balance		2,000,000±	
Annual Interest Rate		13%–15%	
Payment Am't. & Frequency		Monthly	
Remaining Term		25–30	
Assumption Provisions			
Prepayment Penalties			
Personal Endorsement		Yes/Possible No	
Release Clauses			
Subordination Clauses			
Balloon expected year 10			

a) WHAT ALTERNATIVE FINANCING APPROACHES ARE AVAILABLE?

___Cash - participation financing, pension fund___

b) WHAT IS THE LIKELY FINAL FINANCIAL STRUCTURE OR APPROACH THAT WILL BE USED TO CLOSE THE SALE?
___Leaseback of at least 1 or 2 floors with 2 - 3 lease___

DEVELOP TARGET MARKET

1. How does the property relate to the market? Based on market price, property characteristics and financing, what are the best uses that will result in the highest price in Owner's time frame?

   Office use highest and best use/user property ideal

   To convert to multi-tenant needs plans completed

2. What use "need" is most sought after based on Market Conditions that the property could meet?

   Office space - multi-tenant, not major floor user

   A 7,000 square foot user is rare in Clearwater

   2,000 - 3,000 square feet normal

3. Describe and define size and scope of market for Subject Property. Local, State, Out Of State, World, Investment/ User, etc.

   Scope is national on full leaseback or soft terms.

   Local user if sold noninvestment

4. What use or user is missing or limited in the market?

   School Board has need for space, State Life has need for space.

5. What are the benefits this property offers?

   Financial institution, 1st floor, largest quantity of prestigious space

   Immediate availability, 16,306 sq.ft. leaseback

   Location, size below replacement cost

   Main street, executive quality space, flexibility on sale/leaseback

6. Define Highest & Best Use of Property.

   Office space for main building, multi-tenant

   Gas station conversion to office or parking lots

7. Given the above thought process, list in order of priority the potential target prospects, in general.

   a. General user targets on mass media

   b. Target investment buyer-look for transaction structure that

      results in a win-win transaction.

DEVELOPING MARKET PROGRAMS

(1) Marketing programs should be developed based on Time and Cost.

(2) Primary focus on Target Prospect/Market.

(3) Develop plan based on needs that property can satisfy.

(4) List ALL of various programs that logically should facilitate a sale.

(5) Develop Marketing Budget:
- What is estimated FEE?
- What is percentage probability of co-brokerage?
- What is total dollar to be expended in marketing?

	Allocate to Programs:	
	Gross Fee	$ _____
	Co-brokerage	$ _____
Total 30 day Budget	In-house Salesperson	$ _____
$5,000	Company	$ _____
See Ad Schedule	Classified	$ _____
	Direct Mail	$ _____
	Signage	$ _____
	Other (special publications, etc.)	$ __5,000_____

(6) Schedule Programs:
   a) Highest probability first.
   b) As schedule is developed, choose programs with highest probability that fall within Budget until allocated funds are exhausted.

LIST PROGRAMS BEST SUITED FOR PLAN — HIGHEST PROBABILITY VS. COST.

1. Complete new ad and distribute
2. Contact specific new targets
3. Re-contact Tampa contacts
4. Set up leasing program for Federal
5. Have architect design Floors 3 & 4
6. Challenge real estate assessment
7. Develop lease for Federal
8. National CCIM list
9. Study disc
10. Develop plan on sale/leaseback
11. Lunch w/ P. Federal new team
12. Work up operating cost reduction
13. New American Network computer
14. Direct mail investors in computer
15. Develop new flyer
16. Feature again in monthly newsletter
17. Pat Bear at State contact
18. Contact MAI for new prospect
19. Lunch w/ Mr. Broker and prospect
20. Top commercial broker mailing
21. Open house - wine - at Federal
22. Prospect leasing dept. (The Square, Smith Building, First Bank)
23. _____
24. Press release
25. Media blitz - Wall Street Journal,
26. Fla. Trend, St. Pete Times, Tampa
27. Tribune, Miami Tribune, National R/E
28. Investor, Southeast R/E News, Tampa
29. Bay Business
30. _____
31. _____
32. _____
33. _____
34. _____
35. _____
36. _____
37. _____
38. _____
39. _____
40. _____

8. Based on needs that can be fulfilled by property, what prospects come to mind?

1	Dime Corporation	41	
2	School Board	42	
3	Tom Corporation - financing	43	
4	City - Ted Mack	44	
5	Bert Singer - State Power	45	
6	State Rep. Joe James and Tom Jones	46	
7	U.S. Developer	47	
8	Dr. Boyd	48	
9	Dr. Cooper	49	
10	S. Jones of Western and Life	50	
11	Bob Albert	51	
12	Joe Smith Corporation	52	
13	Top broker mailing	53	
14	Bob Harr	54	
15	Dr. Pear	55	
16	Bill Cook, CPA	56	
17	John Kite	57	
18	CPM List	58	
19	Frank Keer	59	
20	Don Deer	60	
21	C-100 mailing list	61	
22	Real Estate Company - New York	62	
23	Attorney Bates	63	
24	Sam Case	64	
25	Dick Boyd - Hall of Fame	65	
26	Cook Office Center	66	
27	Sonic Corporation	67	
28	James Corporation	68	
29	Pat Lee	69	
30	Investors	70	
31	Home Office Concept	71	
32	Attorney Kane	72	
33	Attorney Capp	73	
34		74	
35		75	
36		76	
37		77	
38		78	
39		79	
40		80	

Architectural Advice

At our expense, we had engaged an architectural firm to design and make recommendations as to a multi-tenant conversion of Floors 3 and 4. We felt as though the user market was the obvious best target; however, we also felt that it was necessary to work the investment market in an effort to mitigate the potential of not finding the absolute perfect target. Hence, we were attempting multi-tenant conversion plans and estimates of cost for those floors which could not be easily leased in our market to a single tenant.

We gave specific information on marketing with heavy emphasis on various programs that were working well and brief descriptions of those programs which we had attempted and in fact, had not resulted in good responses. At this stage of our marketing effort, we increased our national marketing penetration with numerous ads. We split up the local marketing effort. My emphasis was on the Tampa developer/rehab market and my associate's, REALTOR® Joel Parker, emphasis was on the local county market. These efforts were described in our marketing report.

Because of the delays we were having in finding a user for the entire building, we were considering making recommendations to our client as to the multi-tenant lease-up of the property. We were taking steps toward that effort in the event we were unsuccessful in finding either an investor to design, modify and lease the building multi-tenant or a single tenant user.

As we explained in our marketing report, a considerable amount of energy was now being spent to work with architects to design a space utilization plan within the building in the event we were unsuccessful in finding a single user. We had spent considerable amounts of time and money with architects designing a multi-tenant conversion of the subject property. The services of three different architectural firms were used before we were satisfied we had the optimum multi-tenant space utilization. A summary of one of these presentations is contained herein for reference.

June 21, 1982

Broker
Real Estate, Inc.

Re: Clearwater Federal Savings Main
    Building Space Utilization

Dear Broker:

In accordance with our meeting of June 16, we have prepared an analysis of level 3 and 4 at the Pioneer Federal Savings & Loan building in Clearwater.

Attached please find the following:

1. Statement of design objectives for reuse of levels 3 and 4

2. Area summary analysis

3. Suggested scope of interior improvements and preliminary cost

We will discuss this information during our meeting on June 21. If you have any questions or concerns, we can make modifications to the document during the week of June 21. Thank you for the opportunity to provide service for this project.

Sincerely,

Robert Aude, AIA

Design Objective for Reuse of Levels 3 and 4

1. Determine the most efficient use of levels 3 and 4 for multi-tenant occupancy.
2. Provide tenant space in blocks of 900 to 1500 square feet with minimum conflict by building columns. The space should offer maximum potential for interior space utilization by tenants. Spaces should be simple, rectangular, and offered in bays of 25 to 30 feet.
3. Maximize the use and effect of the three story open "atrium" area in the existing building by:
   a. providing views through glass walls for the tenant space to the atrium,
   b. providing seating and circulation areas through the atrium for building users,
   c. creating a visual amenity through planting, color and art work.

Area Summary Analysis Levels 3 and 4

	Gross Area	BOMA Rentable	BOMA Useable	Difference Rentable/Useable
Third Floor	8324	7140	5746	1394
Fourth Floor	7869	6701	5133	1569
Total	16193	13841	10879	2963

Analysis
A) Efficiency of rentable to gross: Level 3 = 85.8%
   Level 4 = 85.2%
   Total   = 85.5%
B) Efficiency of useable to gross: Level 3 = 69%
   Level 4 = 65.2%
   Total   = 67.1%
C) Atrium shaft opening on Level 4 is not included in gross or rentable/useable.

Suggested Improvements and Preliminary Costs

There are three areas of improvements that can be made to the interior space. Below is a preliminary assessment of the scope of work in each category.

1. Base Renovation: These are basic improvements to bring the space to a marketable condition, and assume that existing office areas and finishes will not be preferred by prospective tenants. Base renovation will include:

    a. demolition of existing partitions and column chases,

    b. new suspended ceiling and lighting,

    c. new flooring (commercial grade carpet),

    d. new corridor partition (one-hour rated to the underside of existing structure),

    e. new doors, frames, and hardware in corridor partitions,

    f. modifications to the existing air conditioning and heating system to provide additional ductwork and outlets to tenant spaces,

    g. atrium enclosures where appropriate.

2. Tenant Improvements: A tenant improvement allowance should be created in order to provide:

    a. interior partitions, doors, frames, hardware,

    b. electrical switches and outlets,

    c. telephone outlets,

    d. telephone and distribution.

3. Atrium Allowance: An allowance should be created to make improvements to the atrium space. Preliminary assessment is as follows:

    a. building code modifications (enclosures, smoke vent or sprinkler),

    b. seating and lighting,

    c. planting, art work accessories, or other features.

Preliminary Cost

Base renovation, levels 3 and 4: 13,841 sf × $8.96	= $124,000.00
Tenant improvement, levels 3 & 4, provided over useable area only: 10,879 sf × $5.00	= $ 54,395.00
Atrium allowance: preliminary estimate pending discussion with Building Code officials	= $ 9,000.00

Drawings of Possible Renovations

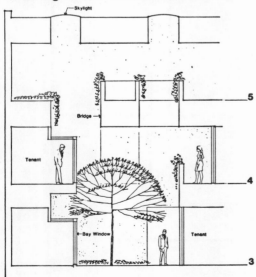

SECTION THRU ATRIUM

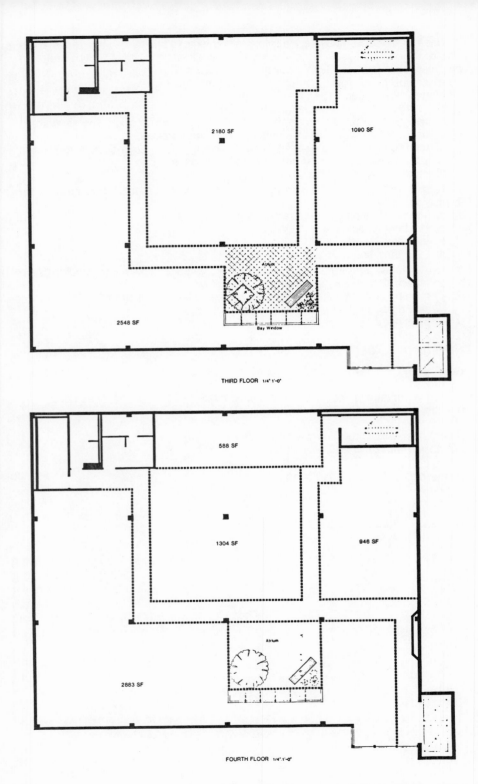

2180 SF

1090 SF

2548 SF

ATRIUM

Bay Window

THIRD FLOOR 1/4" 1'-0"

588 SF

1304 SF

946 SF

Atrium

2883 SF

FOURTH FLOOR 1/4" 1'-0"

Division of Property

We were also considering the division of the property into multiple sales in an effort to reduce the purchase price and to induce a user type purchaser. Therefore, we had additional calculations completed relative to parking lot ratios in the event a subdivision of the parcel was proposed.

Clearwater Federal Cleveland Plaza
Parking Analysis

July 15, 1982

	Gross Sq. Ft.	
1A. First Floor	8,138	
Second Floor	8,469	
Third Floor	8,163	
Fourth Floor	7,703	
Fifth Floor	7,060	
Total	39,533 sq. ft. 99 parking spaces.	
1B. First Floor =	4,000	
Second Floor =	4,000	
	8,000 sq. ft. 20 parking spaces	
2. One Floor =	1,200 sq. ft. 3 parking spaces	
3. One Floor =	5,000 sq. ft. 13 parking spaces	
4. One Floor =	725 sq. ft. 3 parking spaces	
Total Sq. Ft. 54,458		

Present parking by count = 177 spaces

Parking required per gross area = 136 spaces.

Parking requirements established per city ordinance #2254 Jan. 8, 1981 at one space per 400 sq. ft. of gross floor area for offices located in the CBD eastern corridor.

Letters of Intent

The architectural work referred to herein was paid for by us as listing agents in an effort to better understand the property we were marketing and to solve marketing problems that we were encountering. Many times it is better to spend marketing budget monies on solving problems than advertising for prospects. Emphasis is placed on this step because working with architects to better understand a listed property is not often perceived to be an important step in the marketing effort.

In this marketing effort it was extremely important when making presentations to investors, who ultimately made a series of letter of intent offers, to have estimates of cost to convert and net useable estimates. A synopsis of two of the letters of intent that were submitted during this period in the marketing effort are contained herein to show the types of cash flow concerns the investor market expressed. These letters of intent also emphasize the importance of soliciting offers from potential qualified buyers in an effort to better inform the seller as to his marketing options.

Following the synopses is our letter to the Federal with our recommendations on these letters of intent.

Synopsis of Harr Letter of Intent

Purchase Price: $2,700,000
Cash: $ 540,000
Purchase Money Mortgage: $2,160,000 (20 year amort., terms to be determined)

Leaseback

Pioneer Federal to lease back Floors 1 and 2 and drive-in facilities for ten years, with two, five year renewal options. Seller to also lease back remaining space on month-to-month basis for two years or until space is leased.

Purchaser to acquire fee interest in landlease portion for $100,000.

Synopsis of Boom Letter of Intent

Purchase Price: $2,600,000 (does not include 5,000 square foot building and gas station)

Cash at Closing $ 520,000
Purchase Money Mortgage: $2,080,000 (13%, 20 years)

Leaseback

Seller and purchaser to enter into a two year lease of top four floors at $7.25 per square foot with no escalation.

Pioneer Leaseback

Pioneer to lease back Floor 1 of main building, entire South building and drive-in facilities. Term for a period of ten years (two five-year options).

Floor 1—Main Building $14.00 per square foot
South Building $ 8.50 per square foot
Drive-in Facilities $30,000 per annum

Rent to be adjusted on annual basis to 80 percent of Consumer Price Index on each anniversary.

Seller to be responsible for any additional payments due under landlease.

June 22, 1982

Harlan Merhige, President
Pioneer Service Corporation
5770 Roosevelt Blvd.
Clearwater, Florida 33520

Dear Harlan:

Enclosed you will find two new letters of intent and architectural work on the downtown

Pioneer Federal building. The first letter of intent received in our office from Joseph Harr of New York is in the amount of $2,700,000. This letter of intent is predicated on a month to month leaseback for a two year period of the entire building or until a third party leases the vacant space. It is also interesting to note that the purchaser has requested an option or a right to acquire the fee interest in the landlease portion of the sale for $100,000. The proposed letter of intent has the normal inspection contingencies.

Also enclosed is a copy of a proposal from the Wood Property Company based in Tampa. Our contact is the President, Mr. B. E. Boom. Mr. Boom has spent a considerable amount of time with us analyzing the property in an effort to prepare the enclosed letter of intent dated June 8, 1982. It is a very thoughtful letter of intent and should be taken quite seriously. Our experience with Mr. Boom goes back many years and he is quite qualified to perform the acquisition of this property. The new wrinkle or difference in this proposal is that he believes the Federal's interest would be best served by utilizing the two story building for the trust department and not continuing to renovate the second floor. He would like to see the Federal utilize the two story structure including the ground floor for its facilities rather than utilizing the second floor as it is now under construction. It is an interesting concept and, in retrospect, enhances the value of the building. The two story structure is more difficult to lease in the long run and by taking that structure as opposed to the second floor, it reduces the risk associated with the acquisition of the total project. The amount of dollars expended so far on the second floor could be shifted into your lease negotiations for the two story building with the new purchaser. The terms of the leaseback seem reasonable. Please do not let the confusing windfall profits language confuse the intent. It would be my expectation that you would pay the $7.25 a square foot leaseback for a two year period.

It is interesting to note how close the two proposals parallel each other, both on price and terms. The Boom proposal does not include the freestanding 5,000 square foot building or the gas station site and at $2,600,000, it would be the highest total gross purchase price we have generated yet.

We had meetings with the Smith group this morning and are quite pleased with their response. We were advised that we will have a definitive "go, no go" decision by 5:00 tomorrow afternoon. It looks very good for the Smith group to acquire the property; however, we have not seen any formal, firm proposals to date. We have had numerous meetings and feel that they are a qualified user/investor prospect. If Mr. Smith makes a positive decision tomorrow afternoon, we should be under contract by the end of the week.

At our expense, we hired the architectural firm of Prindle, Patrick and Associates, Inc. As you know, we have had three different architects look at the property in an effort to create the highest possible space utilization plan. We believe we have now successfully established division parameters which will be acceptable to potential purchasers. After several redrafts of their proposals, we have come up with a plan which maximizes aesthetic value of the atrium while also maximizing the rentable space. I have enclosed calculations for your inspection and your future reference. We have also enclosed a copy of the space planning information for your inspection.

It is our recommendation that we not respond to the letters of intent we currently have until the Smith group makes their final decision. The Smith group is quite capable of acquiring the property on more favorable terms to the Federal. If you are in agreement, we will wait until Wednesday or Thursday to continue serious discussions of the proposals before you. We think it is important that you have all the information and proposals that we are currently generating in order to better analyze the Smith proposal when it is made. Keep your fingers crossed.

Sincerely,

Broker, CCIM

The Final Contact

With all the various marketing programs at work, it is always interesting to reflect on how the actual buyer was identified and contacted and which programs were the most successful. In reviewing this case study and this marketing effort, it is clear that all of the steps leading up to the actual offer played important roles in both informing us as brokers as well as our seller. It was completely necessary to go through the process of several different offers, contracts and in-depth analysis of the property if we were to consummate this transaction. Merely submitting a contract one week into the transaction without having the vast detailed information in order to best present our proposals would have been impossible.

How the Contact Was Made

Joel Parker was contacted by the ultimate buyer after the buyer saw a company sign on an industrial property several miles north of the downtown market. One of our other associates had made contact with the prospect and shown him several properties, but failed to see the potential match of the Federal's building with this prospect. Because of Joel's keen involvement in the listing, he saw the potential and set up the first showing. The person in the prospective buyer's firm who generated the initial contact was the comptroller of that firm. The comptroller was a member of our Rotary Club and personal friends with the author and the co-listing agent, Joel Parker. The comptroller was also known to most members of our firm. The ultimate buyer was located within a ten-mile radius of the property.

After numerous showings, the first contract proposal was made with the following salient terms and conditions:

- Purchase Price: $2,600,000
- Escrow Deposit: $ 100,000 $10,000 cash deposit; $90,000 cash within five days of acceptance of contract.

- Cash at Closing: $ 420,000
- Purchase Money Mortgage: $2,080,000 14 percent interest; said mortgage providing for releases of Parcels 1, 2, 5 upon payment of specific sums.

- Contract to close September 1, 1982.
- Buyer to take assignment of landlease. Pioneer Federal to pay any increases over the $21,000 per annum.

- Long-term Leaseback—Pioneer Federal to lease back Floors 1 and 2 and drive-in facilities on long-term basis. Lease to be for a term of 20 years, commencement of term to be date of closing. Common use of parking, lobby, elevators and common area.
- Base rent: $250,000 per annum plus sales tax, payable in equal monthly installments. Base rent shall increase eight percent per annum during years two through ten. Base rent shall increase annually by percentage increase in Consumer Price Index during years 11–20; however, minimum increase shall be six percent and maximum increase shall be ten percent.

As is our policy, we prepared a written synopsis of the transaction and the contract as well as formal recommendations to the seller. The following are our recommendations on the first contract offer. We were pleased that the ultimate purchase price was close to our recommended listing price as well as our various in-depth presentations on value. It was also extremely close to the MAI appraised value. We had found what we felt to be the ultimate target, a user for the entire building, who was financially capable of acquiring the property. The recommendation letter to the Federal, while rather extensive, is necessary when dealing with major corporations so that there is not a communication breakdown between the broker and various decision makers.

Recommendations on Sterile Design Offer

July 1, 1982

Harlan Merhige, President
Pioneer Service Corporation
5770 Roosevelt Blvd.
Clearwater, Florida 33520

RE: Pioneer Federal's Cleveland Street Properties

Dear Harlan:

Enclosed please find a Contract to acquire your Cleveland Street property. The purchaser, Craig Turtzo, Trustee, is attorney for Sterile Design Incorporated. Sterile Design is a user who will use at least 12,000 square feet of the building initially. The other principles and beneficiaries of the trust, we are advised, are directly connected with Sterile Design. At least two of the individuals can demonstrate very good financial strength.

Purchase Price
The purchase price is at $2,600,000. It is consistent with the MAI appraisal of $2,615,000, roughly, $55.00 a square foot. Our recommendations in the past have indicated we felt the building would be sold at $2,600,000, plus or minus, based on the Federal financing the property. Therefore, the gross sales price would seem acceptable.

Closing Date
The purchaser would like to close the property on or before September 1, 1982. Specifically, they have indicated they would like to close on August 31, 1982, as an outside date, in order to pick up one more month of depreciation. Further, we believe

they will close in late July or early August if this is acceptable to the Federal. However, we would recommend that we leave the outside closing date of September 1, 1982.

Earnest Money Deposit—Paragraph 7
Paragraph 7 should be clarified in that the total earnest money deposit shall be liquidated damages in the event of default of the Buyer. Paragraph 7 now reads "the deposit, this day" which could indicate the $10,000 is all that is at jeopardy as liquidated damages. We would not want to take the property off the market at this time since there are four letters of intent before you and the contract specifies just $10,000 in jeopardy. The entire $100,000 should be liquidated damages in the event of default.

Date for the Agreement to Be Executed by All Parties—Paragraph 17
The agreement calls for an acceptance by July 2, 1982. Obviously, we will not have it accepted until after July 4th and we need to modify the acceptance date.

Purchase Money Mortgage
The purchase money mortgage of $2,080,000 is at 14 percent interest. At 20 year amortization, the constant is 14.2 percent. The four letters of intent you have before you now indicate interest rates to be negotiated up to a high of 15 percent constant. Frankly, the 14 percent seems extremely reasonable considering the feedback we have been receiving from the market and the actual offers we have in hand at this time. Our computer projections in the past have used 12 percent and 13 percent which results in substantial negative cash flows even when 100 percent leased.

The purchase money mortgage provides for a $125,000 release in Parcel 1 which is the freestanding brick building to the east, $75,000 for the gas station and $50,000 for the out parcel parking lot which is located behind Cleveland Plaza. We spent a considerable amount of time discussing the releases and their effect on the overall transaction. We have buyers for Parcel 1 at $200,000 and a potential buyer for Parcel 5 (with Bob Tom) at a price we believe to be $80,000. It is our recommendation that when the release amounts are granted as desired by the Buyer, that all proceeds, after release amount and direct cost of closing, be applied towards a reduction in the Federal's security deposit called for under the lease. For example, if we were to sell the freestanding brick appraisal office for $200,000, the entire proceeds less closing costs would apply first against the release amount, then the security deposit called for under the lease. It would also be our recommendation that if the gas station is sold, that the remote parking lot not be sold and be available for parking and vice-versa, if the remote parking lot is sold, the gas station be provided for additional parking to the main structure.

Landlease—Paragraph 24
The request for the seller to pay the increase in the landlease payments is consistent with our representations. However, we believe that the buyer was intending to cover all increases including the renegotiation every ten years. It is an area which should be faced or will be faced during the final lease documentation. As we have stated on numerous occasions, a sales price between $48.00 a square foot and $55.00 a square foot is reasonable depending on the final terms. At that price, one would expect that the property would be acquired in fee simple. In fact, we are not able to deliver the property in fee, but subject to a landlease. The landlease has consistently been a barrier in our negotiations. If the Federal is capable of moving the landlease or substituting the landlease for mortgages, then the income stream associated with the landlease would accrue to the benefit of the Federal. Specifically, if you were to agree to these terms—of paying all increases over the $21,000 per annum from the new buyer—you could, in fact, avoid any increases under the landlease by negotiating a

final resolution with lessor over an exchange of mortgages for the landlease interest. We therefore feel that Paragraph 24 should be accepted based on our discussions relative to selling of the landlease.

Leaseback Contingencies
The sale is contingent upon a final execution of the Federal/Buyer lease at closing consistent with the terms contained in Exhibit B. We believe you will not have a great deal of difficulty finalizing the lease with the buyer once the lease increases provided in the landlease are handled by the Federal.

Purchase Price Allocation
Please note that there has been an allocation between the land and the buildings. This should not cause any adverse tax effect to the Federal. However, we would strongly recommend you consult with your C.P.A. relative to an allocation in the event you have taken accelerated depreciation in previous years.

Improvements in Working Condition—Paragraph 28
We believe that the improvements are in working condition; however, your plant personnel should be advised of that contingency.

Personalty
There is no reference to personalty or inventory contained in this offer. We would suggest there are several areas which could be of potential conflict that should be addressed at this time. The file cabinets which are built in on Floor 5 should be included with the modular desk units and should, in good faith, be personalty conveyed with the sale. There are vault doors on Floor 3 that are relatively old and permanent. We would suggest, also, unless there is a need for those doors, that they be included in the sale as a gesture of good faith. We have not been showing the key/telephone switch system for the telephones which is now operating the building. Therefore, the buyer has no reason to believe that it is included in the sale. The final contract should clearly state that the key/telephone switch system is the personal property of the Federal and will not be conveyed in the sale. The air conditioner for the computer room is a permanent improvement and should stay with the building.

Lease Terms—Exhibit B
The area to be leased is consistent with that identified by the architects, Prindle, Patrick & Associates, who recently have been involved in the architectural work on our behalf relative to your building. The term of 20 years is consistent with your original expectation of ten years and two, five year renewal options. Please note that there is no reference to the renewal option and you may want to go with a ten year or 15 year lease with two, five year renewal options. However, if the 20 year term is acceptable, it would be a favorable negotiating position not to try to alter that concept.

Minimum Rent
Minimum rent is $250,000 per annum. Rather than being allocated on a per square foot basis to individual floors and having disputes over rentable versus gross, they have indicated the rent they need to obtain for the space being leased back by the Federal. We do not believe that the rent is inconsistent with the marketplace for the quality of space the Federal is acquiring. The first floor at 7,918 square feet of rentable gross space at $14.00 a square foot is $110,852. The second floor at 8,373 square feet at $13.00 a square foot is $109,148. The drive-in facilities at $30,000 adds up to a total of $250,000. This rental is certainly much more favorable than any of the sales requiring the Federal to either lease back the entire building or various floors. It is consistent with what prime space, such as you are leasing, would be worth in the marketplace. The base rent is subject to an eight percent per annum increase during the first ten years of the lease. Thereafter, the minimum rent shall increase at a mini-

mum of six percent not to exceed ten percent (based on CPI adjustment). We have been advised that the rent increases are in order to meet their cash flow needs associated with this building. They needed this amount of rent increase guarantee. Given the marketplace today, which might dictate a slightly lower rent base but a complete pass through of all operating expenses including power, maintenance and taxes, we suggest that the eight percent is probably consistent with reality. If you were leasing in the First Bank building, they are now quoting $13.00 a square foot plus and they pass through all expenses in totality on a pro rata basis. Therefore, when one considers that the Lessor is paying the power bill, maintenance expenses and base year taxes out of his rental income, the eight percent annual increase seems very reasonable. The only increase which would be borne by the Federal is based on a pro rata share of tax increases. Note that we believe the taxes will be lowered on the building in 1982 because the assessment is $3,300,000 and we will be selling it at $2,600,000. All in all, the eight percent increases and the operating expense conditions seem reasonable.

Use of Office Space—Paragraph 4
The use is consistent with the language we used in the previous contract.

Lessor Services—Paragraph 5
This language is consistent with our previous contract.

Service and Utilities—Paragraph 6
This language is consistent with our previous contract.

Signs and Alterations—Paragraph 8
This language is consistent with our previous contract.

Parking Areas—Paragraph 9
This language is consistent with our previous contract. You will note, again, that as per Mr. Nodine's request, the parking contiguous to the building will be used by the owners' and tenants' invitees and not by employees other than two parking spaces for the owners of the buildings.

Maintenance and Repairs—Paragraph 10
This language is consistent with our previous contract.

Lessee's Maintenance—Paragraph 11
In this case, the Lessee is required to maintain the property at the Lessee's expense and accepts the premises in "as is" condition. This clause seems reasonable.

Lessee's Insurance—Paragraph 12
This language is consistent with most leases and should not pose a problem.

Prepaid Rents—Paragraph 13
The intent of the prepaid rents clause was not prepaid rents, but functionally a security deposit. The C.P.A. who dropped off the contract indicated to us they had intended them to be security deposits and none of their people had picked up the difference between prepaid rents and security deposits. Prepaid rents have an adverse effect on the Lessor and this language will have to reflect a security deposit. The monies placed in the security deposit will be utilized to cover operations, negative cash flow and construction and renovations within the building. In order to protect the Federal's interest in the security deposit, the Lessor has agreed to provide a letter of credit in the amount of the security deposit. These monies will be used to meet the negative cash flow which we projected to be well in excess of $125,000 from operations in year one and upwards to $150,000 for construction improvements totalling somewhere in the

neighborhood of $250,000 to $300,000 negative cash flow year one. This is on top of the substantial down payment which they are bringing to closing.

Conclusions
Pioneer Federal has now received four letters of intent and two formal contracts. This is the second contract and the first legitimate user contract which we have been able to procure. Our company has spent hundreds of hours and many thousands of dollars marketing the property. We believe these users to be bona fide, qualified purchasers. We recommend this contract for some or all of the previous comments. The leasing market has deteriorated and we believe the absorption rate is down from nine months ago when we began the project. As you know, Joe Smith is no longer interested in the property. All of the other contracts and prospects we have are investor prospects with very soft terms which should be considered work-out terms. The Federal is looking at a lease-up status which, at best, is going to be slow. Operating expenses will run the Federal $180,000 to $250,000 over the next 12 months. We believe the Federal is in a much stronger position to accept an offer under these terms and conditions then to attempt a lease-up in today's marketplace. Our architects' estimate of construction costs on Floors 3 and 4 is over $157,000. The Federal would also have to invest these dollars along with considerable marketing expense to realize a leased up building which would probably not sell much higher than our current asking price. We believe we have negotiated an excellent opportunity for the Federal and can document it with extensive computer runs and investment analysis, if necessary.

Time is of the essence. We need to respond as quickly as possible to this contract so that we do not lose the enthusiasm we currently have from Sterile Design. In this economic climate, we have seen buyers cool off very quickly with just one evening news report or one of their business contracts being cancelled. We had an opportunity to see Mr. Nodine at lunch today and he has granted us time on Tuesday to discuss this offer in person. We would appreciate your conveying a copy of our recommendations and the contract to Mr. Nodine prior to our meeting.

We propose to counter their contract with a simple addendum indicating acceptable terms. We should not change the buyer's contract format if at all possible.

Thank you for your assistance in this offer.

Sincerely,

Broker, CCIM

B/sbd

The Seller's Response

Within a rather short period of time, the seller verbally made a proposed reaction to the offer as follows:
- $2.6 million dollar purchase price
- 20 percent down or $520,000
- 30 year amortization at 15 percent with a 15 year balloon
- Leaseback terms of $200,000 base rental
- $100,000 deposit upon execution.

The Federal did agree to extend an additional $100,000 to $150,000 for construction improvements. They accepted our recommendation that no prepaid rent or deposit refund be made to the purchaser. The Federal also indicated that the future landlease increases over $21,000 would be paid by the Federal and that the base landlease of $21,000 would be paid by the purchaser. We presented our counter-proposal in writing on our letterhead in the following format.

Federal Verbal Response to Sterile Design Offer

$2,600,000 Purchase price
       20% Down
$ 520,000
$2,080,000 30 years, 15%
$26,300.44 15 year balloon

Leaseback—$200,000 base rental

$100,000 Deposit upon execution

Credit approval of principal and terms of Trust Agreement
Assign with prior written approval

Will give second mortgage for construction improvements $100,000–$150,000

No prepaid rent or deposits

Federal will pick up all future landlease increases over $21,000 (as long as Federal's lease is in force)

An Alternative to Federal Proposal

$2,600,000
$ 400,000 Master landlease with option to buy
$ 280,000 For parking lot remote, freestanding office building
$1,920,000 Improvements purchase price
       20% Down
$ 384,000 Cash at closing
$1,536,000 30 years at 15%, $19,421.85, 15 year balloon

Payments on landlease—$60,000 per annum

Monthly payment $19,421.85
Master landlease   5,000.00
Center landlease   1,750.00
                  $26,171.85

Federal leaseback $16,666.00 per month

Further Suggestions

We suggested to the buyer that certain parcels of the property would be sold off reducing the required cash at closing spread that we currently knew existed. We also suggested an alternative that all the land be leased to the purchaser until such time as they were in a position to acquire the land for $400,000. This was in an effort to reduce the overall purchase price and the spread between the payments the purchaser was willing to pay and the down payment.

During this period of time, we went through several problem-solving forms in an effort to find alternatives. The landlease alternative which reduces the amount of the purchase price as well as the cash required on down payment and the payments initially was Problem-Solving Technique Number 83, page 85. In our discussions, it became clear that the amount of cash available for acquisition by the purchaser would, by necessity, require that the brokers defer a portion of the fee over a two year period. Further, the purchaser requested that the seller accept a short term note for a portion of the down payment, commonly referred to as a "split down payment." Problem-Solving Technique Number 25 helped solve this problem by guaranteeing the note with an irrevocable noncontingent letter of credit in a form acceptable to the seller. We were, in effect, reducing the cash required at closing while not in any way reducing the actual collateral to the purchaser. The brokers were absorbing part of the risk and the purchasers were using their banking strength to guarantee the split down payment over the next two years.

The flow of the recommendation letter that follows is self-explanatory and illustrates the complexities of the negotiations.

July 13, 1982

William E. Nodine, Chairman
Pioneer Federal Savings and Loan
5770 Roosevelt Blvd.
Clearwater, Florida 33516

RE: Pioneer Federal Cleveland Street Properties/Sterile Design Offer

Dear Mr. Nodine:

Enclosed you will find a contract offer from Craig Turzo, Trustee, for Sterile Design Beneficiaries. The recapitulation of the first offer relative to the second offer is as follows. The Pioneer's gross sale price is $54,000 greater and the net proceeds estimated from sale without adjustments for taxes is over $203,000. A considerable increase over the previous offer.

First Offer

Sales Price	$2,600,000
Brokerage Fee	182,000
Subtotal	$2,418,000
Doc Stamps ($.45/$100)	11,700
Est. Title Insurance ($3/$100)	7,800

Cash Down	$ 520,000	
Less Deposit	250,000	
Less Doc Stamps	11,700	
Less Title Insurance	7,800	
Less Brokerage Fee	182,000	
Estimated Net to Federal	$ 68,500	(No adjustment for real estate taxes)

New Offer

Sales Price	$2,600,000
Brokerage Fee	50,000
Subtotal	$2,550,000

Cash at Closing:

Cash Down	$ 272,000
Doc Stamps	11,349
Title Insurance	7,566
Brokerage Fee	50,000
Estimated Net To Federal	$ 203,085

Your request for the earnest money deposit upon execution of the Contract has been met with the full deposit within twenty-four (24) hours of execution of all parties. It is reasonable not to move a great deal of funds around until we have a meeting of the minds.

Paragraph 8. Please note that Pioneer will only be obligated for $50,000 of the brokerage fee. We have agreed to take the balance of our fee in a personal note from the Purchaser for $50,000 to be paid out over two years at $25,000 on each anniversary of the closing, plus 13 percent accrued interest. There will be no collateral for our note other than the personal endorsements of the Purchaser.

Paragraph 24 addresses the $130,000 short-term note which is actually part of a split down payment that will be guaranteed by an irrevocable noncontingent letter of credit in a form acceptable to you. This letter of credit will provide that, in the event of a default, you can demand for immediate disbursement of the $65,000 plus accrued interest owed on each of the first two anniversaries of the sale.

The purchase money mortgage called for under the Contract recites interest rates for the first two years at 13 percent, second two years at 14 percent and then 15 percent thereafter. The capital the Pioneer currently has invested in the building which is free and clear is very similar and resembles the status of capital you have invested in old mortgages which cannot be called. If $2,080,000 was invested at 1950's, 1960's and 1970's rates, you would jump at the opportunity to realize a blended or new rate of 13 percent overall on capital which is buried in nonproducing assets. It seems reasonable to allow a 13 percent rate on this capital which, on August 31st, the closing date, can immediately turn a higher and much more profitable return to the Federal. Originally, we had quoted 14 percent based on staff representations of management's expectations.

The additional logic for accepting the escalating interest rate would be to consider cash flows for the next 90 days or an assumed period of time necessary to consummate another acceptable contract. With an annual operating expense of approximately $200,000, one quarter is going to cost the Federal $50,000 in direct cash flow.

Interest loss associated with the first 90 days of the 13 percent interest mortgage will be $67,584. Income associated with the cash proceeds from sale invested at 15 percent is $2,634 for one quarter. The total opportunity cost of this decision is $120,218 over the next quarter. The rent to the Lessor at the higher rent associated with the additional space to be used by the Federal is $60,000. The net loss associated with rejecting the proposed plan is $53,968 if it takes an additional quarter to negotiate a contract. Additional time to negotiate reduces the spread between this opportunity and future unknown opportunities. We recommend terms similar to those contained in the Contract with adjustments made for the correct payments based on the prescribed interest rates offered in the Contract. There is obviously an error in the calculation on the payments.

The releases called for in the mortgage under Parcel 1 refer to the freestanding brick appraisal building. Parcel 2 refers to the gas station and Parcel 5 refers to the out parcel parking lot. Please note that we have obtained a Contract from Bob Tom for $64,000 cash, closing on the 31st day of August. Releases are anywhere from 50 percent to 60 percent of value of the real property.

Paragraph 26 refers to the landlease. It was my understanding that they had agreed to the $21,000 a year fixed landlease. I was advised that one of their consultants had felt that was an unacceptable rate and they choose to come back with $9,600 per annum with you picking up any increases. There may be some middle of the road; you start out with $15,000 as the minimum base and pick up all increases over $15,000. They are also interested in trying to work out a purchase price with landlease lessor.

The sale is contingent upon the seller and the buyer consummating a formal lease under the terms and conditions contained in Exhibit B. Exhibit B parallels the original offer with a $40,000 annual concession made on the base rental. This is consistent with your instructions. Please note that the Lessor is providing you with almost all your services except janitorial. This is within the base rent.

The final paragraph refers to the intent to lease at $2,500 per month the second floor of the wing. If it was necessary for you to use more than the second floor for some limited period of time, I am sure a satisfactory rental can be consummated.

We recommend that you accept the contract terms subject to final legal and C.P.A. approval. Our company now has slightly over six months in the project. We have shown the property to numerous qualified potential buyers. We are familiar with its positive features and also its negative features. We have resolved numerous negatives for potential buyers and are now confident it is being presented in its most advantageous light. The decision before the Federal is an opportunity cost decision. Does this opportunity cost more than an alternative opportunity? The obvious decision to hold the property is not an inexpensive decision in light of the capital you have invested. You have $2,600,000 invested in this project and obviously, the benefit you are receiving is a value of $210,000. Or, alternatively, you have invested $2,600,000 for an 8.07 percent return. In other words, the revenue you would receive for renting the building to the Federal at this time as an outside investor with an all cash investment of $2,600,000, is $210,000 or eight percent. The obvious alternative is to look for a more advantageous opportunity. How long will it take to procure a user/buyer with alternative terms more advantageous? Many of the interest rates we have seen have been lower and the purchase price and down payments have been soft. I would also expect the Federal to be asked to have pass throughs of a pro rata share of all operating expenses if negotiations were being handled by professional real estate people. It is my professional opinion that you have an excellent offer before you that should not be taken lightly. It is not often that we will take a $50,000 personal note payable over two years for a fee. We are cognizant of the nature of the market and the amount of time we have spent trying to locate a qualified buyer. With the soft lease market, we highly recommend this proposal with certain adjustments.

Sincerely,

Broker, CCIM

B/sbd

The end result of the negotiations is the following contract.

Contract Summary and Checklist

1. *Buyer:* Craig Turtzo, Trustee, for an investment group.

   Buyer's attorney: Craig Turtzo, 2323 Belleair Road, Clearwater, Florida, 33516, (536-0458).

2. *Seller:* Pioneer Federal Savings and Loan Association

   Seller's attorney: Emil Pratesi, 1253 Park Street, Clearwater, Florida, 33516, (443-3281).

3. *Date contract executed:* 7/20/82

4. *Closing date:* On or before 8/31/82

5. *Purchase price:* $2,522,000 (Craig Turtzo Escrow Account)

Cash Deposit	$ 10,000	(Deposited 7/21/82)
Additional Deposit	90,000	
Cash at Closing	162,000	
Short-term Note	130,000	
Purchase Money Mtg.	2,080,000	
Broker's Commission	50,000	(Additional $50,000 due over 2 yrs)
Total	$2,522,000	

6. *Title insurance commitment:* (Seller) — Provided at the expense of the Seller on or before ten days prior to closing. (Delivered by Real Estate, Inc., to Buyer 7/20/82)

7. *Commission payable by buyer:* (Buyer) — $50,000 note payable to Real Estate, Inc., guaranteed by all Buyers and Sterile Design Corporation. (To be prepared by Craig Turtzo and approved by Real Estate, Inc.)

8. *Extermination inspection:* (Buyer) — Buyer, at Buyer's expense, may have property inspected no later than ten days prior to closing.

9. *Survey:* (Buyer) — Buyer, at Buyer's expense, may survey the property prior to closing.

10. *Lien waiver:* (Seller) — Seller shall furnish Buyer with a lien waiver as to construction.

11. *Maintenance contract:* (Seller)	Seller shall provide Buyer with a copy of all maintenance contracts.
12. *Utility deposit:* (Buyer)	Buyer should make arrangements prior to closing to transfer all utility accounts into the Buyer's name.
13. *Short-term note:* (Buyer)	The Buyer, at Buyer's expense, shall prepare the $130,000 short-term note for Seller's approval.
14. *Purchase money mortgage:* (Seller)	Seller, at Seller's expense, shall prepare the $2,080,000 mortgage and note for the Buyer's review.
15. *Approval of land trust:* (Buyer)	Buyer shall furnish to Seller all documents and evidence of the Land Trust.
16. *Letter of credit:* (Buyer)	Buyer shall provide the Seller with the form of the Letter of Credit for Buyer's approval.
17. *Personal endorsement:* (Buyer)	The purchase money note and mortgage shall be personally endorsed by the principals.
18. *Assignment of landlease:* (Seller)	Seller, at Seller's expense, shall provide to Buyer an assignment of landlease.
19. *Parking spaces:* (Buyer)	Buyer, at Buyer's expense, shall provide to Seller a parking agreement for the sole use of four specific parking spaces.
20. *Lease:* (Buyer)	Buyer, at Buyer's expense, shall submit to Seller a proposed lease, for the property to be leased back, within 14 days from date of Contract.
21. *Purchase price allocation:* (Buyer)	Buyer, at Buyer's expense, shall prepare for Seller's approval an agreement allocating the purchase price as per the Contract.
22. *Note:*	All personalty shall be removed from unoccupied floors by Seller prior to closing. Seller's personalty not to be conveyed or moved shall include, but not be limited, to telephone switch equipment and individual telephones. Personalty includes the built-in lateral files on the fifth floor.

The Close

Ultimately the property closed in a timely fashion within one percent of the MAI appraised value and three percent of the price we recommended in our mid-listing report. The lessons to be observed in this marketing process are the consistent, well-scheduled marketing programs. Probably the most important single variable in working with a major corporation is the information process. Hence, the considerable amount of detail reflected in this case study was also reflected in our various presentations to the Board of Directors through its corporate officers. Less than this type of approach when dealing with major corporations has unsatisfactory results.

Observing the all important process of team coordination with architects, attorneys, engineers and the seller is clearly demonstrated in this marketing effort. Even though the ultimate buyer did not result from one of the planned marketing programs, it should be clear that all of those steps and programs leading up to the actual contract assisted in, if not facilitated, the ultimate sale. Remember that the definition of marketing is the sum total of all activities performed by the company necessary to consummate the sale and satisfy the client.

Appendix to Chapter 7:
Appraisal of the Headquarters Property of Clearwater Federal Savings and Loan*

This appraisal was prepared at the request of the savings and loan. The appraiser was Warren Hunnicutt, Jr., CRE, MAI, and the following digest of the appraisal is used with his permission.

The entire table of contents is included so the reader can see the various elements that make up a complete, thorough appraisal. However, because this is a specific appraisal about a particular property and therefore includes the extensive detail necessary to the client, it has been condensed from the original 108 pages. There is a note in the text indicating wherever an item has been deleted. The table of contents indicates both sets of page numbers. The first set of numbers is the original, which will enable the reader to see the number of pages devoted to various topics; the numbers in parentheses refer to the page numbers in this book. Hopefully, this will make it easier for the reader to absorb the necessary information and realize the valuable part played in the marketing process by an excellent appraisal.

---

*Pioneer Federal Savings and Loan, Clearwater, Florida

Table of Contents

January 15, 1981

Mr. Parker J. Stafford
Senior Vice-President
Clearwater Federal Savings
 & Loan Association
Post Office Box 4608
Clearwater, Florida 33518

Dear Mr. Stafford:

As requested by you and Mr. Harold Robert Welch, Vice-President, Clearwater Federal, we have appraised the headquarters property of Clearwater Federal, commonly known as Cleveland Plaza in Clearwater, Pinellas County, Florida.

A complete investigation and thorough analysis were conducted to estimate market value of those property interests of the aggregate parcel and improvements thereon for the specific purpose of internal use by Clearwater Federal. As briefly outlined in our introduction and more thoroughly discussed in the appraisal, portions of the aggregate parcel are under long-term lease in which Clearwater Federal has other than a total fee interest. In a concluding section, further investment analyses were made as a closer examination of our estimates of the property and market value.

The report, containing a total of 108 pages, including numerous pertinent exhibits, presents our reasoning and analysis of salient information on which estimates of value were predicated. All data collected in the analysis, not appearing in the report, have been retained in our files and are available for inspection upon request.

The opportunity to conduct this assignment is appreciated.

Very truly yours,

Warren Hunnicutt, Jr., CRE, MAI

David A. Brett, Vice-President

WHjr/DAB:mas

Certificate of Valuation

This is to certify that, upon request for valuation services from Mr. Parker J. Stafford, Senior Vice-President, Clearwater Federal Savings & Loan Association, Cleveland Plaza, Clearwater, Florida 33518, we have personally inspected, collected and analyzed various data, and appraised the fee simple and other interest held by Clearwater Federal in their Cleveland Plaza headquarters location in Clearwater, Florida.

In our estimate, as of January 9, 1981, the properties and interest appraised had market values of:

Main Building	$2,200,000
(Two Million Two Hundred Thousand Dollars)	
Administrative/Appraisal Buildings	$210,000
(Two Hundred Ten Thousand Dollars)	

Parking Lot Facility	$95,000
(Ninety-five Thousand Dollars)	
Leasehold Value	$110,000
(One Hundred Ten Thousand Dollars)	
Total Market Value Estimate	$2,615,000
(TWO MILLION SIX HUNDRED FIFTEEN THOUSAND DOLLARS)	

We have no personal interest in these properties, either present or contemplated, and employment in and compensation for making the appraisal are in no manner contingent upon the values reported.

Warren Hunnicutt, Jr., CRE, MAI

David A. Brett, Vice-President
Appraiser

(Exhibits 1 and 2, the state map and county map, have been deleted.)

Purpose and Date of Appraisal

Purpose of the appraisal herein is to estimate, with the highest degree of accuracy possible, market value of the undivided fee simple interest of those properties held in fee by Clearwater Federal Savings & Loan Association and market value of those leased interests created by lease agreements (described more fully in the text of this report) inuring to Clearwater Federal. Date of our reported value is January 9, 1981.

Market value is defined as, "The highest price in terms of money which a property could bring in a competitive and open market, under all conditions requisite to a fair sale; the buyer and seller, each acting prudently, knowledgeably, and assuming the price is not affected by undue stimulus."[1]

We have included accepted definitions of two additional terms referred to in our report. Clarity of the definition of "investment value" and "value in use" should be understood by the client, although these values are not the specific or intended purpose of our analysis.

Investment value is defined as, "Value to a particular investor based on individual investment requirements, as distinguished from the concept of market value, which is impersonal and detached."[2]

Value in use is defined as, "The value of an economic good to its owner-user which is based on the productivity (privacies in income, utility, or amenity form) of the economic good to a specific individual; subjective value may not necessarily represent market value."[3]

(An aerial photograph has been deleted)

Introduction and Discussion of Appraisal Problems

This appraisal has been completed for our client's use with the specific application of exposing the property and/or negotiating sale of its corporate headquarters in the market.

Clearwater Federal's Cleveland Plaza offices are on the eastern periphery of the downtown business core area in Clearwater. The site is an assembled city block

---

1. Byrl N. Boyce, *Real Estate Appraisal Terminology*, (Cambridge, Massachusetts: Ballinger Publishing Co., 1975), p. 137.
2. Ibid., p. 119.
3. Ibid., p. 216.

consisting of the southeast quadrant formed by the intersection of Lincoln Avenue and Cleveland Street and detached parking. Existing improvements include a five-story office complex with a two-story wing extending south along Lincoln Avenue. Rehabilitated strip office space is on the northeast corner of the block and is used for ancillary services by the Association. A service station structure is sandwiched between the office spaces along the southern right-of-way of Cleveland. A remote drive-in facility has been constructed in the southeast corner. Public rights-of-way front all sides of the assembled block. Three unassembled parcels constitute the balance of Clearwater Federal's property interest for the Cleveland Plaza location.

Historical development of the Cleveland Plaza offices has spanned from 1956 to present. Under lease agreement, the original two-story facility at the southwest corner of the block was constructed for the association in 1956. In the early 1960s Clearwater Federal constructed the first two floors of the adjoining main building on acquired portions of the block. In 1973, work began on an addition of three floors to the main structure. Numerous additional lease amendments from the commencement date during this same period added parking facilities south of the assembled block. Additional remote parking was acquired in 1973 and the improved office space currently occupied by administrative and appraisal services in 1974, completing the assemblage of the Cleveland Plaza block.

Legal or ownership interest held by Clearwater Federal in the properties are held in fee and as a leasehold. Those areas are indicated on Exhibit 7. Leased portions provide both improved office space and parking facilities to the association. Three additional lots encumbered by the same lease are not currently being utilized by the Federal. These have been specifically deleted from our valuation by direction.

Appraisal Problems

In our analysis one of the major concerns was treatment or applicability of an assembled parcel constituting a platted block versus individual sites constituting the same block. Market reactions frequently reflect value increments by an assemblage function. However, this added value would be limited to assembled parcels with identical or consistent use relationships. We are of the opinion that an implicit assemblage value is not applicable to the appraised property due to the distinctive physical and economic division on the entire property. Our analysis is based on the contention that collective values of freestanding units or properties within the assemblage are most reflective of market value.

Appraisal Methodology

A brief statement regarding applicable appraisal techniques is noted in this introduction, followed by a more detailed discussion in each respective section. An outline of basic concepts will hopefully aid the reader and the continuity of the report. Any apparent redundancy was intentional to restate or emphasize important elements.

All of the typical appraisal approaches to value were considered in this assignment. The cost approach, where a summation of land and depreciated improvement values are made, was initially considered inapplicable. In addition to the subjective and often inaccurate estimates of various depreciation forms, a further limitation of this approach is the inability to value divisional interest of the fee. A market approach is the most meaningful method when similar market data are available and properly weighted for physical and economic characteristics. A number of urban, west coast office sales were analyzed in our study. Most sales were office buildings acquired for investment, typically oriented to multi-tenancy office suites. Acquisition by owner-occupants or those intended for larger space leasing were limited; this type would have been more consistent with physical and economic features of Clearwater Federal's property.

Valuation by income analysis is also responsive, given actual market activities.

When available, the income analysis of office sales can isolate buyer's/seller's investment criteria and motivations by a relationship of price to income or a capitalization rate. Office properties that have not sold provide additional sources of market information by analyzing actual operating statements, proposed operating budgets, pro forma statements, and rental schedules of current available space. Two principal drawbacks with an income approach for the appraised property is the current owneroccupancy or lack of a market accepted rental rate and the requirement to forecast or estimate absorption if portions or all space occupied by the Association are vacated at sale. We attempted to quantify supply of competitive space and demand for additional space.

To estimate the value of Clearwater Federal's interest in the leased premises, separate valuations were made of the fee interest, as if unencumbered, and the leased fee. Any marginal or residual value remaining was attributed to the leasehold. If this marketable value exists, it should be included as an addition to market value of other fee interests of our client.

Other interests are created by the lease, which may not directly relate to a market value concept. Duration of remaining term and ultimate property control exercised by the tenant may be indirect values not appropriately accounted for in a strict market concept. Value stability of the tenants' interest also requires forecasting; lease payments are based in part on operation qualities of the savings and loan in time deposit dollars, which may not be related to actual market rents.

Additionally, lease provisions call for a reevaluation at ten year increments, which could easily change the proration of value of the fee simple interest between a tenant and lessor.

Investment Considerations and Analysis

Following our conclusions of market values of the various interests, we have attempted to test these conclusions in a number of investment scenarios. The principal technique used was a mortgage-equity analysis. The effects of leveraging through mortgage financing and tax consequences created by the investment ownership were also analyzed in a pre- and after-tax cash flow analysis. Similar forecasts were made for subsequent years during an ownership period. Relationship of market to possible investment values and any further recommendations or considerations for prospective negotiations were made in concluding remarks.

(The legal description of the property has been deleted.)

The Florida Market

Florida is part of the "sun belt." This region, and Florida in particular, has grown and is expected to continue growing at a faster rate than national averages. This is due primarily to the favorable climate characteristics but also attributed to the sudden migration of industry to the southeastern areas where nonunionized labor is more prevalent. This south Atlantic region has shown almost a ten percent increase in population over the five year interval from 1970 and 1975 and is expected to grow at a similar rate over the next ten to 15 years. This would result in a net increase for the entire region of slightly more than six million people over that same period.[4]

(This discussion has been condensed.)

---

4. Data Sources: *Statistical Abstract of the United States,* 1976, U.S. Department of Commerce, Bureau of Census; *Florida Outlook,* a periodical published by the Business and Economic Research Department, University of Florida; *1977 Statistical Data Publication of Tampa and Hillsborough County,* published by the Committee of 100, Greater Tampa Chamber of Commerce; and the *Kiplinger Washington Letter,* entitled "The 80's a Fresh Look," dated July 7, 1978.

Regional Market

The Florida Market has been divided into five major areas: Jacksonville, Miami, Orlando, Pensacola and Tampa. The Tampa marketing area consists of 17 counties (of Florida's total 68 counties), located approximately half way down the west coast of Florida and extending from Lee County on the south, to Marion County on the north, and from Polk County on the east to Florida's West Coast. Pinellas County is centrally located in this entire marketing region.

A further geographical breakdown and one more representative of Pinellas' central location is known as the Tampa-St. Petersburg Metro Area encompassing Pinellas, Pasco and Hillsborough counties (this area coincides with the Standard Metropolitan Statistical Area or SMSA). This metro area ranks with Atlanta and Miami in population and households and ranks either second or third with other metro areas in the 12 southeastern states in the more significant marketing measurements. Table A briefly outlines these market segments.

Table A

Segment	1978	1970	% Change	Southeast Ranking	U.S. Ranking
			TAMPA-ST. PETERSBURG METRO AREA		
Population	1,439,900	1,088,600	+ 32	3	24
Households	630,100	413,000	+ 46	2	21
Effective Buying Income ($000)	8,908,082	3,374,159	+164	3	29
Bank Deposits ($000)	5,504,365	2,445,142	+125	—	—
S & L Deposits ($000)	5,997,408	1,488,279	+303	—	—
Property Valuation ($000)	21,043,900	6,179,800	+241	—	—
Retail Sales ($000)	6,221,521	2,286,359	+172	3	24
Food Sales ($000)	1,280,457	499,713	+156	2	23
Furniture, Home Furnishings, Appliances ($000)	392,750	99,574	+294	3	17
Building Materials ($000)	345,536	84,387	+309	2	19
Eating & Drinking ($000)	633,796	199,401	+218	3	21

In population, the Tampa-St. Petersburg metro has outpaced other Florida metropolitan areas in actual numbers of population growth including Ft. Lauderdale, Miami, Orlando, West Palm Beach areas. The metro area is the second largest in the state after Miami and comprises 16 percent of the state's total population. Distribution of the

Table B

EMPLOYMENT DISTRIBUTION	
Retail Trade	22%
Services	21
Government	16
Manufacturing	14
Contract Construction	7
Finance, Ins., Real Estate	7
Trade, Communication, Utility	6
Wholesale Trade	6
Agriculture	2
*Due to rounding	101%*

employable population in the metro area is broken out in categories and related percentages in Table B.

(The discussion of regional markets has been condensed. The discussion of the county and its economic base has been deleted. Exhibits 3 and 4, the business district map and the census tract map, have been deleted. Also, Tables C and D have been deleted.)

Clearwater Central Business District and Peripheries

A general locational description of the appraised property would be the eastern peripheral of downtown Clearwater's Central Business District in mid-Pinellas County. The core Central Business District (CBD) is formally described by the City as that area between Drew Street on the north and Chestnut Street on the south, between Myrtle Avenue on the east and Clearwater Harbor on the west. Cleveland Street, or State Road 60, traverses east and west through the center of the core area, westerly to Clearwater Beach and easterly to its merging with Gulf-to-Bay. Clearwater Federal Savings & Loan is approximately eight platted blocks east of the eastern periphery of the core area or Myrtle Avenue.

Clearwater, over the past ten years, has been one of Pinellas County's fastest growing areas. This has particularly had an impact on the downtown business district and the area further west along the beaches. One of the principal economic factors affecting growth has been location of both City and County Government in the core area of downtown Clearwater. (Another major growth factor was the residential population increase in condominium development. A number of high-rise condominium projects were completed between the east side of the Intracoastal Waterway and the core area or Governmental complex along Fort Harrison.) The most pertinent growth factor in downtown Clearwater was the development or expansion of professional office space. In 1973 the "1100" Building was completed, a 13-story, 135,000 gross square foot office building, five blocks nearer downtown. In late 1976 the Bank of Clearwater completed its new 11-story home office, with available space. This added another 150,000+ square feet of gross office area to downtown supply.

The area immediately surrounding Clearwater Federal is a composite of shopping center and strip commercial along principal frontages, minor strip office and fast food facilities, and a mix of single and multi-family residential properties. Older and dated commercial is the largest percentage of Cleveland frontage. Drew Street, one-quarter mile north of Cleveland, and Court Street, a similar distance south, are similar although less densely developed commercial frontages. Between these east-west arteries are a blend of older single-family and low density apartment complexes.

Other developments in the area include a major General Telephone switching center, occupying an entire block in the northeast quadrant of Cleveland and Betty Lane. The City has acquired and occupies an annex facility, formerly a freestanding department store, on the southwest corner of Cleveland and Missouri.

Historical development of Clearwater was centered principally in the core area. Rail facilities created a major industrial center between Fort Harrison and Myrtle, in the southerly portion. Business and commerce developed in the center. Later in the 1940s and 1950s, more remote and freestanding commercial development spread easterly along Cleveland.

From a general inspection of the neighborhood and commercial properties, development probably peaked in the mid-1960s. Some sites were noted where improvements are serving only on an interim basis, and others are near the end of a useful life. A number of alternative uses or recycling of original structures were noted. From indicated redevelopment potentials and the close proximity to a viable downtown core, we feel the area may be emerging in a new life cycle. Success of redevelopment would be entirely dependent upon both public and private response. Property values in general appear to be consistent with other downtown locations in Pinellas County. Property values should increase at or slightly above expected inflationary rates currently experienced by the overall real estate market. This trend should have a positive effect on Cleveland Plaza.

(The transportation section has been deleted.)

Population

Present and projected population studies were conducted by the Pinellas County Planning Department to assist the County's administration. This demographic analysis is used as a planning tool for provision of future public service demands. Using census tract data (historic), the analysis extrapolates, through a forecasting technique, population estimates to year 2000. This study separates the county into various planning elements or divisions conveniently allowing a more sensitive investigation of a specific area.

Taken into consideration in their forecasting is the existing type of development, availability of undeveloped properties, adopted land use plans, and projected capital improvements or public service in support of growth.

The application of this brief analysis is simply to forecast what portion of expected growth can be anticipated for the immediate area, supporting either the existing development or potential for new development. Since the immediate area around Clearwater Federal has been a historic development, percentage increases of population or new residents cannot be compared to more remote county locations which have a higher absorbancy. We simply regard this analysis as an additional quantitative tool. Figures are estimated, based on forecasting techniques or models, and undoubtedly have inherent errors in their estimates.

(The statistics from this study have not been included due to their specialized nature and the entire section has been condensed.)

A larger planning sector encompasses most portions of northern Clearwater. Again, because of the stage of development, small increments of population were added for 1975 to 1980. Overall growth is forecasted at a modest 35 percent over the 1975 figures by year 2000.

These figures are estimates based on forecasting techniques or models as stated. 1980 census data, although collected, were unavailable for refinement of these forecasts. It is important that they are included as indications of growth and development trends and further that they are related to other similar developed areas using the same data. These same stagnant trends shown in the table for the Clearwater core area are also experienced in other city cores in Pinellas County.

The Office Building/Space Market

The general real estate market can be classified into two broad categories, residential and nonresidential. The nonresidential market can further be divided by property type. The sub-category of professional office interacts in its own market and is briefly discussed. The major office environment of Florida is along the east coast, extending from Fort Lauderdale south to Miami. Other major office areas include Jacksonville, Orlando, and, most important to our analysis, the St. Petersburg/Tampa SMSA (Standard Metropolitan Statistical Area). Larger urban core properties in major markets would be competitive with one another, regardless of geographical boundaries. Geographic location would be more important to the property type being appraised and more responsive to a local market.

Florida's west coast, extending south from Pinellas to Lee and Collier Counties, is, in our opinion, a competitive area for the office market. Two areas were emphasized in our survey of office buildings, Tampa and Pinellas County. Tampa is currently experiencing a surge of new office construction, with a strong underlying occupancy of existing space. Two favored office locations in Tampa are downtown and the West Shore area. The downtown area has 21+ existing office properties which reportedly contain 1.9 million square feet of net rentable space. The West Shore area has a reported 1.7 million square feet of net rentable area in a combination of freestanding and office complexes. Public and private activities are indicative of Tampa's favorable location for new office construction. Downtown, the new 39-story Tampa City Center is well underway with a reported 725,000 square feet; Tampa Electric is in initial phases of a 292,000 square foot, nine-story headquarters building; Paragon Plaza has proposed a 24-story office tower with approximately 250,000 square feet, joint venture with Metropolitan Life. Two other major centers proposed are the 14-story, 150,000 square foot Dean-Rowe Arch building and the 275,000 square foot Metropolitan Bank building.

In the West Shore area, latest construction includes the recently completed Kennedy Center and Paragon Building; the Austin Center Twin Towers is nearing completion. These properties add approximately 500,000 square feet to the West Shore market.

On the west side of Tampa Bay, the Pinellas County office market has been considerably slow, relative to Tampa. The most noted new construction countywide included the 1979 completion of The Plaza in downtown St. Petersburg. This core area development is 15 stories with a combined 170,000 square feet in office and retail space. The Justice Corporation has recently broken ground with the addition of the Arbor Shore Office Center to the existing Arbor Office complex. Five buildings, in low-rise construction, will add 152,000 square feet, planned for 1981 completion. In central St. Petersburg, the Wittner Companies completed the Wittner Center with over 65,000 square feet and an additional 75,000 currently under construction in Tyrone Square area. Koger Properties, in the Gateway area, have continually added more buildings to their existing office park inventory, with the most recent building completed in late 1980.

With limited new construction, the existing inventory of countywide space was reviewed in *St. Petersburg Times'* 1981 Business Office Space Spotter. Eighty-four properties were listed ranging in size of net rentable space from 8,000 to 306,000 square feet. Summarizing in outline form:

Area	Net Rentable Sq. Ft.	Available Space	Occupancy %
St. Petersburg/Pinellas Park	1,530,843	212,562	86.1%
Largo/Seminole	591,550	159,154	73.1%
Clearwater/Belleair/Dunedin	1,634,264	435,606	73.3%
Total County	3,756,657	807,322	78.5%

The above summaries include space proposed or under construction. A lower occupancy results from the inclusion of uncompleted space, although it should be considered in the competitive market. Pinellas office space is discussed more in depth in our income approach; this is supported by published and individually researched figures.

(Exhibit 5, which identifies major office areas in the county, has been deleted.)

Property Description

Public Utilities

All utilities are available to the site. Electricity is provided by Florida Power Corporation, telephone service by General Telephone Company; water and sewer are provided by the City of Clearwater, as is police and fire protection.

Zoning

The property, consisting of the assembled Block "B" and two detached parking facilities, is zoned under three different districts by the City of Clearwater.

(Exhibit 6, Zoning Map, has been deleted. For zoning map, see page 150.)

General Business District-CG
This district "permits apartment-type development, retail, and professional uses."

DUPLEX-APARTMENT RESIDENTIAL DISTRICT—RM-12: This district "permits single-family and/or duplex units and/or apartment units at a maximum density of 12 dwellings per net acre."

HIGH-DENSITY MULTI-FAMILY USE DISTRICT—RM-28: This district provides "for high density apartment development use. The maximum density permitted is 28 dwelling units per net acre."

Comments follow regarding various zoning districts and the appraised property conformance with the ordinance. Major improvements on Block "B" conform in all regards to the general business district. Two slight deviations exist. The residential property on Betty Lane which is a prohibited use (although grandfathered in). The service station is a permitted use for CG although additionally regulated by a subsequent section. The remote parking facility zoned CG is also permitted. Parking zoned multi-family (under lease) is allowed by special exception which states "non-commercial off-street parking (not operated as a separate business) or spaces of vacant lots or portions thereof for parking passenger motor vehicles."

Under the residential zoning, reference is made in our highest and best use to the nonconformity of the site with its controlling district for apartment construction.

Assessment, Tax Rate and Taxes

For 1980, the property was assessed for $2,118,295. The appropriate tax rate for properties in the City of Clearwater is 19.665 mills. (A mill is one-tenth of one cent or one dollar of tax for each thousand dollars of assessed value.) Tax bills paid in November (or the date of receipt) receive a four percent discount, decreasing one percent per month until March, when a penalty is assessed.

1980 Assessment

Parcel Number	Land	Improvements	Total
15-29-15-38574-002-0010 through 15-29-15-38574-002-0440 (Inclusive of Assembled Block "B")	$323,310	$1,717,490	$2,040,820
15-29-15-38574-010-0010 through 15-29-15-38574-010-0030 (Remote southwesterly parking facility)	$28,210	$ 2,240	$ 30,450

15-29-15-38574-004-0060 & 0070	$ 43,545	3,500	47,045
15-29-15-38574-004-0150 & 0160			
(Leased southerly parking facility)			
Total Assessments	$395,065	$1,723,230	$2,118,295
1980 Millage Rate			19.665
1980 Taxes*			$41,656.27

*This figure represents an undiscounted tax amount which disregards time of payment.
NOTE: Figures do not include Lots 1, 2, and 3, Block "D", under lease.

Site Data and Description

Sources of information relating to the site were aerial and ground inspections, recorded plats and surveys completed at various dates. The latest survey provided by the client was dated October, 1980, by Carl S. Courson, Land Surveying Inc., Job No. 1516. A reduced site plan is included as Exhibit 7 and modified to show various ground areas and building improvements.

The total site consists of three parcels formerly mentioned. Lots 1 through 44 of Block B constitute the assembled Cleveland Plaza. Two additional remote parcels are utilized as parking facilities. The main assemblage is on the south side of Cleveland Street, an 80 foot right-of-way; Lincoln Avenue borders the westerly and Betty Lane the easterly sides of the property with 70-foot and 60-foot rights-of-way, respectively. Park Street, a 60-foot right-of-way, borders the south property line. The Cleveland frontage lots are all 20' by 120', except for Lot 1 which is 35' × 120'. Park Street lots are 20' × 100', except for Lot 44 which is 35' × 100'. A 20-foot vacated alley separates the two sets of frontage lots. Measured frontage along Cleveland and Park is 455 feet; and along Lincoln and Betty, 240 feet. The remote leased parking facility occupies four lots (and 5 feet + on the eastern side of a fifth lot) on the south side of Park Street, directly south of Lots 28 through 32, Block B. This parcel has a measured 95-foot frontage on the south side of Park and the north side of Pierce Street, again a 60-foot right-of-way. Slight discrepancy is shown between the measured and platted dimensions of this lot but are approximately 95' × 203'. The second remote parking area is at the southwest corner of intersecting Pierce and Lincoln Avenue. The lot is comprised of three irregular shaped lots conforming to the right-of-way of Pierce and Hibiscus Circle.

The following insert is a summary of the various lots and related data:

Parcel	Lots	Block	Dimensions	Sq. Ft. Area	Sq. Ft. Vacated Alley Area	Total Area	Interest
Main Blk	1–5	B	115' × 120'	13,800	1,150	14,950	Fee
	6–13	B	160' × 120'	19,200	1,600	20,800	Fee
	14–22	B	180' × 120'	21,600	1,800	23,400	Fee
	23–31	B	180' × 100'	18,000	1,800	19,800	Leased
	32–44	B	275' × 100'	27,500	2,750	30,250	Fee
Subtotal				100,100	9,100	109,200	
Parking Lot	6–8	D	100.21' × 103.78'			10,399.79	Leased
	15–16	D	95' × 100'			9,500	Leased
Subtotal						19,899.79	
Parking Lot	1–3	J	Irregular			20,720	Fee
Leased Area			39,699.79	.91 Acres			
Owned Area			110,120.00	2.53 Acres			
Total Area			149,819.79	3.44 Acres			

*NOTE: Lots 1 through 3, Block D are 50' × 103.78' or a total 15,567 square feet. Lots are part of lease agreement and not isolated by payment. This had to be considered in our lease analysis.

The main parcel is slightly above road grade along Cleveland and Lincoln and appears level extending east and southeasterly. The site slopes along the eastern part of Park and the west side of Betty Lane, caused by a fall in road elevation following the natural contour. The parking facility on the south side of Park Street gradually slopes from the center toward both road surfaces. Parking at Pierce and Lincoln is generally level, sloping along the eastern edge to Lincoln Avenue. Drainage or run-off from the sites would appear to be excellent because of the variation in site and adjoining road elevations.

Natural vegetation is limited to a number of soft and hard wood trees on the southeast corner of the main parcel. Both parking lots have been cleared and surfaced, with some ornamental plantings.

(Exhibit 7, the site plan, has been deleted.)

Site Improvements

These improvements consist primarily of parking and drive pavement, concrete walkways and curbing, minimal amounts of fencing and landscaping. Access routes through the parking areas extend south from Cleveland to Park between the main building and service station, easterly along the vacated alley easement to Betty Lane, physically dividing the parking areas. There are approximately 27 parking spaces on Lots 25 through 30; another 27 in the southeast corner of the block, from Lots 32 through 40. Approximately ten spaces are situated along the west and south sides of the administrative building and approximately 18 spaces east of the main building. The service station area has 21 marked spaces with an excessive amount of unutilized space.

The southern leased parking lot has four parking rows and paralleling access drives; this site is improved with 60 parking spaces. The parking lot at Pierce is similarly improved with 43 counted spaces.

The main block is attractively landscaped along the southeast corner at the drive-in facility. The fronts of the main building along Cleveland and Lincoln Avenue also have extensive landscaping, with two ornamental fountains along the north side.

It appears that the site is not fully utilized in its efficiency of parking design and layout. Excessive curbing and parking islands have limited the maximum number of possible spaces although presenting an uncongested and more scenic appearance. Green space along Park Street could be converted to additional parking, if required, in addition to the service station area.

(The ground photographs have been deleted.)

Building Improvements

All building improvements are confined to the main assembled block. From an aerial and ground view, the overall development of the block is not consistent with its components. The westerly portion appears as institutional office and the eastern portion as a strip office front, interrupted by a service station in between. The drive-in facility at the southeast corner is not visible from the principal road frontage and visually tied with the main structure. This inconsistency of development of the assembled block is again supportive of individual valuations of the physically divisional building structures.

The two-story building located in the southwest corner is the original structure, constructed in the early 1950s. Built on a concrete slab, exterior walls are masonry with a brick face along the west and southern sides. Eastern exterior is covered with cotico tile panels. Copper was used for all roof flashing, rain gutters, and downspouts. A glass atrium area, converted to useful space, is recessed in the southwest corner of the building. Roof support system is steel beam with a flat, built-up tar and gravel roof cover. A number of mechanical systems are roof-top mounted, including the elevator shaft. Main access of the two-story structure is through the main lobby area on the north side of the building. Currently, personnel and accounting departments occupy the first and second floors, respectively. Spaces have been remodeled with fixed and freestanding partitioning and a number of built-in work spaces. All floors are carpeted; wall surfaces are covered in various wall coverings, and ceiling, with older style acoustical tile. Lighting is generally recessed fluorescent fixtures. A passenger elevator on the west side and stairs on the east connect ground with second floor space.

The main structure is a two-phase development; the first two floors, built in 1963, are on a former service station site and a three-story addition, in 1973.

The building is constructed on a reinforced concrete foundation; framing is poured concrete with rebar to specifications. Exterior walls are concrete block with exterior face brick on the ground floor and cotico tile panels on Floor 2 through 5. Finished floor elevations vary from 12 to 13 feet for the top four floors and 16 feet for the ground level; floor structures are pre-cast or poured reinforced concrete. Central air conditioning system is chilled water and heat by water heating coils. Mechanical and electrical systems include a roof mounted lightning protection system, central fire alarm system and communication system for both intercom and video T.V. screens.

Passenger elevators are situated at the southwest corner of the main structure incorporated with the entrance lobby on the ground level and reception areas on Levels 2 through 5. Emergency, fireproof stairwells are at the northeast and southeast corners of the building for all floor levels. Extensive interior rehabilitation and remodeling have tastefully been completed on all floors. Depending on date of construction, walls are finished drywall or plaster covered in a variety of vinyl or suede wall covering. Floor covering is wall to wall carpeting, very good quality commercial grade. All ceilings are dropped acoustical tile on aluminum support with various lighting fixtures. In general open work areas, luminous ceiling panels with light diffusers have been installed. In aisles and individual offices, adjustable flush fixtures or recessed spots are common. Over the fifth floor atrium, skylight panels provide direct sunlight.

Interior space, including the ground floor teller/lobby areas, is high quality and fashionably appointed in contemporary design. Extensive utilization of fixed and freestanding partitions have been made; built-in office fixtures are also typical. Open or vaulted ceilings over the third and fourth floor is consistent with contemporary design, offering an extremely attractive appearance for executive offices.

We have analyzed, from plans, the division of various space by floor, for both the main and southern building. This study is based on our interpretation of plans provided and divisional categories shown. Even with extensive lobby areas on the first floor, common areas on the second and loss of floor space on the fourth and fifth, the efficiency of usable to gross area ranged from 84 percent to 85 percent. As noted later in our market section, this efficiency is in line with other office structures. The south building is very efficient if considered in a single-tenant use although substantially reduced when common areas are accounted for.

Those buildings currently occupied by administrative and appraisal services are atypical construction for smaller storefront office space. Improvements consist of two freestanding buildings, although appearing to be a single unit. Built on concrete slabs, both structures are concrete block with face brick along the frontage and western side. Rear portions are painted with a textured coating. Roof construction is flat with built-up tar and gravel covering. A roof mounted system provides heating and air conditioning to the easterly appraisal section and a separate ground mounted system for administrative services. Each space has completely remodeled interiors of average quality, including carpeting, fixed nonbearing partitioning, panelled walls, and acoustical tile ceilings.

The service station is also typical construction of a two-bay facility built for one of the major oil companies in the 1960s. Block walls on a concrete slab are exposed in the rear and covered with a painted porcelainized aluminum front. Canopies extend off the front and rear of the main structure.

Drive-in banking facility at the southeast corner is concrete block construction with cotico tile panels for exterior cover. Two extensive canopies extend north and south over four drive-in lanes.

(Exhibit 8, a number of property sketches, has been deleted.)

Highest and Best Use

Highest and best use is defined, for purposes of this report as, "That reasonable and profitable use that will support the highest present value, as defined, as of the effective date of the appraisal." A second definition specifically used for the highest and best use of land is, "Alternatively, that use, from among reasonably probable and legal alternative uses, found to be physically possible, appropriately supported, financially feasible and which results in the highest land value." The text further clarifies this latter definition by stating, "in cases where site has existing improvements on it, the highest and best use may very well be determined to be different from the existing use. The existing use will continue, however, unless and until land value in its highest and best use exceeds the total value of the property in its existing use."[5]

In selecting the highest and best use, an analysis of other possible uses or alternatives must be considered. In other words, what use of the property would yield to an owner the highest present value. Consideration must be given first to lawful uses under existing governmental restrictions—zoning, including type and density of development, second, to the economics of the environing area. The highest and best use concept, as defined above, can be applied to properties as improved or vacant. Further determinations can be made of improved properties as if unimproved where improvements contribute little or marginal value to the land component.

The first point dealt with in our analysis was the question of an assemblage or premium value for the consolidated block. Presented in the introduction, overall development of the property is inconsistent from both a physical and economic sense.

Each building component has a particular in-use value to the current occupant, Clearwater Federal. These uses may have little, if any, value to the market of typical office occupants. Legally, each property within the block can be considered freestanding, meeting building and parking requirements either by grandfathered clause or ordinance. Briefly to summarize this point, land and building figures for each property result in adequate parking as required by code.

With the exceptions of the service station and deteriorated residence, improvements to the land have substantial contributory value. Determination of highest and best use of these portions, as if vacant, would be fallacious. Considering the physical, economic and legal characteristics of the improvements, the present use as office space is our opinion of that current highest and best use.

The residential property is both physically and functionally obsolete. Extensive rehabilitation would be required for a structure that encumbers a more efficient use as parking for the administrative building. In our opinion, the structure adds no value and is even considered a cost or expense to demolish.

Again, the service station improvements have a particular value to Clearwater Federal with its large fleet of rolling stock. This value would not be recognized by a more typical user. Over the past few years there has been a strong trend for service station conversion to alternative uses. Major oil companies have been limiting their operation to a number of key locations. Operating independents have periodically relied totally on gasoline allocations rather than location or land value. We have indi-

---

5. Byrl N. Boyce, *Real Estate Appraisal Terminology*, (Cambridge, Massachusetts: Balinger Publishing Co., 1975), p. 107.

cated three alternative uses for the site. The first is a continued special use for fleet maintenance; a second is the reimprovement of the site with compatible office space more efficiently utilizing the site. The last alternative would be for expanded parking after improvement demolition. Each of these alternatives would be based on land value and any contributory value the site improvements (not building improvements) may have.

Leased parking south of Park Street is zoned residential although, by exception, allows noncommercial parking. Two alternative uses for the site as zoned would be the existing use or duplex and/or apartment construction. Because of varying dimension regulations, a maximum of three duplex units could be placed on the site. The total land value for these units is lower than an actual return from rental parking facilities (although not allowed by the code). More important is simply demand for additional parking facilities in lieu of additional residential units.

The remote parking on Pierce Street is zoned general business and may have many future adapted uses. In our opinion, the parking facility has value-in-use to Clearwater Federal and, as an interim use, will continue until the demand for Lincoln Avenue frontage outweighs value as a parking lot.

In this section, we have addressed which specific tenancy for the main building would most effectively utilize the space and in turn be willing to pay the greatest amount for this use. The ground floor of the main building was specifically designed for an institutional lobby. High ceilings (functionally unalterable) and extensive interior improvements in addition to the walk-in vault make it a specialized space. In our study we have concluded that ground floor space would be reemployed by an institutional tenant (commercial or savings and loan) or by a capital market securities firm. Drive-in facilities could be used in conjunction with an institutional tenant or fully utilized as a freestanding unit in the event of another type tenant.

Interior or structural design of the second through fifth floors also limits respective tenants. The second floor has a number of general areas including the community room and employees' dining facility. Mechanical, storage and an open mail room are other major spaces on the floor. Main space is divided into individual office suites with common corridors. As currently improved, the second floor is the only space suitable for multi-tenancy. Floors three through five would facilitate a tenant per floor or a single tenant.

The southern building appears to be extremely flexible, suitable for either single or multi-tenancy. This space could either be used in association with the main building or could be completely independent.

Introduction to the Appraisal Process

In real estate appraisal, there exist three traditional approaches or indications of market value for real estate. Ideally, each of the three approaches should be used in value estimation. Practically, however, often one or more of these approaches is inappropriate or inapplicable to the subject property. The three traditional approaches follow.

Cost or Summation Approach

This approach is based on the principle that an informed purchaser would pay no more for a property than the cost of producing a suitable substitute property with the same utility. Methodology used in this approach generally consists of estimating replacement cost of the subject improvements and subtracting from that figure any depreciation which might be caused by physical deterioration, economic obsolescence or functional obsolescence. The resultant figure is then added to the estimated market value of land, obtained usually through use of the market data approach. This approach is considered particularly applicable when the property being appraised

Table E

AREA EFFICIENCY RELATIONSHIP

Floor	Exterior Gross Area	Interior Gross Area	Common Spaces	Open/Vaulted Ceiling Areas	Stairwells	Mech. Equip. Space	Elevator	Net Rentable Floor Space	Efficiency Ratio
Main Building:									
1st	8,344	8,042	610	—	401	—	150	7,031	84.3%
2nd	8,344	8,042	(A)None (B) 689	—	401	837	150	(A) 6,804 (B) 6,115	(A)81.5% (B)73.3%
3rd	8,071	7,769	—	—	401	—	150	7,368	91.3%
4th	8,071	7,769	—	527	401	602	150	6,239	77.3%
5th	7,205	7,039	—	527	401	75	150	6,036	83.3%
Totals	40,035	38,661	(A) 610 (B)1,299	1,054	2,005	1,514	750	(A)33,478 (B)32,789	(A)83.6% (B)81.9%
South Building:									
1st	3,895	3,544	—	—	245	270	52	(C) 2,977 (D) 3,544	76.4% (Multi-tenant) 91.0% (Single-tenant)
2nd	3,895	3,544	160	—	175	—	52	(C) 3,157 (D) 3,544	81.1% 91.0%
Totals	7,790	7,088	160	—	420	270	104	(C) 6,134 (D) 7,088	(C)78.7% (D)91.0%

(A) & (B) Area analysis if considered individual suites with common areas or an entire leasable floor.
(C) & (D) Same as (A) & (B), if used for multi-tenant vs. single-tenant leasing.

involves new or almost new improvements which represent the highest and best use of land.

Market Data or Direct Sales Comparison Approach

The market approach is based on the principle of substitution; in other words, it is believed market value of a property is predicated on prices paid in actual market transactions for similar, substitute properties. Methodology used in this approach consists of gathering and analyzing recent sales of similar properties. These comparable sales are then compared to the appraised property and adjustments made based on market information to provide an indication of probable sales price, i.e., market value of the subject property. This approach is dependent upon availability of suitable comparable sales and absence of atypical market conditions affecting the sales price.

Income or Capitalization Approach

This valuation approach is based on conversion of anticipated benefits to be derived from ownership or purchase of property into an estimate of its present worth or value. Methodology in this approach can take many formulations; however, it is generally the process of converting a series of anticipated future benefits, in the form of income or reversions, into a present value. This process is known as "capitalization" and depends upon alternative market investments to provide an indication of an applicable capitalization rate. The income approach is considered most applicable in appraising "income producing" properties. It can, however, also be applied to properties generally considered nonincome producing on the basis of the alternative opportunity costs of the intended occupancy.

Market Approach

As indicated in the introduction to the appraisal process, a market approach is based on the principle of substitution; market value of a property is predicated upon prices paid for similar substitute properties. Although it is impossible to find properties which are exactly equivalent to those being appraised, there are generally sales available, in an active market, which display the same general locational or physical characteristics. Because of the differences in both physical, locational and economic characteristics of these sales, adjustments must be made to more accurately reflect the properties appraised.

Examinations of sales of the most similar office buildings in the same general competitive area were made. Sales used in the analysis were limited to those properties with approximately the same quality of construction, general condition, size, efficiency of space utilization, parking and access and typical land to building ratio.

Further consideration was given to mortgage terms of the sale, whether extended by the seller or acquired independently of the transaction. We further attempted to isolate success of the sale by reviewing trends of rental rates before, at and subsequent to the sale date. Existing occupancy levels on the date of the sale were also considered.

The office sales found have been categorized as larger or smaller types for comparison to Clearwater Federal's main building and the administrative/appraisal buildings. Additional service station and vacant land sales were analyzed to estimate market value of these remaining parcels. We were unsuccessful in locating any sale comparable to the drive-in facility.

Market Approach—Main Building

We limited sales used to those most recent and negotiated at arm's length. Each sale was investment quality and, individually, represented an investment value to the respective buyer and/or seller. The composite of sales or sales transactions in this market segment represents market value. When available, we have commented on the market data, pointing out any direct relationships found in our interpretation of the data.

Larger Office Building Sale Number 1

Date of Transaction:	January, 1980
Recorded In:	OR Book 1398, page 1508 Lee County
Grantor:	Pate Industries, inc.
Grantee:	Ed Leerdam
Location:	Southeast corner of South Tamiami Trail (U.S. 41) and Sunrise Boulevard, about 1.5 miles south of Lee County Airport and 8 miles south of downtown Fort Myers.
Parcel Area/Size:	Site is rectangular shaped and contains 94,090 square feet or 2.16 acres.
Road Frontages:	Site has excellent frontage on east side of U.S. 41 and secondary frontage along access road.
Building Size/Description:	Five-story, masonry and glass structure building containing 51,000 square feet of gross area and net rentable of 47,676 square feet.
Land to Building Ratio:	1.85:1
Efficiency Ratio:	93.5%
Date Constructed/Rehabilitated:	Built in 1972
Indicated Consideration:	$2,559,000

Sales Analysis:		
Price Paid per	Gross Building Sq. Ft.	$50.18
(Unit price for land	Net Rentable Sq. Ft.	53.68
& improvement)		
Gross Rent Multiplier		
(Sale Price/Gross Income)		6.98
Overall Rate		
(Net Income/Sale Price)	(Actual)	8.4%

	Total	Avg Net Sq. Ft.
Gross Income	$366,634	$7.70
Expenses	151,678	3.18
Expense Ratio	41.4%	
Net Income	214,956	4.51

Comments:
This sale is the most applicable market transaction found for the property under appraisement. At date of sale, the ground floor was occupied by Palmetto Federal Savings & Loan with approximately 3,600 square feet. The savings and loan acquired the abutting southerly site for $5.05 per square foot in January, 1980, for construction of a new office building. This sale recognizes this near term vacancy, reflected in the sale price. Ninety-eight percent of the space was occupied at the date of sale, with the savings and loan occupying approximately eight percent. Under lease for the 3,600 square feet at $3,000 per month or $36,000 per year, Palmetto Savings & Loan pays rent equivalent to $10 per square foot.

Another major tenant is the State of Florida with regional HRS offices. Based on actual rental figures, average rent per net usable square foot for all space is $7.70 with full service included. Indicated 41 + percent expense ratio appears to be adequate from the excellent appearance and maintenance of the building.

Ample parking on the east and south sides; some covered spaces provided.

(The other six sales in this category have been deleted; however, all the statistics are included in Exhibit 9.)

Summary of Sales

Sale dates ranged from late 1978 to mid-1980, the latest found. Locations of sales were confined to a competitive area, formerly described in the office market section. Site and building areas of sales varied individually. The relationship of site to building area and, further, the efficiency relationship of usable to gross area, were reduced to comparable units. Indicated land to building ratios were derived simply by comparing the overall site requirements to gross building area. The ratio ranged from a low of 1.14 to a high of 2.72. Overall land to building ratio for the entire block, including all structures, is approximately 2.04. The appraised property appears to fall within the indicated range, whatever combination is used.

The second common comparison was the efficiency of useable to gross building area; 93.5 was the highest indicated percentage found in an office park specifically designed for multi-tenants. The lowest was 82.1 percent, again found in a multi-tenant facility. Clearwater Federal's main building indicates an overall efficiency ratio of 83.6 percent, if total area is included on the second floor, and 81.9 percent if excluded. With the specific intended use of Clearwater Federal at time of construction, the building still offers a very acceptable ratio of useable space. If the building was occupied by a single tenant, the entire area would be included.

Sales prices per square foot ranged from a low of $31.22 to $50.18 based on gross square footage and a low of $37.57 and a high of $53.68 based on net useable space. Prior paid per gross square foot would be most applicable if a comparison of a sale with similar size and efficiency of space as the appraised property is made. Figures for net area are already adjusted to exclude any common or wasted space. This unit of comparison would be most applicable to a multi-tenancy building, particularly where common area charges are not prorated to tenants.

Another market comparison is based on actual performance of the property related to the sales price. The gross rent multiplier measures two economic aspects of a property: rental rates and the levels of occupancy. Lower multiples indicate a reduced margin between sale price and gross income, and higher multiples, a greater margin. For those properties where the figures were available, indicated multiples narrowly ranged from a low of 5.69 to a high of 6.98. This unit may have limited application in comparison with the appraised property due to required forecasting of gross or potential gross income. Extracted overall rates are a further refinement of a gross rent multiplier, with consideration given to the efficiency of the operating entity. This rate is applied in an income approach, used directly or supportive of a derived rate.

All of the sales were considered in the analysis, although each limited in some regard to equivalency of the appraised building. The most applicable sale is Sale Number 1 of the Palmetto Federal Savings & Loan Building. Physical and economic properties of the sale were the most comparable found. The building is approximately the same size, although the indicated efficiency ratio is higher. The building was originally designed for multi-tenancy, although some lessees occupy entire floors. The buyer acquired the property with the understanding that a major tenant would vacate space at a future date. This is not, however, as extreme as the possible vacation of the entire building by Clearwater Federal.

Exhibit 9

LARGER OFFICE BUILDING SALES SUMMARY

Sale/Description	Date	Location	Site Area Sq. Ft. (Acres)	Building Area Gross	Net	Land\Bldg. Ratio	Bldg. Effic. Ratio	Sale Price	Price Paid Per Gross Sq. Ft.	Net Sq. Ft.	Indicated GRM	OAR
1. Palmetto Federal Savings & Loan Bldg. Ft. Myers, Lee Co.	1/80	U.S. 41 South	94,090 (2.16)	53,000	47,676	1.85	93.5%	$2,559,000	$50.18	$53.68	6.98	8.4%
2. Gateway Executive Center, St. Petersburg, Pinellas Co.	6/80	4th St. North	108,900 (2.5)	40,101	32,915	2.72	82.1%	1,300,000	32.42	39.50	6.37	7.2%
3. International Executive Center Tampa, Hillsborough	1/81	Pan Am Circle	71,438 (1.64)	31,215	28,872	2.29	92.5%	1,350,000	43.25	46.76	5.69	10.28%
4. Transworld Center Tampa, Hillsborough	8/79	West Kennedy Blvd.	84,283 (1.94)	46,000	40,482	1.83	88%	2,024,100	44.00	50.00	—	—
5. 1900 Main Bldg. Sarasota, Sarasota Co.	7/79	Main St.	39,850 (0.92)	35,000	31,370	1.14	89.6%	1,178,500	33.67	37.57	6.65	8.3–9.0%
6. Belcher Executive Center, Clearwater, Pinellas	4/79	Belcher Road	60,209 (1.38)	31,155	26,482	1.93	85%	1,050,000	33.70	39.65	—	—
7. Freedom Executive Center, Tampa, Hillsborough Co.	11/78	South Dale Mabry	59,460 (1.365)	51,248	42,435	1.16	82.8%	1,600,000	31.22	37.71	—	—

The physical condition of the sale was reportedly excellent at date of sale as well as at our inspection. The exterior appearance is more contemporary and appealing than Clearwater Federal. Interior space and improvements are inferior to Clearwater Federal. In fact, no properties inspected during this assignment were equivalent.

The most appropriate adjustment to the sale property would, first, be upward for the date of sale. Over the past year, the general office market has maintained if not increased occupancy levels at constantly increasing or renegotiated rental rates. The scarcity of available space and prospective, adequate returns to investors in professional office properties have continually pushed prices upward.

Sale Number 5, although historical, showed an annual increase in excess of 20 percent per year over slightly less than a two year holding period. Because of the Palmetto sale prime location and appeal in its market segment, we have estimated an approximate 12 percent increase over an annual period. A downward adjustment was made for the property's more current date and design of construction and superior appearance. This adjustment would also include the design function of more effectively utilized space. An upward adjustment for the interior improvement of Clearwater Federal offsets the former adjustment.

The sale property is located in a rapidly expanding market. General price levels are trending in the same way, although felt to be below more established values for the Clearwater area. Because we have not been able to specifically value difference for the two locations, we have considered the sale location equal to Clearwater Federal, making no adjustment.

The adjusted sale price indicates a price paid of $56.20 per square foot of gross building area and $60.12 of net useable. Applying a gross square footage rate of $56.00 to the 40,035 square feet, a value is indicated of $2,242,000. If the $60.000 price per square foot of net useable space is applied against 33,478 square feet, the indicated value is $2,008,000.

In our opinion, the main structure of Clearwater Federal's Cleveland Plaza office has a market value by a sales comparison or market approach of $2,100,000. This value includes all of the land occupied by the main building and the southeasterly portion of the block. Specifically excluded is the drive-in facility which is an added value measured in our income approach.

Market Approach—
Administrative/Appraisal Property

All of the same techniques or methodology discussed under larger office building sales were employed in this analysis. However, the market area from which sales were collected was confined to Clearwater's downtown or peripheral areas. The following sales were confirmed as arm's length and appear to be reflective of market values for these freestanding Clearwater Federal properties. A number of additional sales were analyzed; and, although not specifically included, certain data were used for our analysis.

Small Office Building Sale Number 1

Date of Transaction:	September 13, 1980
Recorded in:	OR Book 5077, page 1590, Pinellas County
Grantor:	Robert E. Burbank
Grantee:	William Trickel, Jr.
Location:	North side of Cleveland Street in downtown Clearwater, approximately one mile west of Cleveland Plaza.

Parcel Area/Size:	Rectangular shaped parcel, 112′ × 125′; total area 14,000 square feet.
Road Frontages:	112′ on north side of Cleveland Street.
Building Size/Description:	One-story office building with 5,757 square feet of space. No central heating/cooling system was installed at date of sale. Eight thousand square feet paved parking is on site.
Land to Building Ratio:	2.43:1
Date Constructed/ Rehabilitated:	Built in 1940
Indicated Consideration:	$183,000
Sales Analysis:	Price paid per gross building square foot—$31.79.

Comments:

Purchaser indicated that the sale was negotiated at arm's length at the indicated consideration of $183,000. The building was structurally sound at date of sale, but extensive renovation and remodeling was completed for their own use, as a retail jewelry store and combination office. Space had formerly been occupied by Clearwater-Largo Realty, although no rental rates were involved.

(The other three sales in this category have been deleted; however, all the statistics are included in Exhibit 10.)

Summary of Sales

Sales 1 and 2 are the most recent and in the immediate area of downtown Clearwater. Sales 3 and 4 are late 1979 sales, and both had considerably less space than Sales 1, 2 or the appraised properties. The market clearly indicates that smaller building sales are being acquired by individuals who intend to occupy the space. Each sale was purchased with anticipation by the buyer for extensive rehab or remodeling. Sale 2 was the only property that was generating income at date of sale, with a portion leased to Lawyer's Title.

We have concluded that the acquisition of smaller office properties is not principally for investment purposes but rather to provide a fixed cost base for an owner/occupant. Investment consideration is given, however, by the purchaser, over a holding period in anticipation of increased property value.

The most important unit of comparison found was price paid per square foot of total building area. In addition to acquisition price, the buyer estimates his cost for remodeling or alteration for a specific use. Price per square foot ranged from a low of $31.28 to a high of $48.08. The latter was paid for the smallest property and utilized for a single tenancy. Excluding this sale, the average price paid was about $31.50 to $32.00 per square foot. Each sale was adjusted upward from its respective date of sale. A further upward adjustment was made for conditions of the properties. Costs were estimated for remodeling in each sale. The administrative and appraisal service buildings, as formerly described, have been completely updated both in exterior and interior remodeling. It was necessary to make these possibly subjective estimates of cost to compare the sales with the existing structures of Clearwater Federal. After consideration of adjustments for time and physical condition of sale properties, indicated prices per square foot ranged from $41.00 to $56.00; again, the higher indicated price was for Sale 3 or the smallest building area.

Our estimate of value via market approach for this portion of Clearwater Federal's holding was $41.00 per square foot of gross building area or: 5,026 sq. ft. @ $41.00 = $206,000. We rounded our estimate to $210,000.

SMALL OFFICE BUILDING SUMMARY

Sale No.	Location	Date	Site Area	Building Area Gross	Building Area Net	Land/ Bldg. Ratio	Sale Price	Price Paid Per Gross Sq. Ft.	Price Paid Per Net Sq. Ft.	Intended use of Property
1	714 Cleveland Street	9/80	14,000	5,757	—	2.43	$183,000	$31.79	$ —	Owner occupied retail/office
2	500 S. Garden Avenue	8/80	15,725	9,000	8,300	1.75	284,000	31.56	34.22	Tenant occupied and proposed owner occupancy
3	311 S. Osceola Avenue	10/79	13,500	2,600	2,000	5.19	125,000	48.08	62.50	Owner occupied office building
4	1280 Court Street	1/79	16,300	3,200	—	5.09	100,100	31.28	34.76	Owner occupied retail/office

VACANT LAND SALES SUMMARY

Sale No.	Location	Date	Site Sq. Ft. Area	Frontage	Sale Price	Price Paid Per Sq. Ft.	Price Paid Per Fr. Ft.	Proposed/ Existing Use
1A	Missouri Avenue	3/80	6,617	43' (Brown St.)	$ 50,000	$7.55	$1,162	Branch bank location
1B	Same	3/80	29,600	150' (Missouri)	120,000	4.05	800	Same
Total			36,217		170,000	4.70	1,133	
2	Druid & Ft. Harrison	2/80	21,589	107' (Druid)	80,000	3.70	747	Possible medical office
3	Cleveland & Main	12/79	30,000	150' (Cleveland)	100,000	3.33	666	Branch bank location
4	Court & Lincoln	11/79	12,000	120' (Court St.)	52,000	4.33	433	Undetermined
5	Park & Greenwood	10/79	33,210	135' (Cleveland)	160,000	4.82	1,185	Parking lot for 1100 Building

Market Approach—Service Station

As formerly stated, we feel the service station improvements on Lots 6 through 13 add little if any value to the site in a market value concept. Two service station sales, both on Drew Street north of the appraised property, are presented. Both sales sold at arm's length for a confirmed $110,000. From former studies completed for service station type properties, this price is typical for well-located service station packages, including land and buildings. Allocation of purchase price between land and buildings for properties acquired for alternative uses showed a very small percentage of value attributed to improvements. These two recent sales are outlined below.

From the vacant land analysis (in the following section), we have estimated a land value for Lots 6 through 13, or the 20,800 square feet, at $5.00 to $5.50 per square foot. This indicates a value for the underlying land from $104,000 to $114,000. If the property was valued as a service station, the typical market would be willing to pay approximately $110,000. This use, as formerly illustrated, would violate our estimate of highest and best use for the site. Our land value indication shows that most if not all of the value would be attributable to the land. We should possibly consider the cost to remove the building structure, although this expense would be offset by the contributory value of site improvement such as paving, curbs and fencing, which would be added to land value. We have estimated the value of the property at $110,000. We conclude that this is entirely representative of land and site improvement values and not allocated to the building. For discussion purposes, Clearwater Federal or a subsequent owner may attribute some value to the improvements, although in a value in use concept.

Service Station Sale Number 1

Date of Transaction:	September 15, 1980
Recorded in:	OR Book 5078, page 2198 Pinellas County
Grantor:	C. E. Powell, Jr.
Grantee:	Clair J. Vetter
Location:	Southeast corner of Drew Street and Jupiter Avenue, approximately five blocks north of Cleveland Plaza, Clearwater.
Parcel Area/Size:	Rectangular shaped parcel, 102' × 155'; total area, 15,810 square feet.
Road Frontages:	155' on east side of Jupiter Avenue, 102' on south side of Drew Street.
Building Size/Description:	Service station building with 524 square foot office, 918 square foot service area. Typical canopy covers service island. 5,800 square feet of the site are paved.
Land to Building Ratio:	10.96:1
Date Constructed/ Rehabilitated:	Built in 1958
Indicated Consideration:	$110,000
Estimated Land Value:	$79,000 (15,810 sq. ft. @ $5.00)
Contributory Value of Bldg.:	$31,000
Per Square Foot of Building:	$21.50

(The other service station sale has been deleted; no summary was included.)

Market Approach—Fee Parking Lot

The most appropriate and, in fact, only method of valuing a noncommercial parking facility (one not used for profit) is by a market approach in which the value of land is added to any contributory value (usually depreciated cost) of the site improvement. A review was made of a number of sales of similar size, locational qualities and allowable use by zoning. The following six sales are presented in support of our conclusion of land value.

Land sales were also used in our estimate of market value for the land underlying the service station along the south side of Cleveland (formerly discussed) and later in our valuation of lease interest.

Vacant Land Sale Number 1A

Date of Transaction:	March, 1980
Recorded in:	OR Book 4996, page 117 Pinellas County
Grantor:	Cornelius B. Jackson
Grantee:	Gulf Coast Bank of Pinellas
Location:	North side of Brown Street, just west of Missouri Avenue.
Parcel Area/Size:	Irregular, 6,617 square feet; .15 acre. Almost rectangular with indentation at southeast corner.
Approximate Frontages:	43' on north side Brown Street.
Zoning:	C-G
Indicated Consideration:	$50,000
Verified by:	Mr. Baynard, Grantee, Executive Vice-President.
Price Paid per	Square Foot—$7.55
	Front Foot—$1,162
Comments:	Mr. Baynard indicated that Sale 1A and 1B were arm's length and acquired for a branch location on the west side of Missouri. Sale 1A was a single lot assembled with a major parcel, 1B. We have considered the overall acquisition cost.

(The other five land sales were deleted; however, they are all included in Exhibit 11.)

Summary of Sales

All sales were between late 1979 and mid-1980 and in the immediate area of Cleveland Plaza. Prices paid per square foot ranged narrowly between $3.33 and $4.82. Sales 1A and B were the assemblage for a branch bank location, and 3, a single transaction for a recently completed bank facility. The highest price paid per square foot was for proposed parking expansion of the "1100" Building.

Based on this information and the fact that the Clearwater Federal's lot is more remote or less exposed, we have estimated a $4.00 per square foot value for the general business district property. Costs and depreciation estimates were made for parking surfaces, curbing, and minimal landscaping. These site improvements had a value of about $0.48 per square foot or $9,945, rounded to $10,000. Land value for the 20,720 square feet was estimated at $4.00 per square foot or $82,880. Land value plus the $10,000 site improvements indicates a market value of $92,880, rounded to $95,000.

Summary of Market Approach Values

Clearwater Federal's Main Building	$2,100,000
Administrative and Appraisal Services	$210,000
Service Station Property	$110,000
Parking Lot	$95,000
Total Estimate	$2,515,000

These value estimates specifically exclude any lease interest or value contribution of the drive-in facility. Separate valuations are made for each.

Income Approach

As previously discussed, income is based on conversion of anticipated benefits to be derived from ownership or purchase of a property into an estimate of present worth or value. Methodology used in this approach can be in many formulations, each of which relates income to be derived from the property (either an operating income or reversion) to present value, using a market derived discount or capitalization rate.

To evaluate Clearwater Federal's fee interest in the various properties, an examination of several elements was made. First an examination of market rents, that is, the rent being paid in the open market for space similar to the subject's occupancy. Based on available rents, at any given level, the absorption of available space must be anticipated over a reasonably forecasted period. This absorption or occupancy is the generative factor for potential gross receipts. Another element is the structuring of fixed and operating expenses associated with an office building complex. A number of methods are currently utilized in actual office property management; these will be reviewed. Gross income less applicable expenses is a net residual amount attributable to ownership. Net income is a composite return to equity and mortgage positions. By capitalizing or discounting this undivided return (net income), the resultant figure is an indication of property market value.

Market Rents

Discussion of the office market segment included both Hillsborough and Pinellas Counties. Other market data obtained in our analysis of sale properties were also used wherever applicable.

Tampa Market:

A survey was conducted for a number of downtown and West Shore area office complexes. In addition to finding current rates of available space, we collected historical rental schedules to provide some insight of rental escalations in this market segment. In conjunction with rental rates, Exhibit 12 also presents current and, if available, historical occupancy levels.

Briefly summarizing the Hillsborough County office market, more attractive properties in the downtown and West Shore areas are experiencing extremely high occupancy levels. After the 1975–76 slowdown, available space became quickly absorbed, while at the same time, quoted and negotiated rental rates consistently increased. Percentage increases in these rates may be somewhat misleading, for properties experiencing high occupancies had little or no space available. Historical rent levels were tied to leases from one to three years, negotiated under lower per square foot rates.

Pinellas Market

This market was briefly described in an introduction section; and, in contrast to the Tampa market, it is not as clearly distinguished by location. In this analysis, we have considered the entire county to be a competitive market and used it for our estimates of an applicable rental schedule and forecast absorption. Twenty-plus buildings were surveyed by personal interview and published information. A summary of the survey follows in Exhibit 13.

As indicated in the Pinellas survey, current rental rates quoted ranged from a low $6.00 to a high of $12.00 per net square foot, principally in multi-tenant buildings. A much more narrow spread of from $8.50 to $11.00 was indicated in space, which in our opinion was more competitive.

There was a variety of methods used in leasing space for the properties listed. Space was calculated on interior to interior wall of individual suites, or interior space plus a prorated portion of common hallways, restroom facilities and storage. In some properties, even common entry areas were prorated to tenants. Another observation was that, although full services were provided by the landlord, almost every property had expense escalators in addition to base rent ranging from basic real estate taxes to all expense items. A few office properties had a complete pass-through of all expenses incurred in the operating entity and prorated as additional rent, based on a year end expense statement. The most typical base rent adjustment found was a stop provision for property tax and utility charges. Adjustments to base rent, based on the Consumer Price Index, were also common. Typically, this adjustment had a cap or ceiling of seven or eight percent annually.

The data gathered in our sales analysis of office complexes were also used in estimating appropriate rentals for the appraised property. Other market data, not presented, were also used.

Our estimate of potential gross income was based on a division of net leaseable area into two types of space. The first type would include all of the ground floor level currently occupied by the Association's lobby and teller facilities. The second type was the balance of the second through fifth floor space. In accord with our comments on highest and best use, the ground level or highly improved lobby area is limited to a few prospective tenants. This space would either be 1) retained by Clearwater Federal, 2) occupied by another financial institution, or 3) possibly adapted to a securities brokerage firm. An abundance of lease information regarding financial institutions was not found, although one recently negotiated lease to a commercial bank was analyzed. Briefly outlining the agreement, approximately 6,200 square feet of space was leased under a ten year original term with three, five year renewal options. Base rent for the first year was $60,000 and $75,000 for the subsequent eight years. An adjustment by CPI, limited to a maximum of seven percent per annum, was made to base rent after the third year. Rent equates to $9.70 per square foot in year one and $12.25 in years two through ten. High quality interior improvements are provided by the landlord and included in rent. The unusual provision of this lease is the fact that all expenses incurred in the operation of the property are passed through to the tenant, as a proration of space occupied. Total expenses to be passed through were estimated by the developer at $3.50 to $4.00 per square foot of rented area. This would equate to a range of $15.00 to $16.25 over the ten year term (excluding CPI changes).

Potential gross income for the subject's ground floor, if leased to one of the most probable tenants, is estimated at $14.00 per square foot of net rentable area. This figure excludes the common entrance area from Lincoln Avenue and rear parking. It further anticipates that more typical expense items would be the responsibility of the landlord to a base amount and not totally passed through to the tenant in a *net* lease agreement.

Exhibit 12

HILLSBOROUGH COUNTY SUMMARY

Property Name & Location	Total Net Rentable Space	Current Rate Quote	Historic Rates Quoted 1979	1978	1977	Avg. Ann. % Change	Current Occup.	Space Leased & Annual Percentage Gain 1979	1978	1977
Lincoln Center Westshore	190,000	10.50–12.00	10.00–11.25	8.00–9.50	7.50–9.25	10.8%	97%	Minimum	3,200 1.7%	5,000 2.6%
Mariner Square Westshore	45,897	9.50+	8.50–9.50	9.50 7.50	6.75	11.3	95	Minimum	6,500 14.2%	1,920 4.2%
Metropolitan Bank Westshore	30,000	No quote	9.00	8.25	8.00	4.2	100	N/A	2,000 6.7%	28,000 93%
5200 Kennedy Westshore	81,550	No quote	7.50	6.95	6.75	3.1	100	N/A	7,440 9.1%	4,792 5.9%
Kennedy Square Westshore	80,000	No quote	9.25	7.95–8.75	7.95–8.75	4.5	100	N/A	14,400 18%	26,179 32.7%
Florida Federal Westshore	35,000	No quote	8.00	7.50	7.25	3.5	100	N/A	N/A	2,500 7.1%
Austin Center Westshore	310,000	9.00–9.50	7.75–8.75	7.00–8.00	6.50–8.00	10.7	97	Minimum	857	—
Executive Square Westshore	125,000	No quote	7.25	6.50	6.50	3.8	99	N/A	2,516 2%	12,175 9.7%
Flagship Bank Bldg. Downtown	140,000	8.00–9.00	—	—	—	—	100	—	—	—
First Florida Tower Downtown	489,067	11.00–12.50	—	—	—	—	100	—	—	—
Barnett Bank Bldg. Downtown	156,517	8.00–10.50	—	—	—	—	100	—	—	—
Madison Office Downtown	87,000	8.00–8.50	—	—	—	—	100	—	—	—
Exchange National Bank, Downtown	218,712	9.50–11.00	—	—	—	—	100	—	—	—
Freedom Federal Office, Downtown	75,340	9.50	—	—	—	—	100	—	—	—

Exhibit 13

PINELLAS OFFICE SUMMARY*

Property Name & Location	Total Net Rentable Space	Quoted Rate Per Sq. Ft. Current	Quoted Rate Per Sq. Ft. 1980	Annual % Change	Property Type	Lease Terms Minimum Term/Yrs	Lease Terms Services	Lease Terms Interior Allowance	Current Occupancy	Space Leased & Annual % Gain 1980	Space Leased & Annual % Gain 1979
Koger Executive Ctr, St. Petersburg	360,000	10.50–	9.50–	10.5	Multi-tenant Park	5 yrs	Full service	By landlord	97.2	N/A	N/A
Palms of Pasadena Prof. Bldg., South Pasadena	43,000	8.00	7.50	6.7	Medical multi-tenant	3 yrs	Partial	By landlord	100.00	—	—
The Plaza, St. Petersburg	170,000	10.25–11.75	10.00–12.00	—	Multi-tenant & retail	3–5 yrs	Office full service; retail, net	Negotiated	93.2	1,900 1.1%	33,500 19.7%
Tyrone Towers, St. Petersburg	70,000	9.50–11.00	8.50–9.50	12.6	Multi-tenant	3–5 yrs	Full service	By landlord	100.0	2,000 2.9%	—
Attner Center, St. Petersburg	64,000	9.00 (Net lease)	12.00	N/A	Multi-tenant	5 yrs	Pass-through	By landlord	100.0	2,700 4.2%	6,500 10.2%
Arbor Office Ctr, Clearwater	71,000	11.50	10.25	12.2	Multi-tenant	3 yrs	Full service	Basic allowance	86.9	—	—
Bank of Clearwater, Clearwater	137,575	9.00–11.50	8.50–10.00	12.5	Institutional & Multi-tenant	3 yrs	Full service	Basic allowance	98.2	—	3,118 2.3%
Belcher Plaza, Clearwater	95,000	9.00–9.50	8.75	8.5	Multi-tenant	3 yrs	Full service	Negotiated	84.2	—	—
1100 Building, Clearwater	115,000	7.50–8.00	7.25–7.75	10.0	Multi-tenant	1 yr	Full service	Basic allowance	78.3	(15,000) (13%)	20,000 17.4%
Largo Office Ctr, Largo	45,125	8.75	8.00	9.4	Multi-tenant	3 yrs	Full service	Basic allowance	75.6	(11,000) (25%)	4,133 9.2%
U.S. Homes Bldg, Countryside	72,000	10.00	8.75–10.00	—	Multi-tenant	1 yr	Full service	Basic allowance	100.0	—	10,000 13.9%

*Due to space restrictions, the summary has been condensed.

Main Building —
Ground Level
7,031 sq. ft. @ $14.00 = $98,434

The remaining four floors would generate the balance of gross income. The most ideal leasing arrangement for these floors, if not occupied by a single tenant or owner-occupant, would be by floor. The only suitable multi-tenant floor would possibly be the second floor, where hall and restroom facilities are common to all office areas. Floors three, four and five have logical reception areas in the southwest corner with private and open work spaces over the balance. The fifth, or executive floor, because of location, view, and exclusive access, would possibly be leased at a slight premium. The following outline estimates potential gross for floors two through five.

2nd Floor—
   6,115 sq. ft. @ $10.00 = $61,150
3rd Floor —
   7,368 sq. ft. @ $10.00 = 73,680
4th Floor —
   6,239 sq. ft. @ $10.00 = 62,390
5th Floor —
   6,036 sq. ft. @ $11.00 = <u>66,396</u>
Total Gross $362,050

Consideration is given for the drive-in banking facilities. We had no method of analyzing this value in our market approach and have relied completely on prospective income the facility could generate through a lease arrangement. If a financial institution occupied the ground floor of the main structure, these drive-in facilities could logically be used. In conjunction with the commercial bank lease described above, a five-lane drive-in facility was also leased on the same site, under separate lease agreement. Generally, the term coincided with the original lease for ten years with three, five year renewal options. Base rent for year one was established at $40,000, year two at $50,000, and year three at $60,000. After the fourth year, base rent is adjusted at the same CPI or ceiling rate as the main bank lease. We have estimated from this lease information the additional gross income attributed to the drive-in facility as:

Drive-in Facility $ 35,000
Total Potential Gross Income $397,050

Size of the drive-in was not considered a major element in establishing an appropriate rate; more important was the adequacy and access to the facility.

Absorption

Based on the available figures from both Hillsborough and Pinellas Counties, occupancy levels, in general, for office space are high. Good quality space is almost unavailable unless through proposed construction. Most buildings reviewed in downtown Clearwater were 95 to 100 percent occupied. At these higher rates, any indication of vacancy is probably created by tenant turnover. One exception was the "1100" Building which currently has 25,000 square feet available. A major two-floor tenant recently vacated space, accounting for most of that available. Leasing agents are optimistic that the space will soon be committed.

Under our premise that the ground floor be occupied by a financial institution, we have concluded that this tenant would be in place at date of sale. This appears to be a reasonable forecast based possibly on Clearwater Federal's continued occupancy after sale or the aggressive infiltration of new institutions to the Pinellas County market. The drive-in facility would be simultaneously leased.

The balance of upper floor space is estimated to be leased over a two year period or about 12,900 square feet per year. Because actual lease commencements will be unscheduled, neither falling at the beginning or end of the fiscal year, we have estimated that 25 percent of the available space will be leased semiannually, or 6,440 square feet per period.

In addition to vacancy during the absorption period, some allowance for vacancy and credit loss is applicable after a more stabilized occupancy level. This amount is reported after the second year in the reconstructed operating statement.

Expenses

As stated, income and expense patterns varied, based on terms of lease. Two types of leasing arrangements would be most applicable for the Clearwater Federal property. All electrical and mechanical services are common to the building and not feasibly divisible. A new concept to the Pinellas County market is the triple net lease for multi-tenancy with total expense pass-through provisions. Again, any expenses incurred in the operation are passed through to the tenant based on a proration of space occupied. A second method, and the one utilized in our analysis, would be a full service lease with all typical expense items paid by the landlord up to and including the amount established by a base year (year of lease commencement). Any increases over a base amount for each expense item such as real estate taxes, insurance, maintenance, janitorial and utility charges, are added to the tenant's base rent in the similar proration of space occupied.

This offers the advantage of efficienctly providing full service by the landlord, although confining his exposure to future unknown cost. From a valuation point, forecast of increasing expense items is unnecessary since, thereafter occupancy and expenses stabilize.

A number of actual operating statements of investment properties for calendar years 1979 and 1980 were reviewed. For consistency, only those statements reporting similar obligations of the landlord or ownership, as presented above, were used. The most common comparison units from these expense statements were expense amounts per gross and net square foot and expenses as a percentage of collected gross income. For these three categories, we found that an average cost to operate a property was about $3.50 per gross square foot and $4.05 per net. Budgeted expense figures for 1981, by property managements, showed an average range of between $4.00 and $4.50 per gross square foot. From figures supplied by Clearwater Federal for fiscal year 1980, total operating expenses were $239,500. Total expenses included all properties, both fee and leased. By allocating the main building expenses (provided as one figure) between the main building and the southern leased property, a summary of these expenses, as allocated, is presented below with indicated rate per gross and net square foot.

Clearwater Federal Expenses

	Amount	Amount/ Gross Sq. Ft.	Amount/ Net Sq. Ft.
Fixed Expense			
Real Estate Taxes	$ 27,000	$0.67	$0.82
Insurance	14,865	0.37	0.45
Operating Expense			
Utilities	$ 59,726	$1.49	$1.82
Janitorial	21,650	0.54	0.66
Maintenance, Repairs, &			
Service	56,090	1.40	1.71
Total Expenses	$179,331	$4.48	$5.47

Both rates fall above those found in other statements and are accounted for in part, by possibly a less efficient ratio of gross to net.

Our estimates of expenses incurred in the operation of the appraised property are given in gross and net areas, with the total amount for the same expense items:

Expense Items	Gross Area	Net Area	Amount
Fixed Expenses:			
Real Estate Taxes	$0.80	$0.98	$32,028
Insurance	0.25	0.30	10,008
Operating Expenses:			
Utilities	$1.80	$2.20	$72,063
Janitorial	0.50	0.61	20,018
Maintenance, Repairs, & Service	0.90	1.10	36,032
Total Expenses	$4.25	$5.19	$170,149

We have assembled, in the following reconstructed operating statement, each of those items discussed: potential gross income, allowance for vacancy and credit and the estimates of expense items incurred in operating the property. Discussing absorption, we stated a two year rent-up period for the balance of unleased space. This statement handles gross income as a constant amount over this rent-up period.

Exhibit 14

CLEARWATER FEDERAL—MAIN BUILDING
CLEARWATER, FLORIDA

January 15, 1981   Income Detail:

Office Building   7,031 Square feet @ $14.00 per year
Irregular Pattern

Drive-in   1 Facility @ $40,000.00 per year

INCOME AND EXPENSE PROJECTIONS

Description	Year 1	Year 2	Year 3	Year 4	Year 5
Gross Sched. Income					
Office Building					
Level Number 1	$98,434	$98,434	$98,434	$98,434	$98,434
Level Number 2	$43,936	$175,744	$263,616	$263,616	$263,616
Drive-in	$40,000	$40,000	$40,000	$40,000	$40,000
Total Gross Income	$182,370	$314,178	$402,050	$402,050	$402,050
Less V&C Losses	$0	$0	$16,082	$16,082	$16,082
Gross Oper. Income	$182,370	$314,178	$385,968	$385,968	$385,968
Deduct Expenses					
Real Estate Tax	$32,028	$32,028	$32,028	$32,028	$32,028
Insurance	$10,008	$10,008	$10,008	$10,008	$10,008
Management	$3,774	$12,368	$15,247	$15,247	$15,247
Utilities	$24,351	$51,859	$68,376	$68,376	$68,376
Janitorial	$6,799	$14,473	$19,080	$19,080	$19,080
Maintenance	$12,229	$26,054	$34,344	$34,344	$34,344
Total Expenses	$89,189	$146,790	$179,083	$179,083	$179,083
Net Operating Income	$93,181	$167,388	$206,885	$206,885	$206,885
Percentage Change	0.000%	79.637%	23.596%	0.000%	0.000%
Expense/GOI Ratio	48.905%	$46.721%	46.398%	46.398%	46.398%

An expense item not included, is the cost of management which is directly related to occupancy. This expense is not incurred or reflected in Clearwater Federal's provided statement. Other operating expenses will also increase in relation to occupancy up to the point where escalators or stop provisions stabilize these costs.

Conversion of Income

Two methods have been employed to convert net income into an indication of value. The first method employed was the simple conversion of net income by an overall rate. This market-related method extracts rates developed by actual market transactions. Rates indicated in the market section ranged from a low of 7.2 percent to a high of 10.28 percent. The sale of Palmetto Federal Savings & Loan generated an overall rate of 8.4 percent.

In deriving an overall rate, either to support market extracted rate or, in the absence of market information, the effects of mortgage financing must be considered. Typically, in investment situations, as much of the purchase price as possible is financed by mortgage funding, thus limiting required cash investment or equity capital. Because the market actually consists of this mortgage-equity combination, the derived capitalization rate should consider both components.

Each position has different requirements; equity requires a greater interest rate or return than the financed position due to the higher risk involved. Today, the investment market in real property is somewhat revised. From sales and general observation of the market, numerous purchases are based on negative cash flows to the equity position during initial periods of ownership. Overall rates found in the market support the acceptance of negative cash flows, as illustrated later. The derivation of a capitalization rate must consider equity return in the form of equity dividends or periodic cash receipts. The mortgage must receive an adequate return in the form of a mortgage capitalization rate or mortgage constant.

The market clearly shows that an eight to nine percent capitalization rate is being accepted by investors. The overall rate, although not identifying various investment criteria, includes all considerations involved in the transaction. Because the overall rate is a cash flow rate, we can estimate mortgage and equity interests comprising the overall rate.

Band of Investment Formula

$$\frac{\text{Mortgage \% } \times \text{ Mortgage Constant}}{\text{Overall Capitalization Rate}}$$
$$+ \text{ Equity \% } \quad \times \text{ Equity Dividend}$$

as transformed—

$$\frac{\text{Overall Rate} \qquad\qquad 9\%}{-75\% \text{ Mortgage} \times 12.6 \text{ Constant} = 9.45}$$
$$25\% \text{ Equity} = .45\%$$
$$\text{Equity Dividend} = -.45\%/25\%$$
$$= -1.8\%$$

Our purpose here is to show that investments are in fact currently trading at negative cash flows; and, conversely, the market's acceptance of negative cash flows is producing substantially lower capitalization rates than formerly expected.

For using nine percent capitalization rate, we stabilize a single estimate of net income for conversion to value.

Stabilized Net Income / Overall Rate
$200,000 / .09 = $2,222,222
Rounded to $2,225,000

The second capitalization technique is discounting. The process relates a series of cash flow payments, in this case net receipts, through a market discount rate to an indication of present worth or value for the property. The benefit of this process allows treatment of uneven income streams generated during the rent-up, thus not requiring an estimate of stabilized net income. The disadvantage is the requirement to estimate reversion at the investment termination from sale or refinancing.

Discount rates ideally come directly from the market or, based on market components of the rate, are derived by a band of investment. This rate anticipates total return including reversion value. Reversion or terminal value was estimated by direct capitalization of a future net income at a considerably higher overall rate, reflecting risk that income may not increase as forecasted.

The following variable income summary discounts future net receipts and estimated reversion at the 11 percent derived discount rate.

Variable Income Analysis

	.110000 Discount Rate	1 Payments/Year	End of per PMTS
Period	Cash flow	P worth F	Present worth
1	$93,181	0.9009009	$83,946
2	$167,388	0.8116224	$135,855
3	$206,885	0.7311913	$151,272
4	$206,885	0.6587309	$136,281
5	$206,885	0.5934513	$122,776
Totals	$881,224		$630,132
Reversion	$2,600,000 ×	0.5934513 =	$1,542,973
Present Worth of Income and Reversion		=	$2,173,106

Summary of Values

The two income techniques employed in estimating market value of the main facility were by a direct capitalization of the stabilized income and a discounted cash flow of the variable income plus reversion. The two values found were $2,225,000 and $2,175,000, respectively. It should be pointed out that both techniques have attempted to measure value of the drive-in facility which was formerly omitted in our market approach.

We have not included in the income section an income analysis for the administrative and appraisal service property. A reflective market value estimate was made for these properties in the market section, which was the basis for our concluded value estimate. An analysis was done, however, based on general parameters of income and expense figures collected.

Because this property type is not principally acquired as an investment vehicle, prices are not as affected by competitive bidding. A buyer would be less willing to pay a premium for the anticipation of increasing rents or increased terminal value at sale, because of his intended self-occupancy. A higher capitalization rate was used than in the income approach for the main structure, reflecting these different considerations. Our estimate of value by converting income was approximately $220,000 compared to the former value reported at $210,000.

Income Conclusions and Summary

Main Structure $2,200,000
Administrative/Appraisal Building $220,000

Lease Interest Evaluation

Preceding portions of this report estimated fair market value of those properties held in fee simple interest by Clearwater Federal Savings & Loan. The following section deals with partial interest held by Clearwater, or leasehold interest. These interests are created by lease agreement dated January 1, 1956, between Clearwater Federal and Dr. Raymond H. and Mildred H. Center.

It is not believed necessary or advisable to include the lease agreement or subsequent amendments as part of this report. Each item was carefully studied to ensure accurate reportings of rental, financial obligations and responsibilities of both landlord and tenant. A brief summary is, however, included. The original agreement included Lots 23 through 28 in the main block and the two-story, southern structure erected by the lessor. Original term of the lease was from 1956 to 2055, 100 years. There is a specific inclusion for cancellation after a 25 year term with written notice to the lessor. Rental for the original lease was based on $150 per month land rent, $4,200 in annual building rent and paid as additional building rent, $100 per million dollars of time deposits generated by this location over a base of $5,000,000. Amended on January 1, 1958, three additional lots, 29 through 31 were added, and land rent increased to $300 per month. Again, on February 3, 1962, Lots 6, 7, 15, and 16, Block D (southern parking) were added to the lease and base land rental adjusted to $400 per month.

On June 29, 1962, portions of Lot 9 were erroneously added to the lease and corrected in June, 1965, to portions of Lot 8, which abut Lot 7 of the parking facility. Further amendment, dated August 12, 1966, basically rewrote the lease under the same provisions of the original 1956 date. Rent, however, was changed by the deletion of any reference to building rents and the inclusion of additional land rent. New figures were based on savings rate or time deposits at this Clearwater Federal location calculated at $75 per million up to $100,000,000 and $50 per million over that figure. The last known amendment was made in September, 1973, which added three residentially improved lots. Base land rent for the entire leased interest was increased to $800 per month with the same provisions for additional land rent.

Valuation

As stated, the lease agreement has created divisional or partial interest, with benefits enuring to both parties. The lessor is entitled to basic net receipts and the lessee to the use of the leased property. An additional interest is possibly created by a marketable value of a leasehold determined by comparison of market value of the unencumbered fee with value of the leased fee interest. The process to value any leasehold is as a residual of value disparity between the fee and leased fee interest.

Lease fee is defined as, "A property held in fee with the right of use and occupancy conveyed by lease to others. A property consisting of the right to receive ground rentals over a period of time, plus the right of ultimate repossession at the termination of the lease."[6]

Leasehold is defined as, "A property held under tenure of lease. The right of use and occupancy of real property by virtue of a lease agreement."[7]

Our first step was to estimate market value of those leased parcels, which was done by both direct capitalization and comparable sales approach. The second step was to estimate value of the leased fee. This value can be estimated by the present worth of the income rights enuring to the owner/lessor as specifically provided by the lease. This income consists of two parts: net lease payments as provided by lease and

---

6. Byrl N. Boyce, *Real Estate Appraisal Terminology*, (Cambridge, Massachusetts: Ballinger Publishing Co., 1975), p. 127.
7. Ibid., p. 127.

property reversion at termination of lease. Both cash flows are discounted to present worth at an appropriate discount rate and added for indicated value of the leased fee interest.

Another method would be to simply capitalize contract rent to a value indication, without projecting property reversion value. The residual value (total value of unencumbered fee less estimated value of leased fee) represents the lessee's partial interest and leasehold.

Unencumbered Fee Value

Those parcels included in the lease are the southern, two-story portion of the main structure and underlying land, southern parking facility, and three residentially improved properties. This latter property is excluded from our reporting; however, it is included in our lease analysis because there is no proration of lease payments for this portion. Methods employed, as mentioned, were income and market approaches. Although we have not included a detailed accounting of these value estimates, our former analysis of improved smaller office building sales indicated an approximate range of $40 to $45 per square foot of gross area for the two-story office building. Considering the age, condition, and extent of exterior improvements, we used a market indication of $42 per square foot, 7,790 sq. ft. at $42 totals $327,180. We have rounded our estimate to $325,000.

Similarly, by an income approach, we estimated gross income generated by a currently negotiated lease at $7 per square foot of gross floor area. This rate is acceptable in the market with an anticipation of the space being quickly absorbed. With single tenant occupancy or at the most two tenant occupancy , our rental rate was applied against gross area for an annual potential income of $54,530. Those typical expenses accepted by an owner under these lease arrangements would be for real property tax, fire and casualty insurance on building improvements and exterior building maintenance. A 35 percent expense ratio (expenses to gross) applied against gross resulted in $35,000 net income. Net income capitalized at a 10.5 percent rate indicates a $333,333 value. Our conclusion of market value of the unencumbered fee for this portion of the leased property is $330,000.

Both the existing parking facility (Lots 6, 7, part of 8, 15, and 16) and the residentially improved lots (1, 2, and 3 all Block D), were valued by a market approach. Based on land sales previously presented, our estimate of value for the two parcels is $80,000 and $47,800, respectively. Value for the improved parking was considered site improvement contributions. Compared to the fee lot of Clearwater Federal, this site is more restrictively zoned and currently occupied under an excepted use. Lots 1, 2 and 3 are improved with older residential properties, representing little value if used either by the lessee or disposed of in market transactions; our estimate is on land value.

In summary, estimated values for the individual parcels, representing the unencumbered fee simple interest are:

Second Story Building	$330,000
(Includes Lots 23–31)	
South Parking Lot	80,000
(Includes Lots 6, 7, part of 8,	
15 and 16)	
Residential Lots	47,000
(Includes Lots 1, 2 and 3)	
Total Value Estimate	$457,000

Leased Fee

Lessor receives two series of receipts; first, income, which assumes the characteristics of an annuity, possibly variable, by receipt of additional land rent. The second portion, reversion, is not realized until the lease terminates or is cancelled. Two points make a discounting process of income difficult. First, the lease was negotiated, in essence, in perpetuity; and second, a renegotiation provision is provided in the 1973 lease for rent every ten years (1976, 1986, etc.).

By examination of the lease and additional rent statement supplied by the client, the following is a summary of actual contract rents received over the preceding five years.

Year	1976	1977	1978	1979	1980
Base Land Rent	$ 9,600	9,600	9,600	9,600	9,600
Additional Land Rent	11,050	11,200	11,250	11,100	11,350*
Total Contract Rent	$20,650	$20,800	$20,850	$20,700	$20,950

*Reported 1980 savings deposits on land: $177,000,000

$$\$75.00 \times \$100M = \$ \ 7,500$$
$$50.00 \times \ \ \ 77M = \underline{\ \ \ 3,850}$$
$$\$11,350$$

The trend line of actual receipts of the lessor is constant. Anticipation of an additional rent is in the form of saving deposits on hand or based on operational quality of the institution. This would be a problem if income was variable and not stabilized. Because of the stability of income receipts, we have used a direct capitalization of net income of $21,000 per year. Considering the security, term and durability of the lease, a capitalization rate, six percent, is felt to adequately reflect this security or riskless annuity. This rate must be competitive to rates found in our market analysis, ranging from 7.2–10.28. These rates are reflective of substantially greater risk inherent in investments without credit tenant, income duration and durability. Forecast of terminal value for reversion was unnecessary.

$21,000 ÷ .06 = $350,000

Leasehold

As stated, the lessee's partial interest in the property has been valued as a residual or a division of the total value corresponding to that interest. Total value of the unencumbered fee was estimated at $457,000, and of the leased fee, at $350,000.

Market Value/Fee Interest	$457,000
Leased Fee Value	350,000
Leasehold Value (Residual)	$107,000

Conclusions and Summaries of Market Value

The appraisal process is one of bracketing values, determining from an analysis of all available facts the lowest unit of value which the appraised property could not realistically fall below. An upper limit is also estimated above which the property would be unrealistically valued. Once these units are defined, the spread is reduced to a final estimate of value.

As stated, the cost approach was not employed in our valuation. The market or sales comparison is dependent entirely upon the market. Available data and sales of similar properties to the ones appraised reflected the degree of accuracy with which this approach may be employed. The income approach is generally accepted as the investor's approach due to reliance on conclusions for commercial investments. There are numerous reasons for this, depending on a particular capital structure of the individual investor. Generally, the buyer is looking for an adequate return on invested equity capital.

All conclusions reached in our analysis were weighted as to their realistic indication of market value. The various approaches used narrowly ranged within accepted parameters.

It is our opinion that the market value of those properties held in fee by Clearwater Federal and of the additional value interests held under lease, as of January 15, 1981, were:

Main Building		
Market Approach	$2,100,000	
Income Approach	2,225,000	
Value Estimate		$2,200,000
Administrative/Appraisal Building		
Market Approach	$210,000	
Income Approach	220,000	
Value Estimate		210,000
Parking Lot Facility		95,000
Leasehold Value		110,000
Total Market Value Estimate		$2,615,000

Investment Analyses

As a follow-up to our market valuation, we have, by means of some basic computer application, analyzed operational characteristics of the property as an investment to a new owner. In our first analysis, a cash flow projection was made, based on constant dollar receipts and expenses over the same five year holding period used in our income analysis. Allocating a purchase price between mortgage and equity capitals, a loan to value ratio was established. Mortgage financing was based on a 25 year amortizing loan bearing a 12 percent annual interest rate. An annual debt service is shown at $199,000+. This analysis considers both pre- and post-tax positions. An individual's tax bracket of 50 percent was used, although any rate, including corporate rates, could have been used. A straight line depreciation method was employed for an estimated depreciable base of $1,800,000.

Two columns are of particular importance, including the middle column—cas! flows—and the last column which is tax-free cash flows. As shown, this investment would have a tremendous impact on an after-tax investment position; substantial tax losses are reported during a rent-up period and sustained tax losses through year five. Pre-tax cash flows would be, essentially, at breakeven after year two, although still sheltering other ordinary income of between $19,000 to $17,000 from year three to five.

More realistically, in a market of rapidly increasing prices, including expense items, investment prospects for increased rental rates in excess of increasing expense items are anticipated. A second cash flow model has conservatively estimated net income to increase at an annual rate of six percent. This is after allowance for increasing expense items. A similar debt structure was assumed. Pre- and post-tax cash flows become more attractive. Pre-tax cash flows are actual losses in years one and two, breakeven in year three, and favorably increasing years four through ten. Tax sheltering effects of the investment diminish after year five, becoming a reportable income liability.

Without a lengthy discussion of the meaning of internal rates of return, two quick analyses were made, using a financial management and a modified rate. Basically, these rates express relationships of required equity capital and the periodic returns, either in positive or negative cash flows, and ultimately a reversion or terminal value. Both of these 11+ percent rates are after debt service coverage and mortgage retirement at sale. The rates are, however, before any tax consideration which could be a principal motivation of the astute investment community.

Cash Flow Projection

CLEARWATER FEDERAL—MAIN BUILDING
CLEARWATER, FLORIDA

January 15, 1981
Projection begins in month 1 of fiscal year
Tax Bracket 50.000 %

	Depreciation	Base	Life	Method
	Building	$1,800,000	30	Strt Line
	Personal	$0	0	N/A

Mortgage(s) Number	Status	Type	Amount	Int. Rate	Beg. Period	Original Term	Period to Mat	Pmts/Yr	Debt Serv/Yr
1	New	Amortizing	$1,575,000	12.000 %	YR 1 MO 0	25 YRS 0 MOS	25 YRS 0 MOS	12	$199,059.36

Year	Net Op Income	Interest Expense	Principal Amortized	Mortgage Balance	Cash Flow	Total Deprec	Total Deduct	Taxable Inc (loss)	Tax Liab (sav)	Tax Free Cash Flow
1	$ 93,181	$188,427	$10,631	$1,564,368	$-105,878	$ 60,000	$ 248,427	$-155,246	$- 77,623	$- 28,254
2	$167,388	$187,079	$11,979	$1,552,388	$- 31,671	$ 60,000	$ 247,079	$- 79,691	$- 39,845	$ 8,174
3	$206,885	$185,560	$13,499	$1,538,889	$ 7,825	$ 60,000	$ 245,560	$- 38,675	$- 19,337	$ 27,163
4	$206,885	$183,848	$15,211	$1,523,678	$ 7,825	$ 60,000	$ 243,848	$- 36,963	$- 18,481	$ 26,307
5	$206,885	$181,919	$17,140	$1,506,537	$ 7,825	$ 60,000	$ 241,919	$- 35,034	$- 17,517	$ 25,342
Totals	$881,224	$926,834	$ 68,462		$-114,072	$300,000	$1,226,834	$-345,610	$-172,805	$ 58,732

Total Cash & Benefits = $127,194

Appraiser's Comments

As a possible assistance to Clearwater Federal, a number of comments are made. The property is in a prime Pinellas County location, near the downtown Clearwater Business District. In addition to location, a number of factors should be considered that possibly assign some premium to value for the disposition. The property was valued in a market value concept as multiple properties. By a redefinition of highest and best use, the property at some point could be redeveloped as a high-rise, urban office building. The fact that Clearwater Federal assigns the block or successors control the entire block, whether by lease or fee interest, could be weighted heavily in a redevelopment proposal. A second premium which should be considered is the perpetual control the Association has over leased properties. Although renegotiations at future date could eliminate any advantage now held by the leasehold, a positive leasehold value will probably continue, because for all practical purposes, the lease is for land only. The lessor has completely recaptured his investment in the building, considering income as land rental. The tenant has, in essence, free occupancy of 7,700 square feet. A sub-leasing arrangement, with Clearwater as a sandwich position, would retain these favorable leasehold interests. Another point observed is that the seller may be able to convey the special use properties at a premium in-use value if similar occupancy or use was anticipated by new ownership.

Contingent Conditions

1. This appraisal represents the best opinion of the evaluators as to market value of the property as of the appraisal date. The term "market value" is defined in the appraisal report.

2. The appraisers have no present or future contemplated interest in the property appraised, and no bias with respect to the subject matter of the report or to the client or other participants or principals.

3. No furniture, furnishings or equipment, unless specifically indicated herein, have been included in our value conclusion. Only the real estate has been considered.

4. This appraisal has been made in conformity with the rules of professional ethics of the American Institute of Real Estate Appraisers.

5. The appraisers herein certify that, to the best of their knowledge and belief, statements contained in this appraisal, and upon which the opinions expressed herein are based, are correct, subject to the limiting conditions set forth herein.

6. No survey of the property was made or caused to be made by the appraisers. It is assumed the legal description closely delineates the property, and was checked with tax records for accuracy. Drawings in this report are to assist the reader in visualizing the property and are only an approximation of grounds or building plan.

7. Sub-surface rights (minerals, oil, or water) were not considered in this report.

8. Description and condition of physical improvements, if any, described herein are based on visual observation. As no engineering tests were conducted, no liability can be assumed for soundness of structural members.

9. All value estimates have been made contingent on zoning regulations and land use plans in effect as of the date of appraisal, and based on information provided by governmental authorities and employees.

10. This appraisal report covers only the premises herein, and no figures provided, analysis thereof or any unit values derived therefrom are to be construed as applicable to any other property, however similar they may be.

11. Certain data used in compiling this report were furnished by the client, his counsel, employees and/or agent or from other sources believed reliable. Data have been checked for accuracy as possible, but no liability or responsibility may be assumed for complete accuracy.

12. A diligent effort was made to verify each comparable sale noted in the report. However, as many principals reside out of the area, or are entities for which no agent could be contacted within the time allowed for completion of this report, certain of the sales may not have been verified.

13. No responsibility is assumed for matters legal in nature, nor is any opinion rendered herein as to title, which is assumed to be good and merchantable. The property is assumed free and clear of all liens or encumbrances, unless specifically enumerated herein, and under responsible ownership and management as of the appraisal date.

14. Employment in and compensation for making this appraisal are in no manner contingent upon the value reported, nor upon the finding of any predetermined or specified value or condition.

15. Consideration for preparation of this appraisal report is payment in full by the employer of all charges due the appraisers in connection therewith. Any responsibility by the appraisers for any part of this report is conditioned upon full and timely payment.

16. The appraisers, by reason of this report, are not required to give testimony in court with reference to the property herein, nor obligated to appear before any governmental body, board or agent, unless arrangements have been previously made therefor.

17. Neither all nor any portion of the contents of this appraisal shall be conveyed to the public through advertising, public relations, news, sales or other media without the written consent and approval of the appraisers, particularly as to valuation conclusions, identity of the appraisers or firm with which they are connected, or any reference to the American Institute of Real Estate Appraisers, or to the MAI designation.

18. Possession of this report or copy thereof does not convey any right of reproduction or publication, nor may it be used by any but the client, the mortgagee or its successors or assigns, mortgage insurors or any state or federal department or agency without prior written consent of both the client and the appraisers, and, in any event, only in its entirety.

(The appraiser's qualifications have been deleted.)

Bibliography

American Society of Real Estate Counselors. *Office Buildings: Development, Marketing and Leasing.* Chicago, 1981.

——. *Real Estate Counseling: A Professional Approach to Problem Solving.* Chicago, 1981.

Anderson, Jerry D., CCIM. *Success Strategies for Investment Real Estate.* Chicago: REALTORS NATIONAL MARKETING INSTITUTE®, 1982.

——. "A Year's Supply of Commercial Sales Meetings: Perk up Your Meetings (and the Sales Force) by Putting Some of These Ideas into Practice." *Real Estate Today* Sept.–Oct. 1981, p. 17–22.

Anderson, Paul E. *Tax Factors in Real Estate Operations.* Englewood Cliffs, N.J.: Prentice-Hall, 1980.

Bates, Dorothy R. *How to Run a Real Estate Office.* Reston Va.: Reston Publishing Company, Inc., 1981.

Boyce, Byrl N., ed. *Real Estate Appraisal Terminology.* Cambridge, Mass.: Ballinger Publishing Company, 1975.

Buell, Victor P., and Carl Heyel, eds. *Handbook of Modern Marketing.* New York: McGraw-Hill, 1970.

Building Owners and Managers Association International. *Downtown and Suburban Office Building Experience Exchange Report.* Washington D.C. Issued annually.

California Association of REALTORS®. *Listing Real Estate.* Los Angeles, 1978.

——. *Real Estate Office Administration.* Los Angeles, 1963.

——. *Successful Real Estate Office Policies and Procedures.* Los Angeles, 1974.

Chase, Cochrane, and Kenneth L. Barasch. *Marketing Problem Solver.* Radnor, Penn.: Chilton Book Company, 1976.

Commerce Clearing House, Inc. *1983 Federal Tax Course.* Chicago, 1983.

Cyr, John E. *Training and Supervising Real Estate Salesmen.* Englewood Cliffs, N.J.: Prentice-Hall, 1973.

Cyr, John E., and Joan M. Sobeck. *Real Estate Brokerage: A Success Guide.* Chicago: Real Estate Education Co., 1981.

Davidson, Les. *Using the Magic of Word Power to Multiply Real Estate Sales.* Englewood Cliffs, N.J.: Executive Reports Corp., 1973.

Digital Equipment Corporation. *Guide to Personal Computing.* Maynard, Mass., 1982.

Dilmore, Gene. *The New Approach to Real Estate Appraising.* Englewood Cliffs, N.J.: Prentice-Hall, 1971.

Dooley, Thomas W. *Real Estate Brokerage in the Eighties.* Chicago: Real Estate Education Co., 1980.

Downs, James C., Jr., CSD, CPM. *Principles of Real Estate Management*. Chicago: Institute of Real Estate Management, 1964.

Fletcher, David R. *Condominium Sales and Listings*. Reston, Va.: Reston Publishing Company, Inc., 1981.

Friedman, Milton R. *Commercial Real Estate Leases*. 12th ed. New York: Practicing Law Institute, 1981.

Friedman, Milton R. *Friedman on Leases*. 3 vols. with 2 supplements. New York: Practising Law Institute, 1974.

Gale, Jack L. *Commercial Investment Brokerage: An Introduction with Case Studies*. Chicago: REALTORS NATIONAL MARKETING INSTITUTE®, 1979.

Getter, Ronald E. *Real Estate Guidelines and Rules of Thumb*. New ed. New York: McGraw-Hill, 1976.

Gillig, Harry. *Gillig's Guide to Turning Unprofitable Real Estate into Money-Makers*. Englewood Cliffs, N.J.: Institute for Business Planning, 1979.

Girard, Weldon. *How to Make Big Money Selling Commercial and Industrial Property*. Englewood Cliffs, N.J.: Prentice-Hall, 1977.

Glassman, Sidney. *A Guide to Commercial Management*. Washington, D.C.: Building Owners & Managers Association, 1981.

Godi, Art, CRB, CRS, and Ken Reyhons, CRB, CRS. *Creative Listing Handbook*. Chicago: REALTORS NATIONAL MARKETING INSTITUTE®, 1980.

Gordon, Edward S. *How to Market Space in an Office Building, Portfolio Number 10*. Boston: Warren, Gorham & Lamont, 1979.

Graaskamp, James A. *A Guide to Feasibility Analysis*. Chicago: Society of Real Estate Appraisers, 1970.

Hanford, Lloyd D. *Feasibility Study Guidelines*. Chicago: Institute of Real Estate Management, 1972.

Heintzelman, John E. *The Complete Handbook of Maintenance Management*. Englewood Cliffs, N.J.: Prentice-Hall, 1976.

Herman, George D. *Real Estate Data: Your Market and Your Firm*. Chicago: REALTORS NATIONAL MARKETING INSTITUTE®, 1980.

Hoven, Vernon, and Harold H. Holen, Ph.D., CPA. *Dramatic Tax Savings through Real Estate Transactions*. Englewood Cliffs, N.J.: Prentice-Hall, 1982.

Institute for Management. *How to Prepare an Employee Handbook*. Old Saybrook, Conn., 1982.

Institute of Real Estate Management. *Income/Expense Analysis: Office Buildings—Downtown and Suburban*. 1982 ed. Chicago, 1982.

————. *Income/Expense Analysis: Apartments*. Chicago. Issued annually in midyear.

————. *Income/Expense Analysis: Suburban Office Buildings*. Chicago. Issued annually in midyear.

————. *Expense Analysis: Condominiums, Cooperatives, & Planned Unit Developments*. Chicago, 1978.

Irwin, Robert. *Protect Yourself in Real Estate*. New York: McGraw-Hill, 1977.

Key, Wilson Bryan. *Subliminal Seduction*. New York: New American Library, 1974.

Kinnard, William N., Jr., et al. *Industrial Real Estate*. 3rd ed. Washington D.C.: Society of Industrial REALTORS®, 1979.

Korb, Irving, SIR. *Real Estate Sale-Leaseback: A Basic Analysis.* Chicago: Society of Industrial REALTORS®, 1974.

Kusnet, Jack and Robert Lopatin, *Modern Real Estate Acquisition and Disposition Forms.* With commentary. Boston: Warren, Gorham & Lamont, 1981.

———. *Modern Real Estate Leasing Forms.* Boston: Warren, Gorham & Lamont, 1980.

Levine, Mark Lee. *Real Estate Exchanges.* Chicago: REALTORS NATIONAL MARKETING INSTITUTE®, 1981.

———. *Real Estate Transactions: Tax Planning & Consequences.* 2nd ed. St. Paul, Minn.: West Publishing Company, 1976.

———. *Realtor's Liability.* New York: John Wiley & Sons, 1979.

Lindeman, Bruce. *Real Estate Brokerage.* Reston, Va.: Reston Publishing Company, 1981.

Luther, William M. *The Marketing Plan: How to Prepare and Implement It.* New York: American Management Association, 1982.

McIntyre, Alice. *Role Playing: A Real Estate Training Tool.* Chicago: REALTORS NATIONAL MARKETING INSTITUTE®, 1982.

McMichael, Stanley L., and Paul T. O'Keefe. *How to Finance Real Estate.* 3rd ed. Englewood Cliffs, N.J.: Prentice-Hall, 1967.

Mader, Chris. *The Dow Jones-Irwin Guide to Real Estate Investing.* Rev. ed. Homewood, Ill.: Dow Jones-Irwin, 1982.

Mandell, Maurice I., D.B.A. *Advertising.* 3rd ed. Englewood Cliffs, N.J.: Prentice-Hall, 1980.

Marcus, Bruce W. *Marketing Professional Services in Real Estate,* Chicago: REALTORS NATIONAL MARKETING INSTITUTE®, 1981.

Mayer, Albert J., III, ed. *Readings in Management for the Real Estate Executive.* Chicago: REALTORS NATIONAL MARKETING INSTITUTE®, 1978.

Messner, Stephen D., et al. *Analyzing Real Estate Opportunities: Market and Feasibility Studies.* Chicago: REALTORS NATIONAL MARKETING INSTITUTE®, 1977.

———. *Marketing Investment Real Estate: Finance Taxation, Techniques.* 2nd ed. Chicago: REALTORS NATIONAL MARKETING INSTITUTE®, 1982.

Metzger, Jerry. *Showcasing Commercial Property.* Chicago: REALTORS NATIONAL MARKETING INSTITUTE®, 1980.

Peckham, John M., III. *Master Guide to Income Property Brokerage.* Englewood Cliffs, N.J.: Executive Reports Corp., 1968.

Petersen, Sandy and Knobby Ross. "Working with Attorneys in Commercial and Investment Real Estate." *Real Estate Today,* Nov.-Dec. 1981, pp. 32–35.

Phillippo, Gene. *The Professional Guide to Real Estate Development.* Homewood, Ill.: Dow Jones-Irwin, 1976.

Professional Real Estate Publishing Co. *Realty Bluebook.* San Francisco, 1977.

Rames, H. B. *The Dynamics of Motivating Prospects to Buy.* Englewood Cliffs, N.J.: Parker Publishing Company, Inc. (Prentice-Hall), 1973.

Randall, William J. *Appraisal Guide for Mobile Home Parks.* Chicago: Finance Division of Mobile Homes Manufacturers Association, 1966.

Real Estate Education Company. "How to 'Market' Commercial Sites to Retail Chains and Franchises." Chicago.

Real Estate Education Company in cooperation with Grubb & Ellis Commercial Brokerage Company. *Successful Leasing and Selling of Office Property*. Chicago, 1980.

————. *Successful Leasing and Selling of Retail Property*. Chicago, 1980.

REALTORS NATIONAL MARKETING INSTITUTE®. *The Competitive Edge in Selling*. Chicago, 1979.

————. *Percentage Leases*. 13th ed. Chicago, 1973.

————. *Real Estate Advertising Ideas*. Chicago, 1973.

————. *Real Estate Office Management: People, Function, Systems*. Chicago, 1975.

————. *Real Estate Sales Meetings: Techniques and Topics*. Chicago, 1976.

————. *RNMI's Guide to Real Estate Forms*. Chicago, 1972.

Reed, John T. *Aggressive Tax Avoidance for Real Estate Investors*. Moraga, Cal.: Real Estate Investor Information Center, 1981.

Ripnen, Kenneth H. *Office Space Administration*. New York: McGraw-Hill 1974.

Roberts, Duane F. *Marketing and Leasing of Office Space*. Chicago: Institute of Real Estate Management, 1979.

Robinson, Gerald J. *Federal Income Taxation of Real Estate*. Boston: Warren, Gorham, & Lamont, 1979.

Rybka, Edward F. *The Number One Success System to Boost Your Earnings in Real Estate*. Englewood Cliffs, N.J.: Prentice-Hall, 1971.

Sayler, James. *Real Estate Exchange Desk Book*. Englewood Cliffs, N.J.: Institute for Business Planning, 1978.

Seltz, David D. *How to Conduct Successful Sales Contests and Incentive Programs*. Chicago: Dartnell Corporation, 1979.

Siegan, Bernard H. *Land Use without Zoning*. Lexington, Mass.: Lexington Books, 1972.

Sirota, David. *Winning in Real Estate*. Reston, Va.: Reston Publishing, 1981.

Smith, Harvey J. *Real Estate Exchanges, Taxation, and Investment: A Systems Approach*. Belmont, Cal.: Harley J. Smith, 1977.

Smith, Keith V. *Guide to Working Capital Management*. New York: McGraw-Hill, 1979.

Steelmacher, Bob H. *Case Studies in Real Estate Practice*. New York: Macmillan, 1980.

Stock, Gerald R., et al. *Professional Real Estate Brokerage: A Guide for Real Estate Executives*. Homewood, Ill.: Dow Jones-Irwin, 1978.

Stone, W. Clement. *The Success System that Never Fails*. Englewood Cliffs, N.J.: Prentice-Hall, Inc., 1962.

Tanzer, Milt. *Commercial Real Estate Desk Book*. Englewood Cliffs, N.J.: Institute for Business Planning, 1981.

Tappan, William T. *The Real Estate Acquisition Handbook: Money-Making Techniques for the Serious Investor*. Englewood Cliffs, N.J.: Prentice-Hall, 1980.

————. *Real Estate Exchange and Acquisition Techniques*. Englewood Cliffs, N.J.: Prentice-Hall, 1978.

Urban Land Institute. *Dollars and Cents of Shopping Centers*. Washington, D.C., 1981.

Wachs, William. *How Sales Managers Get Things Done*. Salt Lake City, Utah: Parker Publishing Co., Inc., 1971.

Wilson, Audrey. *The Marketing of Professional Services.* New York: McGraw-Hill, 1972.

Yorks, Lyle. *Effective Communication in Real Estate Management.* Chicago: REALTORS NATIONAL MARKETING INSTITUTE®, 1979.

Index

Accountants, working with, 14, 198. *See also* Certified Public Accountants, working with

Advertising, 33, 43, 58. *See also* Marketing plan

All-inclusive mortgages: transaction problem solved, #85, 86.* *See also* Financing

American Institute of Real Estate Appraisers, 73n

Amortization: transaction problem solved, #45, 81; #57, 82; #64, 83; #93, 87

Apartments: transaction problem solved, #80, 85

Appraisals, 32, 72

Appraisers, working with: case study example, 207–49. *See also* Member, Appraisal Institute

Architects, working with: case study example, 187–95

Assumptions: transaction problem solved, #73, 84

Attorneys, working with, 14, 15; transaction problem, Y, 77; transaction problem solved, #76, #77, 85

Backwork mortgages: transaction problem solved, #93, 87. *See also* Financing

Billboards, 17

Blanket mortgages: transaction problem solved, #42, 81. *See also* Financing

Board of REALTORS®, 14–15

Bonds: tax deferred exchanges, 103; transaction problem solved, #7, 78

Borrowing: transaction problem solved, #14, #20, 79

Boyce, Byrl N., 56n

Brochures, 17. *See also* Marketing plan

Brokers: appearance, 19; business philosophy, 1–11, 12–21; centers of influence, 14–17; co-brokerage, 3, 8, 37, 60; community involvement, 14; education, 2, 2n, 19, 100n, 104n; ethics, 2–3; fees, 7–8, 60; specializing, 18–19; time management, 10–11, 50, 59; transaction problem, Z, 77. *See also* Commercial-investment real estate brokerage

Broker participation: transaction problem solved, #17, #24, 79, #103, #104, 88

Budget, marketing, 37, 58–60, 65–68

Business cards, 16

Business environment, 13–21

Business philosophy, 1–11, 12–21

Buy-back options: transaction problem solved, #47, 81; #104, 88

Buyer appeal, 30, 32

Buyer's agreements, 4

Buyers, working with: buyer's agreements, 4; identifying, 55; providing property information, 65–68. *See also* specific transaction problem headings

Capital gains: in exchanging, 100–13; transaction problem, T, 77; transaction problem solved, #60, 82

Cash: in exchanging, 109–11; transaction problem solved, #54, #57, #58, 82; #61, 83; #75, 84–85; #80, #82, 85; #84, #86, 86; #100, #104, 88

Cash flows: transaction problem, B, E, 76; transaction problem solved, #5, 78; #25, 79; #29, 80; #45, 81; #59, 82; #67, 83; #85, 86; #93, #95, 87

CCIM. *See* Certified Commercial Investment Member

---

*Entries marked with a # or a capital letter refer to entries in "Common Negotiation and Transaction Problems," Figure 5-2 and "Transaction Structure Solutions," Figure 5-3.